THE COMPREHENSIVE GUIDE TO CYBERSECURITY CAREERS

A Professional's Roadmap for the Digital Security Age

Dr. Jason Edwards, DMIST, CISSP

J.ROSS PUBLISHING

ISBN-13: 978-1-60427-202-4
e-ISBN: 978-1-60427-855-2

Printed and bound in the U.S.A. Printed on acid-free paper.

10 9 8 7 6 5 4 3 2 1

Library of Congress Cataloging-in-Publication Data can be found in the WAV
section of the publisher's website at www.jrosspub.com/wav.

Phone: (954) 727-9333
Fax: (561) 892-0700
Web: www.jrosspub.com

*To Michelle, Chris, Ceylin, Mayra, and
all of my esteemed students,*

*This book is dedicated to you—the bright stars
of my life and the classroom.*

*To Michelle, Chris, Ceylin, and Mayra—you are the greatest gifts
life has ever given me. Each of you, unique in your own right,
has filled my heart with immeasurable joy and pride: Michelle,
with your keen intellect and compassionate heart; Chris, whose
resilience and creativity know no bounds; Ceylin, a beacon of
determination and grace; and Mayra, whose vibrant spirit and
curiosity light up every room. Together, you form a constellation
of brilliance and love that guides me daily.*

*To my students, past, present, and future—you are the reason I
am inspired to teach, learn, and grow continually. Your thirst for
knowledge, diverse perspectives, and boundless potential have
enriched not only my career but my life in profound ways. Each of
you has left an indelible mark on my journey as an educator. I am
forever grateful for the privilege of being a part of your academic
and personal growth.*

*This book reflects my thoughts and experiences and the lessons I
learned and shared with each of you. It is a mosaic of our collective
journey, a testament to the power of learning, and a celebration
of the bonds we have formed. May you always carry the joy of
discovery, the courage to challenge the unknown, and the
strength to pursue your dreams.*

With most profound admiration and love,

Jason (Dad)

CONTENTS

PREFACE

Welcome to a comprehensive journey into the dynamic and ever-evolving world of cybersecurity. This book is more than just a guide; it is a companion for anyone from novices to experienced professionals who are eager to navigate the intricate landscape of cybersecurity. Our core purpose is to offer a detailed and insightful exploration of cybersecurity roles, education paths, skill requirements, and emerging trends in this critical field. Whether you are contemplating a career in cybersecurity, seeking to expand your expertise, or aiming to stay abreast of the latest developments, this book promises to be an invaluable resource in your professional journey. Join us as we delve into the multifaceted realm of cybersecurity, equipping you with the knowledge and tools necessary to thrive in this exciting and indispensable domain.

AUTHOR'S BACKGROUND IN CYBERSECURITY

My journey into the world of cybersecurity began over two decades ago, driven by a blend of curiosity and a profound sense of the critical role that digital security plays in our lives. As a current professor of cybersecurity and a seasoned veteran in this field, my experiences span various sectors, including the military, insurance, finance, technology, and energy. These diverse environments have enriched my understanding of cybersecurity challenges and highlighted this field's universal importance.

Holding key leadership positions throughout my career, I have witnessed the evolution of cyber threats and the need for robust defense mechanisms. My passion for cybersecurity extends beyond professional responsibilities, as I regularly share insights at conferences and seminars, contributing to the broader conversation on digital safety and innovation.

Academically, my foundation in Information Technology, with a Bachelor's and Master's degree, was further solidified by a Doctorate in Cybersecurity.

This academic journey, coupled with certifications like Certified Information Systems Security Professional and Certified in Risk and Information Systems Control, has equipped me with a comprehensive understanding of cybersecurity's technical and strategic aspects. This book is a culmination of my experiences, learnings, and steadfast commitment to advancing the field of cybersecurity.

MOTIVATION FOR WRITING THIS BOOK

The inspiration for this book stems from my extensive experience as a teacher and mentor in cybersecurity. Over the years I have had the privilege of instructing and guiding thousands of individuals in the classroom and through an active and vibrant LinkedIn network. This interaction with a diverse range of aspiring and established cybersecurity professionals has afforded me a unique perspective on the myriad challenges and opportunities that define this field.

I noticed a significant gap in the existing literature—the lack of a comprehensive guide that addresses the technical aspects of cybersecurity and delves into the practicalities of building a successful career in this domain. Many resources cover the *what* of cybersecurity, but there is a scarcity of literature addressing the *how* of navigating a career path in this dynamic industry. This book aims to bridge that gap by offering real-world insights, actionable advice, and a detailed exploration of various career paths, roles, and the evolving nature of cybersecurity work. It is designed to be an indispensable resource for anyone at any stage of their cybersecurity career, enriched by the lessons from my journey and the many voices I have encountered.

CHAPTER SYNOPSIS

The book is structured to provide a comprehensive and practical insight into cybersecurity. Each chapter is meticulously crafted to guide you through various facets of the field, blending educational theory with practical advice:

1. **Introduction to the Cybersecurity World:** This chapter sets the stage, offering a broad overview of the cybersecurity landscape. It addresses the fundamental concepts, current challenges, and the significance of cybersecurity in our digital era.
2. **Paths of Cybersecurity Education:** Here, we explore the different educational pathways one can pursue in cybersecurity. The chapter

emphasizes the importance of continuous learning in this rapidly evolving field, from university programs to self-study routes.

3. **Certifications and Their Significance:** Focused on the role of certifications, this chapter provides a roadmap for obtaining various cybersecurity certifications, highlighting their importance in career advancement.

4. **Personal Development and Soft Skills in Cybersecurity:** Beyond technical skills, this chapter delves into the soft skills necessary for success in cybersecurity, such as teamwork, problem-solving, and stress management.

5. **Building a Strong Portfolio:** Practical tips on creating a compelling cybersecurity portfolio are provided here. It covers everything from showcasing problem-solving skills to leveraging experiences in open-source projects and hackathons.

6. **Navigating the Cybersecurity Job Market:** This chapter offers guidance on job search strategies, resume tailoring, and interview preparation, crucial for a successful career in cybersecurity.

7. **Social Networking Strategies on LinkedIn:** The focus here is leveraging LinkedIn for career growth, including optimizing your profile and networking.

8. **Technical Roles in Cybersecurity:** An in-depth look at various technical roles in the field; this chapter helps readers understand the specific skills and responsibilities associated with each role.

9. **Management Roles in Cybersecurity:** Here, the emphasis is on leadership positions in cybersecurity, detailing roles like Chief Information Security Officer and Security Architect and the pathways to these positions.

10. **Research and Development in Cybersecurity:** This chapter highlights cybersecurity research and development roles, such as Cryptographers and Security Software Developers.

11. **Policy and Training Roles in Cybersecurity:** Focused on roles involving cybersecurity policy and training, it explores positions like Cybersecurity Policymaker and Trainer.

12. **Risk and Compliance Roles in Cybersecurity:** Covering the critical area of risk and compliance, this chapter outlines roles like Compliance Director and Information Security Auditor.

13. **Threat Intelligence Roles in Cybersecurity:** Here, we delve into the world of threat intelligence, discussing roles such as Cyber Counterintelligence Specialist and Threat Intelligence Analyst.

14. **Cloud Security Roles in Cybersecurity:** With the rise of cloud computing, this chapter focuses on roles specific to cloud security.
15. **Artificial Intelligence (AI) Roles in Cybersecurity:** This chapter explores the intersection of AI and cybersecurity, discussing roles like AI Security Analyst and Machine Learning Security Engineer.
16. **Cybersecurity Across Different Sectors:** An overview of how cybersecurity roles vary across finance, healthcare, and government sectors.
17. **Future Trends in Cybersecurity Careers:** The concluding chapter looks at the future of cybersecurity careers, discussing emerging trends, the role of AI and automation, and the importance of adaptability and continuous learning in the field.

TARGET AUDIENCE

This book is meticulously designed to cater to a wide and varied audience, encompassing individuals at different stages of their cybersecurity journey:

1. **Students and aspiring cybersecurity professionals:** This book is an essential guide for students and aspiring professionals embarking on their cybersecurity journey. It provides foundational knowledge, introduces various career paths, and offers guidance on educational routes and certifications. The early chapters are particularly beneficial for those seeking to gain a solid grounding in the basics of cybersecurity.
2. **Established cybersecurity professionals:** For professionals already in the field, this book offers advanced insights into specialized roles, emerging trends, and strategies for career advancement. Chapters focusing on management roles, sector-specific cybersecurity challenges, and future trends are particularly relevant. The book also serves as a refresher on the latest developments in cybersecurity, ensuring that established professionals stay updated in this fast-paced domain.
3. **Career changers and enthusiasts:** Individuals looking to transition into cybersecurity from other fields will find this book extremely valuable. It provides a clear roadmap for acquiring the necessary skills and credentials, making it easier for career changers to navigate this new landscape. Cybersecurity enthusiasts who may not be looking for a professional role but are keen to understand the field will also find the book informative and engaging.

4. **Academicians and trainers:** Educators and trainers in cybersecurity can use this book as a resource to enhance their curriculum. The comprehensive coverage of various roles and the latest trends in cybersecurity makes it an excellent reference for academic purposes.

RELEVANCE IN TODAY'S CYBERSECURITY LANDSCAPE

Cybersecurity is more critical than ever in today's rapidly evolving digital world. The book is acutely aligned with current trends and pressing challenges in the cybersecurity landscape:

1. **Emerging threats and technologies:** The cybersecurity domain continually faces new threats and adapts to groundbreaking technologies. This book addresses these challenges head-on, discussing the latest cyber threats like ransomware, phishing, and state-sponsored attacks. It also delves into cutting-edge technologies such as AI, Machine Learning (ML), and blockchain and their implications in cybersecurity.
2. **Increasing need for cybersecurity professionals:** With the rise in cyberattacks, there is a growing demand for skilled cybersecurity professionals. The book tackles this issue by providing guidance on entering and navigating the cybersecurity field, outlining various career paths and the skills required for each.
3. **The shift toward remote work and cloud security:** The recent shift toward remote work has brought new challenges in securing remote networks and cloud infrastructures. The book includes dedicated chapters on cloud security roles and strategies, making it a timely resource for professionals dealing with these modern complexities.
4. **Compliance and regulatory environment:** As regulations like the General Data Protection Regulation and the California Consumer Privacy Act become more prominent, understanding cybersecurity's legal and compliance aspects is crucial. This book covers these aspects, providing insights into roles like Compliance Officers and Auditors, which are essential in today's regulatory landscape.
5. **Cybersecurity in diverse sectors:** This book acknowledges that cybersecurity challenges vary across different sectors, such as finance, healthcare, and government. It provides sector-specific insights, making it relevant for professionals working in various industries.

6. **Integration of cybersecurity in business strategy:** Today, cybersecurity is not just a technical issue but a critical part of business strategy. This book covers management roles in cybersecurity, highlighting how cybersecurity knowledge is vital for business leaders and decision makers.

PRACTICAL APPLICATIONS

This book is designed to impart knowledge and serve as a practical toolkit for real-world application:

1. **Career path guidance:** The book provides detailed insights into various cybersecurity roles and paths, allowing readers to identify and pursue careers that align with their interests and skills. For example, someone interested in a technical role can follow the roadmap for becoming a Penetration Tester. At the same time, those inclined toward policy might find the pathway to becoming a Cybersecurity Policymaker more relevant.

2. **Skill development and enhancement:** Each chapter offers actionable advice on developing the necessary skills for different cybersecurity roles. Readers can apply these tips to improve their technical proficiency, soft skills, and overall understanding of cybersecurity concepts.

3. **Certification and training resources:** Recognizing the importance of certifications in cybersecurity, the book includes comprehensive lists and overviews of certifications such as Certified Information Systems Security Professional and Certified in Risk and Information Systems Control. This serves as a guide for readers to choose and pursue certifications that will enhance their career prospects.

4. **Application in diverse sectors:** The book's sector-specific insights equip readers to apply cybersecurity principles in various industries. For instance, a professional working in healthcare can utilize the healthcare cybersecurity chapter to understand and address unique challenges in their field.

5. **Practical tips for the job market and networking:** With chapters dedicated to job search strategies, resume writing, and leveraging LinkedIn for networking, readers can directly apply this advice to enhance their professional presence and increase job opportunities in the cybersecurity sector.

6. **Guidance for continuous learning:** Emphasizing the importance of lifelong learning in cybersecurity, the book provides strategies and resources for continuous education, ensuring that readers can keep pace with the rapidly evolving field.

ENCOURAGEMENT FOR CONTINUOUS LEARNING

In the dynamic and ever-changing field of cybersecurity, continuous learning is not just an advantage; it is a necessity. This book strongly emphasizes the importance of ongoing education and skill enhancement to stay abreast of the latest developments and threats in the cybersecurity landscape:

1. **Evolving cyber threats:** Cyber threats and technologies evolve at a breakneck pace, making continuous learning vital for staying effective in combating these threats. This book encourages readers to be curious, seek new knowledge, and stay informed about the latest cyber threats, security tools, and mitigation strategies.

2. **Adapting to technological advancements:** As new technologies like AI, Internet of Things, and blockchain become more integrated into our digital ecosystem, they bring new challenges and opportunities in cybersecurity. Continuous learning enables professionals to understand and adapt to these technological changes, ensuring they remain relevant and practical.

3. **Professional growth and career advancement:** The book highlights how continuous learning and upskilling can lead to career growth. By acquiring new certifications, attending workshops, and pursuing advanced degrees, professionals can open doors to higher positions, specialized roles, and broader career opportunities.

4. **Engagement with the cybersecurity community:** Networking and engagement with the cybersecurity community are pivotal for learning and growth. The book encourages readers to participate in forums, attend conferences, join professional groups, and engage on platforms like LinkedIn. This community involvement facilitates the exchange of ideas, keeps professionals updated on industry trends, and provides opportunities for collaboration.

5. **Sharing knowledge and experiences:** Continuous learning also involves sharing one's knowledge and experiences. Mentoring, contributing to discussions, and writing articles or blogs help others and reinforces the professional's understanding and perspective.

FINAL THOUGHTS AND ENCOURAGEMENT

As we conclude, I want to leave aspiring cybersecurity professionals with words of encouragement and reflection. Becoming a skilled professional in this field is challenging but immensely rewarding and critically important in our modern world:

1. **Encouragement for aspiring professionals:** Remember that your contributions are invaluable to all those who are embarking on or continuing their journey in cybersecurity. The road may seem daunting sometimes, but your persistence and dedication will pay off. Each challenge you face is an opportunity to grow; every obstacle you overcome is a step toward mastery. Cybersecurity is not just a career; it is a commitment to protecting the digital integrity and security of individuals, organizations, and nations. Your role in this field is not just a job—it is a service to the greater good.

2. **The critical role of cybersecurity:** In today's interconnected world, the importance of cybersecurity cannot be overstated. With the increasing reliance on digital infrastructure, the role of cybersecurity professionals has never been more crucial. You are the guardians of the digital frontier, the defenders against unseen threats, and the architects of safe digital spaces. Your work ensures the safety of digital information, protects privacy, and upholds the very fabric of our digital society.

3. **A call to action:** As you move forward, take the knowledge, skills, and insights gained from this book and use them to make a difference. Stay curious, remain vigilant, and continuously seek to improve your skills and understanding. Remember, in cybersecurity, you are not just building a career; you are shaping the future of digital security and, by extension, our digital world.

ACKNOWLEDGMENTS

As I reflect on the journey of writing this book, I am filled with immense gratitude toward many who have supported, inspired, and walked alongside me.

First and foremost, my heartfelt thanks to the great leaders in the field of cybersecurity. Your vision, determination, and leadership have shaped the industry and have been a guiding light in my career and the writing of this book. Your contributions have been invaluable, and your footprints in the digital sands are what many of us aspire to follow.

To the incredible friends I have made along the way—your camaraderie, insights, and endless debates have enriched this journey beyond words. Our discussions, whether in conference halls or over coffee, have been the breeding ground for many ideas on these pages. Your support and encouragement have been a constant source of motivation.

A special acknowledgment to my family—your unwavering support and understanding have been my backbone. Balancing the demands of writing with personal life is no small feat, and it would have been impossible without your patience, love, and, sometimes, sacrifices. You are my rock, and this accomplishment is as much yours as it is mine.

And last but not least, a peculiar and special thanks to the survivors of the A7 program—you know who you are. Your resilience in the face of our *unique* challenges (and yes, I am using the term *unique* as sarcastically as possible) has been both a source of inspiration and amusement. The A7 program, with all its quirks, has been a memorable chapter in my life, and you, my fellow survivors, made it all the more remarkable. Your ability to navigate the labyrinth of our shared experiences with humor and grit is nothing short of admirable.

Thank you to each of you who has been a part of this journey. Your influence has been the wind beneath this book's wings; for that, I am eternally grateful.

ABOUT THE AUTHOR

Dr. Jason Edwards is a seasoned cybersecurity expert with extensive experience across many industries, including technology, finance, insurance, and energy. His professional journey is enriched by a Doctorate in Management, Information Systems, and Information Technology, along with profound roles that have contributed to cybersecurity resilience and regulatory compliance for diverse organizations. Each role reflects Jason's depth of expertise and strategic approach, demonstrating his capability to enhance organizational cybersecurity frameworks and navigate complex risk and compliance landscapes.

A Bronze Star punctuates his remarkable 22-year career as an Army officer, a testament to his extraordinary service and dedication. Beyond organizational contributions, Jason is a stalwart in the cybersecurity community. He engages a broad audience through insightful publications on LinkedIn and steers a comprehensive cybersecurity newsletter, reaching tens of thousands of readers weekly. Jason is the author of several books and lives with his family in San Antonio, Texas.

Web
Added
Value™

This book has free material available for download from the
Web Added Value™ resource center at *www.jrosspub.com*

At J. Ross Publishing we are committed to providing today's professional
with practical, hands-on tools that enhance the learning experience and give
readers an opportunity to apply what they have learned. That is why we offer
free ancillary materials available for download on this book and all participating Web Added Value™ publications. These online resources may include
interactive versions of material that appears in the book or supplemental
templates, worksheets, models, plans, case studies, proposals, spreadsheets
and assessment tools, among other things. Whenever you see the WAV™
symbol in any of our publications, it means bonus materials accompany the
book and are available from the Web Added Value Download Resource Center at www.jrosspub.com.

Downloads for *The Comprehensive Guide to Cybersecurity Careers* include
a Behavioral Interview Prep Guide for cybersecurity professionals.

1

INTRODUCTION TO THE CYBERSECURITY WORLD

In the ever-evolving digital landscape, cybersecurity has become a cornerstone of technological and organizational strategy. As we embark on a journey through the realm of cybersecurity, it is essential to grasp the current state of this dynamic field.

Recent cybersecurity incidents have starkly highlighted the vulnerabilities and potential impacts of cyberattacks. From large-scale data breaches affecting millions of users to sophisticated ransomware attacks crippling critical infrastructure, these incidents serve as a wake-up call to the importance of robust cybersecurity measures. The fallout from these breaches extends beyond immediate financial losses, encompassing long-term reputational damage, legal repercussions, and a shaken trust in digital systems.

The evolution of cyber threats is a testament to the ongoing arms race between cybersecurity professionals and cyber criminals. Hackers continually refine their techniques, employing advanced methods like artificial intelligence and machine learning to bypass traditional security measures. This constant progression demands an equally dynamic and proactive approach to cybersecurity, where ongoing education and adaptation are nonnegotiable.

Global cybersecurity trends reflect a growing recognition of these threats. Increased investment in cybersecurity infrastructure, the rise of cybersecurity insurance, and the implementation of stringent regulatory frameworks exemplify how nations and corporations respond to these challenges. This global perspective is crucial since cyber threats know no boundaries and can quickly ripple across countries and sectors.

The role of cybersecurity spans various sectors, each with its unique challenges and requirements. In the healthcare sector, for instance, protecting patient data is paramount, while in finance, ensuring the integrity of transactions and financial data is critical. The public sector also faces challenges when safeguarding national security interests and citizen data. Across all these sectors, the common thread is the need for robust, tailored cybersecurity strategies to protect against the increasingly sophisticated landscape of cyber threats. See Table 1.1 for some important cyber statistics.

Table 1.1 Key cyber statistics

From	Description	Key Statistics/Details
Last decade	Data breaches worldwide	Over 300 breaches led to the loss of at least 100,000 files each.
2018	Data breaches in the United States	More than 1,200 breaches, exposing 446.5 million records.
First half of 2019	Breaches resulting in data exposure worldwide	4.1 billion exposed records were reported between January and June.
2021	Record number of breaches in the United States	1,291 breaches between January 1 and September 30, a 17% increase from 2020.
Global costs	Average data breach costs (2019)	Climbed to $3.92 million, up from $3.86 million in 2018.
Common causes	Causes of data breach incidents worldwide	48% due to employee/contractor negligence.
Business impact	Impact on businesses by data breaches	43% of incidents impact small businesses; 95% affect government organizations, retail companies, or technology companies.
Method	Standard method used in breaches	Spear phishing or targeted emails are used in 91% of successful breaches.

Sources:
1. https://www.forbes.com/sites/niallmccarthy/2014/08/26/chart-the-biggest-data-breaches-in-u-s -history/?sh=350e92807735
2. https://www.statista.com/statistics/273550/data-breaches-recorded-in-the-united-states-by -number-of-breaches-and-records-exposed/
3. https://www.forbes.com/sites/daveywinder/2019/08/20/data-breaches-expose-41-billion -records-in-first-six-months-of-2019/?sh=29cea594bd54
4. https://www.securitymagazine.com/articles/96667-the-top-data-breaches-of-2021
5. https://purplesec.us/resources/cyber-security-statistics/

THE IMPORTANCE OF CYBERSECURITY IN TODAY'S DIGITAL AGE

In today's digital age, the significance of cybersecurity cannot be overstated. As we increasingly rely on digital technologies for personal and professional activities, safeguarding data and systems becomes paramount.

Protecting personal and corporate data stands at the forefront of cybersecurity efforts. For individuals, personal data encompasses sensitive information such as financial records, health information, and private communications, all of which are susceptible to breaches. The consequences of such breaches can range from identity theft to financial fraud. For corporations, the stakes are equally high. Corporate data includes proprietary information, customer data, and trade secrets, which are all vital to a company's competitive edge and reputation. A breach can lead to significant financial losses, customer trust erosion, and long-term brand damage.

Ensuring business continuity is another critical aspect of cybersecurity. In an era where businesses operate in a highly interconnected digital ecosystem, a single cybersecurity incident can disrupt operations, leading to downtime and loss of revenue. The ability to quickly recover from cyberattacks is essential for maintaining operational resilience and ensuring the uninterrupted delivery of services. This need for continuity drives the development of comprehensive incident response plans and recovery strategies, providing that businesses can withstand and rebound from cyber incidents.

The legal and regulatory implications of cybersecurity are becoming increasingly pronounced. Governments worldwide enact laws and regulations to protect consumer data and ensure organizations implement adequate cybersecurity measures. Noncompliance with these regulations attracts hefty fines and signifies a failure in corporate responsibility, which can have lasting reputational consequences. These evolving legal frameworks underscore the need for organizations to stay abreast of legal requirements and embed compliance into their cybersecurity strategies.

Cybersecurity transcends technical and corporate realms, emerging as a social responsibility. In an interconnected world, the actions of one entity can have far-reaching impacts on others. Ensuring the security of digital systems is not just about protecting individual or corporate interests but also about safeguarding the broader community. It involves a commitment to ethical practices, a focus on education and awareness, and a collaborative approach to security, recognizing that we are all interconnected and responsible for each other's safety in the digital world. As we navigate the complexities of cybersecurity, it is essential to remember that it is not just a technical issue but a critical component of our social fabric in the digital age.

THE PURPOSE OF THIS BOOK

Cybersecurity is as vast as it is vital, and navigating its waters can be as daunting as necessary. This book aims to serve as a compass in this journey, offering guidance and insight into the multifaceted world of cyber careers. Its purpose is fourfold: to introduce you to the diverse landscape of cybersecurity careers, to assist in preparing you for choosing a suitable career path, to shed light on the art of building professional networks, and to provide strategic advice on the hiring process in this dynamic field.

First, this book provides an introduction to the world of cyber careers. Cybersecurity is not a monolithic field but a tapestry of various specializations and roles, each addressing different aspects of digital security. From frontline defenders like security analysts to strategists and policymakers, this book explores the breadth of career paths available, detailing the skills, responsibilities, and challenges of each. This exploration is designed to give you a comprehensive view of the opportunities in cybersecurity, which will allow you to make informed decisions about where your interests and skills could be best applied.

Second, the book aims to help prepare you to choose a career in cybersecurity. Choosing a career is significantly influenced by personal interests, strengths, and market demand. We delve into the factors that should be considered when making this decision, including the evolving nature of cyber threats, the skill sets required for various roles, and the career trajectories that these roles offer. This guidance will equip you with the knowledge to align your career choice with personal aspirations and industry needs.

Building alliances through networking is another key focus of this book. In the ever-changing world of cybersecurity, professional networks can be a source of opportunities, learning, and support. We explore building and maintaining these networks, engaging with peers and mentors, and leveraging these relationships for mutual growth and learning. Effective networking strategies, both in-person and digital, are discussed, highlighting their role in career development and industry engagement.

This book offers insights into the cybersecurity hiring process. Securing a job in this competitive field requires more than just technical know-how; it demands an understanding of the hiring landscape, the ability to showcase your skills effectively, and the knowledge to navigate job interviews and assessments. From crafting a compelling resume to acing interviews and understanding the expectations of employers in cybersecurity, this book provides practical advice and strategies to increase your chances of landing a job that aligns with your career aspirations in cybersecurity.

This book guides aspiring cybersecurity professionals, offering a comprehensive overview of the field, actionable advice on career selection and preparation, strategies for building effective professional networks, and practical tips for navigating the hiring process. Whether you are just starting to explore the field of cybersecurity or looking to make a more informed career choice, this book aims to be a valuable resource in your professional journey.

THIS BOOK IS A LIVING DOCUMENT

Like the cybersecurity field, this book is a living document. It is an evolving repository of knowledge and insights, shaped not only by the advancements in the field but also by the experiences and contributions of its readers. As you navigate through its chapters, you are encouraged to absorb and actively engage with the information.

First and foremost, I invite you to review the contents of this book and gain your own experiences. The theoretical knowledge provided here is a foundation, but the actual depth of understanding comes from applying these concepts in real-world scenarios. Whether through internships, projects, or professional roles, your experiences will add layers to your foundational knowledge and help you grow as a cybersecurity professional.

Your feedback is invaluable. I encourage you to connect with me on LinkedIn (https://www.linkedin.com/in/jasonedwardsdmist/) and share your thoughts, insights, and experiences. This feedback will help refine and update the book and contribute to the collective learning of the cybersecurity community. Your perspectives, challenges, and successes can enlighten and inspire revisions, making this book a more relevant and practical guide for others.

Paying it forward is a central theme of this book. Cybersecurity is not just about protecting networks and data; it is about building a knowledgeable, vigilant, and supportive community. I encourage you to help others learn about cyber careers and defend themselves in the digital world. Share your knowledge, mentor aspiring professionals, and contribute to forums and discussions. In doing so, you strengthen the entire community against evolving cyber threats.

Building your brand in the field of cybersecurity is also crucial. Your brand reflects your expertise, values, and contributions to the field. Engage with the community through social media, blogs, or speaking engagements. Share your insights, discuss emerging trends, and showcase your achievements. A strong personal brand will open new doors and opportunities in your career.

Finally, remember that the time to start or advance your career in cybersecurity is today, not tomorrow. The field is rapidly growing, with opportunities emerging as quickly as the threats it contends with. Do not wait for the perfect moment; begin your journey now, armed with the knowledge from this book and a commitment to continuous learning and improvement. Your initiative today will shape your professional journey in the dynamic world of cybersecurity.

2

PATHS OF CYBERSECURITY EDUCATION

The journey into cybersecurity is anchored in a diverse array of essential skills and knowledge. These foundational elements are critical for anyone aspiring to make a mark in this field. Technical skills form the backbone of cybersecurity expertise. Networking and system administration proficiency are crucial because these skills provide the groundwork for understanding how systems communicate and function. This knowledge is essential for identifying vulnerabilities, securing networks, and managing systems effectively. A deep understanding of networking concepts, such as Transmission Control Protocol and Internet Protocol, firewalls, and network protocols, alongside practical system administration skills, equips individuals to tackle complex cybersecurity challenges.

In parallel with technical skills, soft skills play an equally vital role in cybersecurity. Critical thinking and effective communication stand out as key competencies. Analyzing situations, thinking logically, and solving problems are indispensable in a field where threats constantly evolve, and each new challenge requires a unique approach. Communication skills are equally important since cybersecurity professionals must explain complex technical issues to nontechnical stakeholders, write clear and concise reports, and work collaboratively with diverse teams.

Understanding the foundations of cybersecurity is another critical area of focus. This includes a thorough grasp of concepts like cryptography, which is fundamental for securing data, and risk management, which is essential for identifying, assessing, and mitigating cybersecurity risks. Knowledge of these areas ensures that cybersecurity professionals can develop strategies to protect against breaches and respond effectively to incidents.

Industry-specific knowledge can significantly enhance a cybersecurity professional's effectiveness. Different sectors, such as finance and healthcare, face unique cybersecurity challenges and regulatory requirements. Protecting financial transactions and complying with standards like the Payment Card Industry Data Security Standard are paramount in finance. In healthcare, securing patient data and adhering to the Health Insurance Portability and Accountability Act regulations are critical. A deep understanding of these industries' specific cybersecurity needs and challenges can make cybersecurity professionals more effective and sought-after in their fields.

UNIVERSITY PROGRAMS

University programs are essential in preparing the next generation of cybersecurity professionals. These programs, offered by leading institutions, blend academic rigor with practical experience, ensuring that graduates are well-equipped to tackle the challenges of the cybersecurity field.

The University of Texas at San Antonio (UTSA) is at the forefront of cybersecurity education and is renowned for its comprehensive approach to cyber-defense education. UTSA's curriculum covers a broad spectrum, from network security fundamentals to cyber operations and threat intelligence complexities. This broad coverage ensures that students are not only versed in current practices but are also prepared to adapt to emerging threats and technologies. UTSA's commitment to research and innovation further enriches the student experience by providing opportunities to engage in cutting-edge projects and to collaborate with leading experts in the field.

Hallmark University distinguishes itself with a curriculum that emphasizes practical skills. Their programs are meticulously crafted to balance theoretical knowledge with real-world application, focusing on making students job-ready. By integrating hands-on training and simulations, Hallmark ensures that graduates are knowledgeable and adept at applying their skills in various cybersecurity scenarios. This approach is invaluable in an industry where practical problem-solving abilities are as crucial as theoretical knowledge.

Georgetown University's cybersecurity program is noted for its holistic education, spanning technical skills, policy, and legal aspects of cybersecurity. This broad-based curriculum prepares students to understand and address cybersecurity challenges from multiple dimensions, a necessity in a field that intersects with various sectors and disciplines. Georgetown's emphasis on policy and legal aspects is particularly crucial, as it prepares students to navigate the complex regulatory landscape and understand the broader implications of cybersecurity measures.

The U.S. Military Academy at West Point and the U.S. Air Force Academy offer unique programs that merge cybersecurity education with military discipline. These institutions focus on developing leaders skilled in cybersecurity and capable of making strategic decisions under pressure. The curriculum at these academies is rigorous, combining technical cybersecurity training with leadership and strategic studies. This comprehensive approach is designed to prepare graduates for critical roles in national defense, where they are tasked with protecting sensitive information and national infrastructure from cyber threats.

The curriculum in these university programs often includes specialized areas such as digital forensics, ethical hacking, cloud security, and cybersecurity management. This specialization allows students to delve deeply into specific areas of interest that will prepare them for niche roles in the cybersecurity ecosystem. These areas of specialization are constantly evolving, reflecting the dynamic nature of the field and the need for professionals who are specialists in their domains.

Internships and cooperative education opportunities are integral to these programs. They provide students with invaluable exposure to real-world scenarios, enhancing their learning and giving them a taste of the professional world. These experiences are crucial for building practical skills, understanding workplace dynamics, and developing professional networks. Internships often lead to full-time employment opportunities because employers value the hands-on experience that these programs provide.

After graduation, the avenues that are open to alums of these programs are diverse and abundant. Graduates find themselves well-positioned for roles across various sectors, including government agencies that play a vital role in national security; private sector companies, where they protect critical data and infrastructure; and nonprofit organizations that contribute to broader societal security. Many graduates pursue careers in consulting where, by leveraging their expertise across different industries or in academia and research, they contribute to advancing cybersecurity knowledge.

University programs in cybersecurity are crucial for developing a skilled and adaptable workforce that is capable of addressing the diverse and complex challenges of the cybersecurity landscape. These programs provide the foundational knowledge, specialized skills, and practical experience necessary for a successful career in this dynamic and critically important field (see Tables 2.1 and 2.2).

Table 2.1   Selected online cybersecurity degree colleges in the United States

Institution	Location	Program Highlights
Regent University	Virginia Beach, VA	BS in Cybersecurity Online; National Center of Academic Excellence in Cyber Defense
Maryville University of St. Louis	St. Louis, MO	BS in Cybersecurity Online Tracks in Offensive, Defensive, and General Cybersecurity
Indiana Wesleyan University–National & Global	Marion, IN	BS in Cybersecurity Online; Prepares for certification programs
Mississippi State University	Starkville, MS	BAS in Cybersecurity Online; Focuses on cyber systems and defense, ethical hacking
University of Illinois at Springfield	Springfield, IL	BS in Information Systems Security Online; National Center of Academic Excellence in Cyber Defense Education
University of Arizona	Tucson, AZ	BAS in Cyber Operations Online; Concentrations in Engineering, Defense & Forensics, Cyber Law & Policy
Franklin University	Columbus, OH	BS in Cyber Security Online; Center of Academic Excellence in Cyber Defense
Hallmark University	San Antonio, TX	BS in Cyber Security Online; MS in Cyber Security Online

Table 2.2   Selected (in-person) cybersecurity degree colleges in the United States

Institution	Location	Program Highlights
University of Maryland Global Campus	Adelphi, MD	Bachelor's and Master's in Cybersecurity, Software Development & Security, Digital Forensics & Cyber Investigation
American Public University System	Charles Town, WV	Bachelor's, Master's, and Certificate Programs in Cybersecurity
Western Governors University	Salt Lake City, UT	Cybersecurity Degrees with industry certifications
Davenport University	Grand Rapids, MI	In-person/Online Cybersecurity Education; National Center of Academic Excellence in Cyber Defense Education
Ferris State University	Big Rapids, MI	Associate, Bachelor's, Master's in Information & Security Intelligence
Drexel University	Philadelphia, PA	Bachelor of Science in Computing and Security Technology, Master of Science in Cybersecurity
DePaul University	Chicago, IL	Bachelor's and Master's in Cybersecurity; National Center of Academic Excellence in Cybersecurity
Rochester Institute of Technology	Rochester, NY	Bachelor's in Cybersecurity; Global Cybersecurity Institute
Community College of Allegheny County	Pittsburgh, PA	Associate in Cybersecurity, I.T. Support Specialist, Cybersecurity Support Specialist certificate
Champlain College	Burlington, VT	Bachelor's in Computer & Digital Forensics, Computer Networking & Cybersecurity

ADULT PROFESSIONAL PROGRAMS

Adult professional programs play a crucial role in the cybersecurity education landscape, especially for individuals seeking to enhance their skills or who wish to transition to a cybersecurity career later in life. These programs are designed to cater to the unique needs of working professionals, offering flexible learning options that include evening and online courses. This flexibility is vital for balancing their education with work and personal responsibilities.

Evening and online courses have become increasingly popular, providing an accessible pathway for continued education. These courses are designed to be flexible and convenient, allowing learners to engage with material at their own pace and on their own schedule. This learning mode is particularly beneficial for those who are managing full-time jobs or family commitments. Online courses often utilize interactive platforms that include video lectures, virtual labs, and discussion forums, creating an engaging and comprehensive learning experience that rivals traditional classroom settings.

One of the leading training programs in this sphere is ThriveDX.com. ThriveDX's Cyber Academy offers a comprehensive training solution that addresses the cybersecurity industry's talent shortage and diversity gap. It provides a dynamic learning platform with over 1,000 hours of hands-on training and 300 real-world simulations, aligned with the National Initiative for Cybersecurity Education/National Institute of Standards and Technology 800-181 framework. The program offers flexible learning options, including full-time and part-time tracks, and emphasizes hands-on learning with real-world applications through immersive exercises and simulations.

The training program is unique in its focus on reskilling high-potential talent from diverse backgrounds, offering industry-driven, government-grade cybersecurity training. It adheres to an accelerated learning methodology and a streamlined curriculum that teaches the specific skills necessary to excel in the cybersecurity industry, regardless of the learner's background.

ThriveDX has graduated over 50,000 students globally and maintains strong partnerships with over 50 universities and 500+ enterprise customers—earning recognition as a global leader in cybersecurity education. The program's duration varies, offering a full-time 12-week track or a part-time 24-week track to accommodate different learners' needs. Graduates are equipped for various roles in the cybersecurity industry, such as Cyber Defense Analyst and Cyber Incident Responder. No prior knowledge or background is required to participate, making the program accessible to individuals from diverse backgrounds, including those from nontechnical fields (see Table 2.3).

Table 2.3   ThriveDX Cybersecurity Bootcamp (online)

Course Title	Brief Description
Introductory Course	Entry-level exploration of networking, Linux and Windows operating systems, and virtualization concepts. Includes real-life cyberattack scenarios.
Microsoft Security	Focuses on managing networks and computers and setting up domain environments using Active Directory, DHCP, DNS servers, and other network services.
Computer Networking	Covers network devices, layers, and protocols, preparing students for the CompTIA Network+ certification exam.
Cloud Security	Involves understanding cloud storage and exploring platforms like Google Cloud, Microsoft Azure, and Amazon AWS. Prepares students for the AWS Certified Cloud Practitioner exam.
Linux Security	Teaches the Linux operating system, especially Kali Linux, and prepares students for the LPI Linux Essentials certification exam.
Network Security	Builds skills in managing, securing, and operating network communication equipment with preparation for the Cisco Certified CyberOps Associate exam.
Cyber Infrastructure & Technology	Explores various infrastructure defenses, secure architecture design, and working with SIEM solutions like Splunk.
Introduction to Python for Security	Provides instruction in basic programming with Python, setting up Python environments, and using tools for automating cybersecurity tasks.
Offensive Security: Ethical Hacking	Offers immersive exercises to understand cybercriminals, covering various cyberattacks and defense strategies.
DFIR & Threat Hunting	Focuses on advanced threat hunting methods, digital forensics, incident response, and the role of Security Operations Center teams.
Game Theory Strategy in Cybersecurity	Teaches innovative ways to solve defense issues by applying cyber tactics and game theory strategies to real-life cyberattacks.
Career Services	Dedicated to job search preparation in the cybersecurity industry, including interview training, networking, and resume writing.

Career transition pathways are a crucial focus of adult professional programs. For many professionals who are looking to shift into cybersecurity from different fields, these programs guide that transition. They often include career counseling, resume workshops, and interview preparation—all tailored toward the specific demands and expectations of the cybersecurity job market. This holistic approach is invaluable for those looking to change careers, providing them with the necessary skills and guidance to navigate the job market.

When considering adult education options, one of the critical decisions is choosing between certificate programs and degree programs. Certificate programs typically focus on specific skills and are shorter in duration, making them a practical choice for those looking to gain specialized knowledge or update existing skills quickly. On the other hand, degree programs offer a more comprehensive education, covering a broad range of topics and often including opportunities for research and specialization. The choice between these options depends on individual career goals, time commitments, and the specific requirements of the roles they aspire to.

Balancing work, life, and education is a significant challenge for adult learners. Adult professional programs recognize this challenge and are structured to provide as much flexibility as possible. Time management is a crucial skill for students in these programs, as is the ability to prioritize and set realistic goals. Many programs offer resources to help students manage these challenges, including counseling services, time management workshops, and peer support groups. This support is essential in assisting adult learners to successfully navigate their educational journey without compromising their work or personal life.

In summary, adult professional programs offer a vital pathway for professionals seeking to enter or advance in cybersecurity. These programs provide the flexibility, support, and specialized training needed to succeed in this dynamic industry. Whether through evening and online courses, career transition support, or balancing education with other commitments, these programs are tailored to meet the diverse needs of adult learners, empowering them to achieve their career goals in cybersecurity.

SELF-STUDY PROGRAMS

Self-study programs in cybersecurity offer a flexible and personalized path for individuals who are eager to delve into the field at their own pace. These programs are particularly suited for those who seek autonomy in their learning process or for professionals looking to upskill alongside their current job commitments. The key to success in self-study lies in identifying and utilizing the wealth of online resources that are available.

One of the most prominent resources in the realm of self-study cyber-security education is Cybrary. Cybrary has carved out a niche as a leading platform, offering an extensive range of cybersecurity courses. Cybrary provides learners with access to knowledge, from fundamental concepts to advanced topics. The platform is renowned for its user-friendly interface and the quality of its instructional content, which is both comprehensive and up-to-date. For those embarking on a self-study journey in cybersecurity, Cybrary stands as a beacon, guiding learners through the complexities of the field with its expertly crafted courses and resources.

Apart from Cybrary, other valuable online resources such as Coursera, Udemy, and MIT OpenCourseWare exist. These platforms host courses ranging from introductory to advanced levels, often designed and taught by experts in the field. They offer a mix of free and paid courses, providing learners with flexibility in terms of content and cost. These resources are ideal for creating a structured learning plan that caters to individual learning objectives and pacing.

Creating a structured learning plan is critical for practical self-study. This involves setting clear goals, choosing relevant courses, and allocating specific times for study. A well-structured plan helps to maintain focus and direction, ensuring that learning is consistent and comprehensive. It also involves balancing various topics, from technical skills like network security to theoretical knowledge like cybersecurity policies, to gain a holistic understanding of the field.

Staying motivated and accountable is another challenge in self-study programs. Without the external structure of a traditional classroom, self-learners need to cultivate discipline and motivation. Setting regular milestones, rewarding progress, and maintaining a dedicated study space can help sustain motivation. Additionally, keeping track of learning progress and continuously challenging oneself with practical projects or quizzes ensures that learning is compelling and engaging.

Joining online communities and forums is an excellent way to complement self-study programs. Communities such as Stack Overflow, Reddit's cybersecurity forums, and LinkedIn groups provide platforms for learners to ask questions, share knowledge, and stay updated with the latest industry trends. These communities also offer networking opportunities, allowing learners to connect with professionals and peers. Engaging in these communities can provide practical insights, peer support, and a source of motivation and inspiration.

Self-study programs in cybersecurity are a viable and effective means of acquiring knowledge and skills in the field. By leveraging resources like Cybrary, creating a structured learning plan, staying motivated, and engaging with online communities, learners can navigate the complexities of cybersecurity and build a solid foundation for their careers or further studies.

IMPORTANCE OF CONTINUOUS LEARNING

In the ever-changing cybersecurity landscape, continuous learning is not just beneficial—it is essential. The field is characterized by rapidly evolving technologies and methodologies, making it crucial for professionals to keep abreast of the latest developments. This ongoing learning process can take many forms, from formal education to self-directed study. Staying updated with technological advancements ensures that cybersecurity professionals can effectively defend against new and emerging threats. It also fosters innovation since understanding the latest trends can lead to developing novel security solutions.

Networking and professional development are critical components of continuous learning in cybersecurity. Engaging with peers, attending industry conferences, and participating in workshops and webinars offer valuable opportunities to exchange knowledge and experiences. These interactions provide insights into current best practices and open doors to potential collaborations and career advancements. Building a solid professional network can be a significant asset, offering support, advice, and access to opportunities that might not be available through formal channels.

The role of mentorship in cybersecurity education and career growth is substantial. Having a mentor offers numerous benefits, including guidance on career development, insights into industry trends, and advice on navigating professional challenges. Mentors can also provide practical support, such as helping with understanding complex concepts or offering feedback on projects. A mentor can be a guiding light for those new to the field, while experienced professionals can gain fresh perspectives and stay connected to the broader community (see Table 2.4).

Table 2.4   Finding a mentor checklist

Step Number	Step Description	Details
1	Identify your goals	Clearly define what you want to achieve in your professional career and what kind of guidance you seek.
2	Research potential mentors	Look for individuals with expertise in your area of interest. Utilize LinkedIn, professional organizations, and your network.
3	Evaluate compatibility	Consider the mentor's background, mentoring style, and availability to ensure a good match with your needs.
4	Prepare your request	Draft a clear, concise, and respectful message or email. Mention your goals, why you chose them, and what you hope to gain.
5	Reach out	Send your request. Be professional and polite. If using email, use a clear subject line like "Mentorship Inquiry."
6	Follow up	Send a polite follow-up if you don't hear back in a week or two. Respect their decision if they're unable to commit.
7	Discuss expectations	Once a mentor agrees, discuss expectations, goals, communication frequency, and methods.
8	Establish a mentorship agreement	Agree on a mentorship plan. This might include regular meetings, objectives, and feedback methods.
9	Engage actively and respectfully	Be proactive in the relationship. Prepare for meetings, be open to feedback, and respect their time.
10	Express gratitude and give feedback	Regularly thank your mentor for their guidance. Provide feedback about what's working and what could be improved.

The importance of continuous learning in cybersecurity cannot be overstated. Keeping up with evolving technologies, engaging in networking and professional development, seeking mentorship, and pursuing certifications and advanced training are all crucial for maintaining relevance and effectiveness in this dynamic field. This commitment to ongoing education ensures that cybersecurity professionals are well-equipped to protect against current and future cyber threats.

3

CERTIFICATIONS AND
THEIR SIGNIFICANCE

Certifications in cybersecurity, recognized and valued across the industry, formally acknowledge a professional's expertise and competencies in specific cybersecurity areas. The concept of certifications dates back several decades, marking a significant evolution in information security and cybersecurity professionalization. The history of these certifications highlights their long-standing importance in the field.

In 1967, the Information Systems Audit and Control Association (ISACA)—now known by its acronym only—was founded, marking one of the early steps toward formalizing the field. This was followed by the foundation of the Association of Better Computer Dealers in 1982, which later became the Computing Technology Industry Association (CompTIA) in 1990. CompTIA introduced vendor-neutral IT certifications in 1992, a significant milestone that set the stage for standardized certifications in the industry.

In 1989, the International Information System Security Certification Consortium (ISC2) was formed to standardize information security certifications. ISC2 launched its most popular certification, the Certified Information Systems Security Professional (CISSP), in 1994. This certification rapidly gained recognition with the 10,000th person receiving the CISSP certification by 2002. The CISSP remains one of the most prestigious and sought-after certifications in the cybersecurity field.

Another major player in cybersecurity certifications is the International Council of Electronic Commerce Consultants (EC-Council), which was founded in 2002. The EC-Council is now the world's largest cybersecurity technical certification body, operating in 145 countries. They offer certifications such as Certified Ethical Hacker (CEH) and Computer Hacking Forensics Investigator (C|HFI). These certifications have been instrumental in training and certifying more than 200,000 individuals globally.

The significance of cybersecurity certifications extends beyond the validation of individual skills. They represent the evolution and maturation of cybersecurity as a profession. Over the years, certifications have become integral to the cybersecurity industry, bridging academic education and practical, real-world skill application. They are a testament to a professional's commitment to continuous learning and staying abreast of the rapidly evolving cybersecurity landscape.

Cybersecurity certifications are diverse, catering to various aspects of the field. Schools and universities, vendor-sponsored credentials, association- and organization-sponsored credentials, and governmental licenses and certifications all contribute to the tapestry of cybersecurity certifications available today. The quality and acceptance of these certifications vary worldwide, from well-known and high-quality examples like a master's degree in cybersecurity, CISSP, and Microsoft certifications to a broad array of lesser-known credentials. These certifications can be obtained through coursework, exams, and, in some cases such as the CISSP, by demonstrating experience and receiving recommendations from existing credential holders.

Certifications in cybersecurity have a rich history and are crucial for professionals in the field. They serve as benchmarks for skills and knowledge, ensuring adherence to industry standards, and play a vital role in career development and progression within the cybersecurity domain.

RECOMMENDED CERTIFICATIONS FOR BEGINNERS

For individuals embarking on a career in cybersecurity, starting with the proper certification can provide a solid foundation and set the stage for future advancement. Entry-level certifications are designed to offer beginners a comprehensive introduction to cybersecurity principles and practices. CompTIA Security Plus, Global Information Assurance Certification (GIAC) Security Essentials (GSEC), and ISC2 Certified in Cybersecurity (CC) are among the most recommended entry-level certifications:

- **CompTIA Security Plus** is widely recognized as an excellent starting point for beginners. This certification covers many topics, including network security, compliance, operational security, and threats and vulnerabilities. It is ideal for individuals seeking a holistic understanding of cybersecurity fundamentals. The certification is vendor-neutral, meaning the skills and knowledge gained are applicable across various systems and technologies, making it a versatile and valuable addition to any cybersecurity professional's credentials.

- **GSEC** is another highly regarded entry-level certification. GSEC focuses on the practical skills and knowledge necessary to understand and address real-world security issues. It covers areas such as cryptography, incident response, and risk management. GSEC is particularly valued for its emphasis on practical, hands-on skills. It is an excellent choice for those looking to demonstrate their ability to apply cybersecurity knowledge in real-world scenarios.
- **ISC2 CC** is a relatively newer certification explicitly designed for entry-level professionals. It provides foundational knowledge and skills in cybersecurity and serves as a stepping-stone to more advanced certifications, such as the CISSP. This certification is particularly beneficial for those who aim to build a long-term career in cybersecurity and seek a pathway for continuous advancement.

For career starters, following structured pathways can be beneficial in navigating the complex world of cybersecurity careers. One such resource is Cyberseek Pathways, which provides detailed information on various cybersecurity roles, the required skills, and the certifications that can help achieve these roles. This resource is invaluable for beginners because it offers a clear and structured approach to building a career in cybersecurity. It helps individuals understand where to start, what certifications to pursue, and how each certification aligns with different career paths.

Entry-level certifications like CompTIA Security Plus, GSEC, and ISC2 CC are excellent starting points for those who are new to cybersecurity. They provide the essential knowledge and skills to embark on a cybersecurity career. Resources like Cyberseek Pathways further aid in mapping out a career path, ensuring that beginners can make informed decisions about their education and professional development in cybersecurity's dynamic and ever-evolving world.

ROADMAP TO OBTAINING A CERTIFICATION

Embarking on the journey to obtain a cybersecurity certification is a significant commitment that requires a strategic and well-planned approach. A comprehensive roadmap to navigate this process is essential for ensuring success. This roadmap encompasses several key stages:

- Setting detailed goals and timelines
- Developing thorough study plans
- Employing effective exam strategies

- Understanding the critical role of maintaining certification and continuing education

Setting Goals and Timelines

The first step in the roadmap to obtaining a cybersecurity certification—setting goals and timelines—is a multifaceted process that demands careful consideration and strategic planning. This step transcends merely picking a certification; it requires a nuanced understanding of how this choice will influence your professional growth and align with your long-term career aspirations. It is about envisioning where you want to be in the cybersecurity landscape and identifying the certification that will catalyze achieving those goals. This decision should be informed by researching various certifications, understanding their relevance in the industry, and recognizing how they align with your areas of interest and expertise.

Once you have selected the certification that best suits your career objectives, the next crucial phase is establishing a clear, realistic, and personalized timeline for your preparation. This timeline is more than just a schedule; it is a roadmap that guides your journey toward achieving your certification goals. It should be tailored to fit your unique circumstances by taking into consideration your current work schedule, personal responsibilities, and lifestyle. This bespoke timeline should be realistic, setting achievable targets without causing burnout. It is about finding a balance that allows you to progress steadily while managing other aspects of your life.

Breaking down your preparation into manageable phases is an effective way to approach your studies. This phased approach involves segmenting your study plan into specific, achievable milestones. For instance, you could divide the syllabus into modules and set targets for completing each module. Incorporating practice exams at different stages of your preparation can provide valuable checkpoints to assess your understanding and readiness for the actual exam. This structured study approach enables you to maintain focus and direction, ensuring that you cover all necessary areas thoroughly. Regularly reviewing and adjusting these milestones based on your progress is crucial. It allows you to adapt your study plan to address areas where you need more focus, ensuring that you are always moving forward in the most effective way possible.

Setting goals and timelines is a critical first step in the certification journey. It involves strategically selecting the certification that is tailored to your career aspirations and creating a personalized, realistic, and phased study plan. This approach ensures that you stay on track, make consistent progress, and adjust your strategy as needed, ultimately leading you to achieve your certification and advance your career in cybersecurity successfully.

Study Plans and Preparation Tips

Developing an in-depth study plan is vital to preparing for a cybersecurity certification exam. This plan is more than just a schedule; it is a comprehensive strategy encompassing every facet of your study journey. The first step in this process is to understand the exam syllabus fully. Scrutinize the syllabus to understand the breadth and depth of the topics covered, and pay attention to the credence given to each topic. This knowledge will allow you to allocate your study time effectively, ensuring that you spend more time on the most significant or challenging areas.

Once you clearly understand the syllabus, the next step is gathering diverse study materials. This collection should include textbooks that provide detailed explanations and insights into various topics. Additionally, augment your study materials with online course materials and video tutorials. These digital resources often offer interactive and engaging ways to learn complex concepts and can be particularly helpful for visual and auditory learners. Do not overlook the value of community forums, where you can interact with other learners and professionals. These forums can be a goldmine of information, tips, and insights not found in textbooks or courses.

To make your study plan truly effective, diversify your learning methods. Different aspects of the syllabus might require different approaches. For instance, theoretical concepts might be best understood through textbooks, while practical skills could be honed through interactive simulations and labs. Complementing self-study with interactive online courses can provide a structured learning environment. At the same time, study groups offer the opportunity to discuss and debate topics that can deepen your understanding and provide new perspectives.

Regularly revising challenging topics is vital for a solid grasp of the material. Don't just move on from a problematic topic once you understand it; revisit it periodically to reinforce your knowledge and ensure it stays fresh in your mind. This regular revision is crucial in converting short-term understanding into long-term retention.

Incorporating practical exercises, such as labs or real-world scenarios, is essential. These exercises allow you to apply the theoretical knowledge you've gained in a practical context. This application is not just beneficial for learning; it is crucial when it comes to preparing for the practical aspects of the exam. Many cybersecurity certification exams include practical components to test your ability to apply your knowledge in real-world scenarios. Practicing these skills enhances your ability to think critically and solve problems—key skills in any cybersecurity role.

Developing an in-depth study plan for a cybersecurity certification requires a multifaceted approach. It involves thoroughly understanding the exam syllabus, gathering diverse study materials, diversifying learning methods to cover different aspects of the syllabus, regularly revising challenging topics, and incorporating practical exercises. This comprehensive approach ensures that you are well-prepared for the exam and the practical application of your knowledge in the field.

Exam Strategies and Practice Resources

Effective exam strategies and the judicious use of practice resources are fundamental components of your preparation for a cybersecurity certification exam. These elements are not just supplementary; they are essential in ensuring that you are fully equipped to tackle the exam with confidence and proficiency.

Gaining familiarity with the format and style of the exam is the initial step in this strategic approach. Each certification exam has its unique structure—encompassing various questions, time allocations, and overall approaches. Understanding these elements in depth is vital. It enables you to tailor your study and practice sessions to mirror exam conditions as closely as possible. This familiarity minimizes surprises on the exam day and allows you to navigate the exam more efficiently.

The utilization of practice exams is a cornerstone of adequate exam preparation. These practice tests offer a multitude of benefits. First, they simulate the actual test environment, allowing you to adapt to the timing and pressure of the real exam. This experience is invaluable in enhancing time-management skills and reducing the anxiety that often accompanies high-stakes testing scenarios. Additionally, practice exams serve as a diagnostic tool, highlighting areas of strength and pinpointing topics where further study and focus are required. By regularly incorporating practice exams into your study regimen, you can track your progress over time, continually refining your understanding and approach.

Developing a nuanced strategy for tackling different questions is another crucial aspect of your exam preparation. For instance, multiple-choice questions often require a technique of elimination, where you systematically rule out the least likely answers to increase your chances of selecting the correct one. Scenario-based questions, on the other hand, demand an application of theoretical knowledge to practical, real-life situations that will test your ability to apply what you have learned in a more contextualized manner.

The skill of carefully reading and thoroughly understanding exam questions cannot be overemphasized. The pressure of a timed exam can sometimes lead to hasty reading and consequent misinterpretation of questions. Cultivating the habit of reading each question methodically, thereby ensuring that you grasp what is being asked before attempting an answer, is crucial. This practice helps avoid common errors, such as overlooking key details or misunderstanding the core requirement of the question.

Applying logical reasoning in determining the most appropriate answer is also a critical skill, particularly in cybersecurity exams, where the questions often involve complex problem-solving or decision-making scenarios. This skill goes beyond mere recall of information; it consists of synthesizing knowledge from various topics, drawing inferences, and making informed decisions based on the information presented in the question.

A comprehensive and well-rounded exam preparation strategy is the key to success in cybersecurity certification exams. This strategy encompasses a deep understanding of the exam format, regular practice with mock exams, tailored approaches to different question types, meticulous reading and comprehension, and applying logical reasoning in answering. With these components in place, you can approach your certification exam with greater assurance and a higher likelihood of success.

Maintaining Certification and Continuing Education

Maintaining your certification and committing to continuous education in the cybersecurity field is an ongoing, lifelong process that is as critical as obtaining the certification itself. Most cybersecurity certifications are not just one-time achievements; they require periodic renewal. This renewal process often involves engaging in professional development activities, undergoing additional training, or sometimes even retaking the certification exam. This continuous renewal process ensures that certified professionals remain up-to-date with the latest advancements and changes in the field.

Accumulating professional development credits is a common requirement for maintaining certifications. These credits can be earned in various ways, such as attending workshops, webinars, or industry conferences. Participating in such events is not just a means to accumulate credits; it is an opportunity to stay current with the evolving trends and developments in cybersecurity. Cybersecurity is dynamic, with new threats, technologies, and best practices emerging regularly. Engaging in continuous learning activities helps professionals adapt to these changes, ensuring they remain effective and relevant.

Undergoing additional training is another way to maintain certification. This training can take many forms, from online courses to hands-on workshops. Additional training not only helps in brushing up on existing skills but also provides an opportunity to learn about new areas within cybersecurity. This can be particularly beneficial for professionals who are looking to specialize in a specific area or to expand their expertise.

Retaking the certification exam is sometimes a requirement for renewal. This may seem daunting, but it is an effective way to ensure that certified professionals have maintained their level of expertise. Preparing for and retaking the exam necessitates thoroughly reviewing the subject matter, thereby reinforcing the professional's knowledge and skills.

Participating in professional groups and attending industry conferences are crucial for staying connected with the cybersecurity community. These gatherings are not just educational; they are networking opportunities, allowing professionals to connect with peers and industry leaders. Networking can lead to new insights, career opportunities, and collaborations. It's an invaluable aspect of professional growth and development in the cybersecurity field.

Online webinars and workshops are another effective way to stay informed and continue your education. These online resources offer convenience and flexibility, allowing professionals to learn from experts around the globe. They provide insights into the latest research, emerging threats, and innovative solutions in cybersecurity.

Maintaining your cybersecurity certification and committing to continuous education is a comprehensive process that involves accumulating professional development credits, additional training, and sometimes retaking certification exams. It is about staying abreast of industry trends and developments, actively participating in professional groups, attending conferences, and engaging in online learning opportunities. This continuous commitment to education and professional development is essential for remaining proficient and competitive in cybersecurity.

COMPREHENSIVE LIST OF CYBER CERTIFICATIONS

In the rapidly evolving cybersecurity domain, professional certifications play a pivotal role in validating the expertise and knowledge of practitioners. The following section provides a comprehensive list of cybersecurity certifications that was meticulously compiled to cater to various professional needs and career paths. This exhaustive list details the multiple certifications available. It delves into the certifying authorities behind each credential, offering insights into the unique focus and value they bring to cybersecurity. Accompanying each certification is information about the recommended audience, helping professionals at different career stages—from beginners to seasoned experts—identify which certifications align best with their career objectives and current skill levels. This list serves as a crucial resource for anyone looking to advance their career in cybersecurity, providing a clear and detailed roadmap of the certifications that can open doors to new opportunities and recognition in this dynamic and critical industry:

- **ISC2:** The ISC2 is a leading organization in information security. Renowned for its comprehensive suite of cybersecurity certifications, the ISC2 focuses on information security, software security, and cybersecurity management. Their certifications are designed to equip professionals with essential skills and knowledge across various cybersecurity domains. ISC2 certifications, including the well-known CISSP and other specialized credentials, are globally recognized and respected. These certifications cater to a wide range of professionals, from those who are new to the field to experienced security practitioners. They are intended to validate the expertise and skills necessary for various cybersecurity roles, ranging from hands-on technical positions to high-level management and leadership roles. The ISC2 is committed to promoting a secure and safe cyber world and supports this mission by providing education, certifications, and thought leadership in information security. Professionals seeking to certify their knowledge and advance their careers in information security often turn to the ISC2 for its rigorous and well-regarded certification programs.

- **CC:** The CC certification is an entry-level certification that is designed for individuals who are just beginning their journey in cybersecurity. It offers foundational knowledge and skills, laying the groundwork for a career in this area. The accreditation covers essential cybersecurity concepts, making it suitable for newcomers to the field or those transitioning from other IT-related roles. The CC certification is a stepping-stone for those who are aspiring to build a robust foundation before moving on to more advanced cybersecurity certifications.

- **Systems Security Certified Practitioner (SSCP):** The SSCP is tailored for IT administrators, network security professionals, and systems engineers who are involved in IT security's hands-on operational aspects. The certification covers access controls, security operations and administration, risk identification, incident response, and cryptography. It is ideal for professionals who have a practical role in their organization's operational IT security and want to validate their skills and experience with a formal certification.

- **CISSP:** The CISSP is one of the most sought-after and globally recognized certifications in information security. It is designed for experienced security practitioners, managers, and executives. The CISSP certification encompasses a broad range of topics in information security, including security and risk management, asset security, security architecture and engineering, communication and network security, identity and access management, security assessment and testing, security operations, and software development security. This certification is recommended for professionals with significant IT security experience who want to demonstrate their expertise on a global scale.
- **Certified Cloud Security Professional (CCSP):** The CCSP is aimed at IT and information security leaders who deal with cloud security architecture, design, operations, and service orchestration. This certification focuses on the advanced technical skills and knowledge that is required to design, manage, and secure data, applications, and infrastructure in the cloud. It is particularly beneficial for those in cloud security roles, such as enterprise architects, security administrators, systems engineers, and security consultants.
- **Certified in Governance, Risk, and Compliance (CGRC):** This certification is for professionals specializing in governance, risk management, and compliance within the information security domain. It addresses the need for a comprehensive understanding of these areas and their interplay in the organizational context. Professionals who would benefit most from the CGRC certification include compliance officers, risk managers, and professionals involved in IT governance. The certification validates their expertise in effectively implementing and managing governance, risk, and compliance strategies.
- **Certified Secure Software Lifecycle Professional (CSSLP):** The CSSLP certification is for professionals involved in the software development lifecycle and are responsible for ensuring software security. This certification covers secure software concepts, requirements, design, implementation, testing, and lifecycle management. It is highly recommended for software developers, engineers, and architects who are focused on building secure software from the ground up.
- **Information Systems Security Architecture Professional (ISSAP):** As a concentration under the CISSP, the ISSAP is designed for CISSP holders who wish to further specialize in the architecture aspects of information security. This certification is ideal for chief security architects and analysts, focusing on access control systems, telecommunications and network security, cryptography, requirements analysis and security standards, and technology-related risk management. It

is tailored for professionals who are responsible for developing, designing, and analyzing security solutions within an organizational framework.

- **Information Systems Security Engineering Professional (ISSEP):** Another concentration under the CISSP, the ISSEP certification is for those who integrate security into projects, applications, business processes, and information systems. This certification is aligned with systems engineering practices and emphasizes the importance of incorporating security into all facets of technology. It is particularly relevant for systems engineers, information assurance officers, and individuals responsible for establishing secure systems.

- **Information Systems Security Management Professional (ISSMP):** The ISSMP certification is a CISSP concentration focusing on information security management aspects. This certification suits individuals in leadership roles, such as chief information officers, chief information security officers, and senior IT managers. The ISSMP covers leadership and business management, risk management, policy development, and incident management—equipping professionals to lead and manage an organization's information security program effectively.

ISACA

ISACA is a globally recognized association focusing on IT governance, risk management, and information systems audit and security. It provides industry-leading certifications that are highly valued in IT governance, risk management, information systems auditing, and information security management. ISACA's certifications are known for their rigorous standards and are often pursued by professionals looking to advance their careers in these specialized areas of IT:

- **Certified Information Security Manager (CISM):** The CISM certification is designed for management-focused professionals who develop and manage an enterprise's information security program. The CISM certification covers information security governance, risk management, program development and management, and incident management. It is important for current or aspiring information security managers, IT consultants, and individuals responsible for overseeing or assessing an organization's information security.

- **Certified Information Systems Auditor (CISA):** The CISA certification is globally recognized as a standard of achievement for those who audit, control, monitor, and assess an organization's IT and business systems. The CISA certification covers domains including information systems auditing process, governance and management of IT, information systems acquisition, development and implementation, information systems operations and business resilience, and protection of information assets. This certification is ideal for IT auditors, audit managers, consultants, and security professionals.

- **Certified in Risk and Information Systems Control (CRISC):** The CRISC certification is aimed at IT professionals who identify and manage risks through developing, implementing, and maintaining information systems controls. The certification focuses on risk identification, assessment, evaluation, response, monitoring, information systems control design and implementation, and information systems control monitoring and maintenance. CRISC mainly benefits IT, risk, and control professionals, and business analysts in risk management and information systems control.

CompTIA

CompTIA is a widely recognized IT industry organization known for its certifications covering various aspects of technology, from foundational IT skills to advanced IT security. CompTIA certifications are valued for their practical approach and are often pursued by individuals looking to establish or advance careers in IT and cybersecurity. These certifications are well-regarded for providing foundational skills and are a common starting point for many IT professionals:

- **CompTIA Security+:** The CompTIA Security+ certification is designed for individuals who are seeking to start or grow their career in IT security. It covers foundational cybersecurity skills and knowledge, including threat management, cryptography, identity management, security infrastructure, and risk management. This certification is ideal for IT professionals seeking an understanding of security concepts and practices, and it serves as a springboard for more specialized security certifications. Security+ is widely recognized and often seen as an essential certification for IT professionals interested in cybersecurity.
- **CompTIA Cybersecurity Analyst (CySA+):** The CompTIA CySA+ certification is tailored for individuals who want to play a more proactive role in cybersecurity through analytics. It uses behavioral analytics skills to detect, prevent, and combat cybersecurity threats. The CySA+ certification covers areas like threat detection, data analysis, and interpretation of results to identify vulnerabilities, threats, and risks. It suits

IT security analysts, vulnerability analysts, threat intelligence analysts, and security operations center (SOC) professionals.

- **CompTIA Advanced Security Practitioner (CASP+):** The CASP+ certification is aimed at experienced IT security professionals and emphasizes advanced-level competency in risk management, enterprise security operations and architecture, research and collaboration, and enterprise security integration. CASP+ is well-suited for individuals in roles such as security architects, technical lead analysts, and application security engineers. This certification is unique in its focus on critical thinking and judgment across various security disciplines in complex environments.

- **CompTIA PenTest+:** The CompTIA PenTest+ certification is designed for cybersecurity professionals tasked with penetration testing and vulnerability management. This certification covers the entire penetration testing process, including planning, scoping, and managing weaknesses, not just exploiting them. It also includes management skills that are necessary to determine the network's resilience against attacks. Suitable for penetration testers, security consultants, vulnerability testers, and network security positions, PenTest+ is recognized for its emphasis on hands-on practical skills, covering both traditional and modern pen testing methods.

GIAC (Sans Institute)

GIAC specializes in certifications for IT security professionals, emphasizing practical, hands-on skills and knowledge. Renowned for their technical depth and rigor, GIAC certifications are recognized and respected worldwide in the IT security industry. These certifications cater to a wide range of specialized roles within cybersecurity, from intrusion detection and incident response to forensics, defense, and penetration testing. Professionals pursuing GIAC certifications often aim to demonstrate their expertise in specific technical areas of cybersecurity and to enhance their practical skills for specialized security roles:

- **GSEC:** The GSEC certification is aimed at professionals seeking foundational knowledge in information security. It covers many topics, including network security, access controls, cryptography, and risk management. The certification is ideal for individuals new to cybersecurity, IT professionals broadening their security knowledge, or those seeking a comprehensive understanding of security principles and practices. GSEC is often pursued as a starting point for careers in cybersecurity, providing a solid foundation for further specialization.

- **GIAC Certified Intrusion Analyst (GCIA):** GCIA focuses on network traffic analysis, intrusion detection, and defensive strategies. Professionals who pursue this certification typically work in roles such as network analysts, security analysts, or intrusion detection specialists. The certification emphasizes skills in monitoring networks, analyzing traffic for suspicious activity, and identifying signs of cyberattacks. It is ideal for individuals actively protecting networks from threats and wanting to deepen their expertise in intrusion detection and analysis.

- **GIAC Certified Incident Handler (GCIH):** The GCIH certification is designed for professionals who manage security incidents. This certification covers the strategies for understanding and defending against attacks, focusing on incident handling and response. Ideal candidates for GCIH include incident responders, SOC personnel, and system administrators. The certification equips professionals with the necessary skills to effectively manage and respond to various cybersecurity incidents, enhancing their ability to protect organizations from threats.

- **GIAC Certified Forensic Analyst (GCFA):** The GCFA certification is tailored for professionals specializing in forensic analysis, particularly in incident response and investigation. This certification is ideal for forensic analysts, incident responders, and IT security professionals responsible for investigating and analyzing data post-intrusion. It delves into advanced techniques for collecting and analyzing data from Windows and Linux computer systems, providing critical skills for uncovering the details of cybercrimes and malicious activities.

- **GIAC Certified Enterprise Defender (GCED):** GCED is designed for security professionals defending enterprise networks. The certification covers network security, defense-in-depth strategies, and security policy implementation. It suits network and system administrators, security consultants, and individuals safeguarding network infrastructure. The GCED certification helps professionals develop a comprehensive understanding of protecting complex enterprise environments from potential threats.

- **GIAC Certified Firewall Analyst (GCFW):** GCFW focuses on the skills required to design, configure, and monitor firewalls. This certification is ideal for network security professionals, firewall administrators, and IT personnel responsible for firewall management. It addresses various aspects of firewall administration, including configuration, policy development, and network traffic analysis, providing essential skills for securing network perimeters.

- **GIAC Web Application Penetration Tester (GWAPT):** GWAPT is designed for professionals securing web applications. It covers methodologies, tools, and techniques for testing web application security, making it suitable for penetration testers, web developers, and security auditors. This certification emphasizes hands-on skills for identifying and exploiting vulnerabilities in web applications, a critical area in cybersecurity, given the prevalence of web-based services.
- **GIAC Certified Unix Security Administrator (GCUX):** GCUX is tailored for the security and auditing of Unix and Linux systems. This certification is ideal for system administrators and security professionals securing Unix/Linux environments. It covers key aspects of Unix security, including user and service security, and is essential for professionals working in Unix-based environments.
- **GIAC Certified Windows Security Administrator (GCWN):** The GCWN certification, similar to GCUX, focuses on securing and auditing Windows systems. It addresses security settings, audit policies, and best practices for Windows security, making it suitable for Windows system administrators and security professionals. This certification is crucial for those responsible for maintaining the security and integrity of Windows environments in organizations.
- **GIAC Certified Penetration Tester (GPEN):** GPEN is for professionals conducting comprehensive penetration tests. It is ideal for penetration testers, ethical hackers, and security consultants, covering planning, scoping, and executing penetration tests. The certification emphasizes practical skills in ethical hacking and penetration testing methodologies, focusing on identifying and exploiting vulnerabilities in networks and systems.
- **GIAC Security Leadership (GSLC):** GSLC is designed for individuals leading or directing an organization's security program. This certification covers governance, security policy, risk management, and legal aspects of information security, making it ideal for security managers and directors. The GSLC certification equips professionals with the knowledge to manage and lead comprehensive security programs within organizations effectively.
- **GIAC Certified Project Manager (GCPM):** The GCPM certification focuses on managing IT projects, particularly those with significant information security components. This certification suits project managers, IT managers, and security professionals overseeing projects. It addresses the unique challenges of managing IT and information security projects, combining project management principles with a strong emphasis on security.

- **GIAC Certified Wireless Analysis (GAWN):** GAWN is tailored for professionals securing wireless networks. It covers wireless security technologies and protocols, making it ideal for network administrators and security professionals working with wireless technologies. This certification provides essential skills for protecting wireless networks against security threats and vulnerabilities.
- **GIAC Certified Industrial Control Systems (ICS) Security Professional (GICSP):** The GICSP certification focuses on securing critical infrastructure systems. It is useful for professionals in environments using ICS, Supervisory Control and Data Acquisition, and other operational technologies, such as in the energy, utilities, and manufacturing sectors. This certification provides skills and knowledge to secure these specialized systems, which are crucial for national and industrial infrastructure.
- **GIAC Critical Controls Certification (GCCC):** GCCC focuses on implementing critical security controls. It is suitable for professionals who are responsible for developing and maintaining a security controls framework, including security professionals, auditors, and IT managers. The certification emphasizes the practical implementation of critical security controls in organizations, enhancing their overall security posture.
- **GIAC Certified Forensics Examiner (GCFE):** GCFE is focused on forensic analysis of Windows systems and is for forensic analysts, incident responders, and law enforcement personnel. The certification covers techniques for collecting and analyzing data from Windows systems, providing skills essential for investigating digital crimes and malicious activities.
- **GIAC Reverse Engineering Malware (GREM):** GREM is designed for professionals analyzing and responding to malware incidents. It covers reverse-engineering techniques for dissecting malware, making it suitable for incident responders, forensic analysts, and IT security professionals. The certification provides critical skills for understanding the inner workings of malicious software and developing effective defenses against it.
- **GIAC Cloud Security Automation (GCSA):** The GCSA certification focuses on securing cloud environments through automation. It suits cloud security professionals and DevOps engineers responsible for implementing security in cloud infrastructures. The certification emphasizes using automation tools and techniques to enhance security in cloud environments, a growing necessity in the rapidly evolving cloud landscape.

- **GIAC Continuous Monitoring (GMON):** GMON is designed for professionals involved in continuous security monitoring. It covers skills and techniques for maintaining awareness of information security, vulnerabilities, and threats. This certification suits security analysts and professionals working in SOCs, emphasizing the importance of continuous monitoring in detecting and responding to security incidents.
- **GIAC Certified Detection Analyst (GCDA):** GCDA focuses on threat detection and analysis skills. It is suitable for security analysts and professionals in threat detection roles. The certification covers techniques for identifying and analyzing cyber threats, providing essential skills for proactive cybersecurity defense.
- **GIAC Certified Security Awareness (GCSA):** GCSA is aimed at professionals who are responsible for developing and managing security awareness programs. It covers the strategies and techniques for promoting cybersecurity awareness in organizations. This certification is ideal for security managers, IT professionals, and anyone educating employees about security best practices.
- **GIAC Security Expert (GSE):** The GSE certification is one of the most prestigious and challenging certifications in IT security and is designed for top-level security experts. It covers various security topics and requires written and practical testing. The GSE is geared toward seasoned security professionals seeking to demonstrate expertise across various security disciplines.

EC-Council

EC-Council is renowned for its cybersecurity certifications, focusing on ethical hacking, penetration testing, forensics, and information security management. Their certifications are designed to provide practical, relevant skills and knowledge to professionals in various cybersecurity roles. EC-Council certifications are recognized globally and are often pursued by those who are seeking to specialize in specific cybersecurity disciplines—from technical hands-on roles to strategic management positions:

- **CEH:** The CEH certification is one of the most prevalent cybersecurity certifications focused on ethical hacking. It teaches professionals how to think and act like hackers (legally and ethically) to identify vulnerabilities and weaknesses in systems. The certification is ideal for security officers, auditors, security professionals, site administrators, and anyone concerned about network infrastructure security.
- **EC-Council Certified Security Analyst (ECSA):** ECSA goes beyond the basic hacking techniques to provide a deeper understanding of

penetration testing methodologies. It covers testing modern infrastructures, operating systems, and application environments. This certification suits IT professionals pursuing a career in ethical hacking or penetration testing.

- **Licensed Penetration Tester (LPT):** The LPT is a step above the CEH and ECSA, offering a more advanced certification in penetration testing. This certification tests the candidate's ability to perform penetration tests in various complex scenarios and environments. It is ideal for experienced penetration testers who want to prove their expertise in finding and exploiting system vulnerabilities.

- **Computer Hacking Forensic Investigator (C|HFI):** C|HFI focuses on the skills required to detect hacking attacks, extract evidence to report the crime, and conduct audits to prevent future attacks. This certification suits police and other law enforcement personnel, defense and military personnel, e-business security professionals, and legal professionals.

- **Certified Network Defender (CND):** The CND certification is designed for network administrators. It focuses on protecting, detecting, and responding to threats on the network. It covers a comprehensive range of network security topics, making it ideal for professionals who are responsible for managing and ensuring the integrity of network infrastructure.

- **Certified Chief Information Security Officer (CCISO):** CCISO is an executive-level certification focusing on the knowledge and skills required to govern and oversee an information security program. It suits current and aspiring C-level executives, particularly those focusing on information security, risk management, and technical strategy.

- **Certified SOC Analyst (CSA):** The CSA certification is designed for current and aspiring SOC analysts and focuses on the fundamentals of SOC operations and procedures. It covers the skills necessary for managing and responding to security incidents, making it perfect for individuals who are working in or aiming to work in SOCs.

- **Certified Threat Intelligence Analyst (CTIA):** CTIA is focused on the skills needed to gather, analyze, and interpret threat intelligence effectively. This certification is ideal for network defenders, SOC analysts, threat intelligence analysts, security architects, and incident response team members.

- **Certified Encryption Specialist (ECES):** The ECES certification covers encryption technologies and how they can be used to secure data in transit, at rest, and in various storage mediums. It suits individuals working in or with data encryption and security responsibilities.

- **Certified Application Security Engineer (CASE):** CASE focuses on application security and is designed for software application developers. It covers critical security principles to fortify applications throughout the software development life cycle, making it ideal for developers responsible for designing and building secure applications.
- **Certified Incident Handler (ECIH):** The ECIH certification is tailored for individuals who deal with incident handling and response. It covers the skills to handle and respond to various security incidents, identify vulnerabilities, and take preventive actions. This certification suits incident handlers, risk assessment administrators, penetration testers, and cybersecurity professionals.
- **Certified Security Specialist (ECSS):** ECSS is an entry-level certification that covers information security basics and best practices. It is suitable for anyone new to cybersecurity, IT professionals looking to gain a broad understanding of security concepts, and individuals seeking a career in cybersecurity.
- **Certified Disaster Recovery Professional (EDRP):** The EDRP certification focuses on developing business continuity and disaster recovery plans. It is for those responsible for creating and maintaining these plans, ensuring the continuation of business processes during a disaster or interruption.
- **Certified Internet of Things (IoT) Practitioner (CIoTP):** CIoTP is designed for IoT technology and security professionals. It covers the essentials of IoT security, including securing IoT networks, devices, and data. This certification is ideal for IT professionals in IoT device development, deployment, and management.

Cisco

Cisco is a leading name in networking and telecommunications, and its certifications are highly regarded in the IT industry. Cisco's certifications, particularly in network and cybersecurity, are designed to equip professionals with the skills needed to design, implement, manage, and secure advanced network systems. Cisco offers a range of certifications from entry-level to expert-level, catering to various aspects of network security and operations:

- **Cisco Certified Network Associate (CCNA) Security:** The CCNA Security certification validates the skills required to secure Cisco networks. It covers core security technologies, installation, troubleshooting, and monitoring of network devices to maintain data and device integrity, confidentiality, and availability. This certification is ideal for network professionals and administrators who want to specialize in network security and is a stepping-stone for higher-level Cisco certifications in security.

- **Cisco Certified CyberOps Associate:** This certification is designed for SOC roles, focusing on cybersecurity fundamentals, policies, and procedures used in SOCs. It covers security concepts, monitoring, host-based analysis, network intrusion analysis, and security policies and procedures. The CyberOps Associate certification suits entry-level cybersecurity professionals and analysts in SOCs.

- **Cisco Certified CyberOps Professional:** Building upon the associate level, this professional certification delves deeper into cybersecurity operations. It focuses on advanced topics such as incident response, threat detection, and system hardening. This certification is intended for cybersecurity professionals seeking to advance their cybersecurity operations and incident response skills.

- **Cisco Certified Specialist—Security Core:** This certification recognizes core security skills. It covers foundational security knowledge, including network security, cloud security, content security, endpoint protection, secure network access, and visibility and enforcement. It suits professionals who want to establish a strong foundation in core security technologies and practices.

- **Cisco Certified Specialist—Identity and Access Management:** This certification focuses on identity and access management within Cisco's security solutions. It includes securing network access, identity management, and access control strategies. Ideal for network security professionals, this certification is crucial for those managing identity and access in Cisco environments.

- **Cisco Certified Specialist—Security Operations:** This specialist certification covers the skills needed in security operations, including incident response, network forensics, and threat hunting. It is designed for security analysts and professionals working in SOCs who want to hone their skills in detecting and responding to cybersecurity threats.

- **Cisco Certified Specialist—Network Security VPN Implementation (SVPN):** The SVPN certification focuses on implementing Virtual Private Network (VPN) solutions in a Cisco environment. It covers VPN technologies, secure communications, remote access, and troubleshooting of VPN connections. This certification suits network engineers and administrators who implement and maintain VPN solutions.

- **Cisco Certified Specialist—Network Security Firepower:** This certification concerns Cisco's Firepower security technologies. It covers the deployment, management, and troubleshooting of Cisco Firepower

Threat Defense and Firepower 6.x. It is ideal for network security professionals who are responsible for managing security solutions using Cisco Firepower.

- **Cisco Certified Specialist—Network Security Identity Management:** This certification focuses on identity management within network security, particularly in Cisco environments. It includes topics like secure access, identity management, and the configuration of identity management solutions. It is geared toward network and security professionals who specialize in identity solutions.

- **Cisco Certified Specialist—Network Security Email Security:** This certification covers the skills required to secure email in a Cisco environment. It addresses topics like email security, threat defense, policy enforcement, and best practices in email protection. Ideal for professionals managing email security, this certification is important for ensuring secure email communication in organizations.

- **Cisco Certified Specialist—Network Security Web Security:** This certification is focused on securing web access in Cisco environments. It includes web security, cloud-delivered security solutions, and advanced threat protection. It is for network security professionals responsible for web security solutions in organizations using Cisco technologies.

- **Cisco Certified Specialist—Network Security Secure Access:** This certification emphasizes secure access in network environments, particularly with Cisco's security solutions. It covers secure access technologies, TrustSec, identity services, and access control policies. It is suitable for network security professionals focusing on secure access solutions.

- **Cisco Certified Specialist—Network Security Firepower Threat Defense:** This certification focuses on Cisco's Firepower Threat Defense technology. It covers this technology's configuration, management, and operation, including threat detection, network visibility, and security intelligence. Ideal for network security professionals, this certification is key for those managing Cisco's Firepower solutions.

- **Cisco Certified Specialist—Network Security ISE:** This certification centers on Cisco's Identity Services Engine (ISE). It covers ISE architecture, implementation, and troubleshooting. This certification is for network security professionals who deploy and manage Cisco ISE solutions.

- **Cisco Certified Specialist—Network Security AMP:** This certification focuses on Cisco's Advanced Malware Protection (AMP) technology. It covers malware protection, file reputation, file analysis, and endpoint security. It suits security professionals who manage AMP solutions for endpoint security and threat protection.

- **Cisco Certified Specialist—Network Security ESA:** Focused on Cisco's Email Security Appliance (ESA), this certification covers email security, threat defense, policy enforcement, and best practices in managing ESA. It is ideal for professionals responsible for email security in Cisco environments.

- **Cisco Certified Specialist—Network Security Web Content Security:** This certification addresses the skills needed to manage Cisco's Web Security Appliance (WSA). It covers web content security, threat defense, policy enforcement, and administration of WSA. This certification is suitable for professionals managing web content security in Cisco environments.

Amazon Web Services (AWS)

AWS is a comprehensive—and the largest—cloud provider in the world, offering over 200 fully featured services from data centers globally. AWS certifications are highly sought after in the IT industry because they validate expertise in cloud architecture, engineering, and operations on AWS. These certifications are designed for IT professionals who are looking to build and validate their cloud computing skills, with a focus on various aspects of AWS services:

- **AWS Certified Security—Specialty:** The AWS Certified Security—Specialty certification is designed to provide a secure production environment for individuals who fully understand AWS security services and features. It validates an individual's ability to demonstrate an understanding of specialized data classifications and AWS data protection mechanisms. The certification also covers data encryption methods, secure Internet protocols, and a deep knowledge of AWS security services and features in order to build and maintain a secure and compliant cloud environment.

This certification is particularly relevant for security professionals with roles such as security engineer, security consultant, security architect, or related positions. Candidates are expected to be familiar with AWS workloads, have a strong understanding of AWS security controls, and have experience securing AWS environments. It is ideal for those looking to demonstrate their ability to design and implement security solutions to secure the AWS platform and who want to validate their advanced skills in managing and securing AWS-based applications.

This specialized certification helps professionals highlight their expertise in AWS security, distinguishing them in an increasingly important field as more organizations move to cloud-based infrastructures. It is a valuable asset for those who are looking to advance their careers in AWS cloud security and to ensure the protection of sensitive data and systems in the cloud.

Google Cloud

Google Cloud is a prominent player in the cloud computing market, offering a suite of cloud services and solutions. Google Cloud certifications are designed to validate professionals' expertise in various aspects of Google Cloud technology, focusing on designing, developing, managing, and administering application infrastructure and data solutions on Google Cloud. These certifications are particularly valuable for IT professionals specializing in cloud computing and security within the Google Cloud ecosystem:

- **Google Cloud Professional Cloud Security Engineer:** The Google Cloud Professional Cloud Security Engineer certification validates an individual's ability to design and implement a secure infrastructure on the Google Cloud Platform. This certification covers a wide range of topics, including configuring access within a cloud solution environment, managing operations in a cloud solution environment, and ensuring data protection and compliance. It suits cloud professionals who are responsible for managing and securing cloud applications and infrastructure. This certification demonstrates an individual's expertise in using Google Cloud security best practices and understanding security controls and techniques in a cloud environment.
- **Google Cloud Security—Identity and Access Management (Specialization):** This specialization focuses on the crucial aspects of identity and access management (IAM) within Google Cloud. It covers managing user identities, access control, and security policies, ensuring that only authorized and authenticated users can access resources. This specialization is ideal for cloud administrators and security professionals who are responsible for managing user access to Google Cloud services, offering in-depth knowledge and skills in securing identities and managing access effectively.
- **Google Cloud Security—Asset and Vulnerability Management (Specialization):** The specialization in Asset and Vulnerability Management on Google Cloud is designed to provide deep insights into asset management, vulnerability analysis, and the associated security protocols within the Google Cloud infrastructure. It involves managing cloud assets, understanding cloud vulnerabilities, and applying best

practices to mitigate risks. Professionals who focus on this area are typically responsible for maintaining the security posture of cloud assets and ensuring compliance with security standards, making this specialization essential for cloud security professionals and system administrators.

- **Google Cloud Security—Security Operations (Specialization):** The Security Operations specialization within Google Cloud targets the operational aspects of cloud security. It encompasses monitoring, logging, incident response, and threat detection within the Google Cloud environment. This specialization is tailored for security operation professionals, including those working in SOCs, who maintain continuous vigilance over cloud-based systems. It gives them the expertise to effectively detect, respond to, and mitigate security incidents in the cloud.

Red Hat

Red Hat is a leading provider of open-source software solutions, including its widely used Red Hat Enterprise Linux (RHEL) platform. Red Hat certifications are respected and recognized in the IT industry for their focus on practical skills and comprehensive knowledge of Red Hat systems and software. These certifications are especially valuable for IT professionals working in environments that rely heavily on Linux and open-source technologies. Red Hat's security certifications specifically target professionals who are responsible for the security of Linux systems and seek to validate their skills in securing Red Hat Enterprise Linux environments:

- **Red Hat Certified Specialist in Security: Linux:** The Red Hat Certified Specialist in Security: Linux certification is designed for IT professionals responsible for implementing and managing security on RHEL systems. This certification validates a candidate's ability to secure RHEL systems against unauthorized access and to configure various security-related aspects of the system, including security-enhanced Linux (SELinux), auditing, and security compliance standards. It covers critical areas such as using SELinux for system control, managing users and passwords, updating software for security, and understanding the mechanisms of system logging and auditing. This certification is ideal for system administrators, security administrators, and RHEL system engineers who wish to demonstrate their expertise in securing RHEL systems.

- **Red Hat Certified Engineer (RHCE) in Security: Linux:** The RHCE in Security: Linux certification is a higher-level certification that builds upon the knowledge and skills covered in the Red Hat Certified System Administrator (RHCSA) and RHCE certifications. This certification is focused on advanced security and networking skills in RHEL environments. It encompasses a deeper understanding of securing network services, advanced firewall configurations, and security policy enforcement. Candidates for this certification are expected to have proficiency in creating and managing secure, robust, and high-availability services on RHEL. The RHCE in Security: Linux certification suits experienced Linux system administrators and engineers who want to validate their skills in securing and optimizing RHEL systems, particularly in complex and large-scale environments.

4

PERSONAL DEVELOPMENT AND SOFT SKILLS IN CYBERSECURITY

In cybersecurity, technical understanding is undeniably crucial, but the importance of soft skills, particularly communication skills, cannot be overstated. Effective communication is a cornerstone of successful cybersecurity practices because it bridges the gap between complex technical issues and various stakeholders who may not have a technical background. This chapter delves into the multifaceted role of communication skills in cybersecurity, encompassing everything from crafting clear reports and presenting findings to mastering interpersonal communication with teams and clients to handling communication during crises and incident responses.

Effective communication in cybersecurity roles involves conveying complex technical information clearly and understandably. Cybersecurity professionals must often explain intricate technical details to nontechnical staff, management, or external stakeholders. Translating these details into comprehensible language ensures that crucial information is understood and acted upon correctly.

Writing reports and presenting findings is another critical aspect of communication in cybersecurity. Reports should be concise, well-structured, and tailored to the audience's level of technical understanding. They should provide clear insights into cybersecurity risks, vulnerabilities, and recommendations for mitigations. Similarly, presenting findings—whether in meetings, conferences, or other forums—requires clarity, confidence, and the ability to engage the audience. This involves a thorough understanding of the content and skills in public speaking and presentation.

Interpersonal communication with teams and clients is equally important. Cybersecurity professionals work collaboratively and must communicate effectively with colleagues, management, and external clients. This involves active listening, empathy, and the ability to negotiate and resolve conflicts. Building strong relationships based on effective communication can enhance teamwork and lead to more successful cybersecurity outcomes.

Crisis and incident response communication is a critical skill in cybersecurity. During a security incident or breach, clear and timely communication is essential. It involves coordinating with different teams, informing stakeholders about the situation, and providing clear instructions on the response plan. Communicating effectively under pressure is crucial in managing the incident efficiently and minimizing its impact.

Communication skills are vital in the field of cybersecurity. They enable professionals to convey technical information, write effective reports, present findings, engage in productive interpersonal interactions, and manage communications during crises. Developing strong communication skills is an essential part of personal development for anyone aspiring to excel in cybersecurity.

TEAMWORK AND COLLABORATION

Teamwork and collaboration are essential components of effective cybersecurity practices. Working well within a team and across various departments becomes crucial in an environment where threats are complex and multifaceted. This section explores the dynamics of building and managing cybersecurity teams, the significance of collaborative problem-solving during cyber incidents, and the importance of cross-functional collaboration with IT and other departments. It reviews case studies that highlight successful examples of cybersecurity teamwork.

Building and managing cybersecurity teams requires a nuanced understanding of the diverse skills and expertise needed to address various cybersecurity challenges. Effective team management involves assembling a group of skilled individuals and fostering an environment where collaboration and communication are prioritized. It is about creating a culture where team members feel valued, their insights are welcomed, and their professional development is supported. Effective cybersecurity teams often consist of members with complementary skills, ensuring a well-rounded approach to tackling security issues.

Collaborative problem-solving in cyber incidents is vital. Cybersecurity incidents often require rapid responses and the ability to work efficiently under pressure. Teams that can collaborate effectively are better equipped to analyze incidents, develop response strategies, and implement solutions swiftly. This collaboration extends beyond the cybersecurity team; it involves working closely with other departments to ensure a comprehensive and coordinated response.

Cross-functional collaboration with IT and other departments is also essential in the broader scope of organizational cybersecurity. Cybersecurity is not a siloed function; it intersects with various aspects of an organization's operations. Effective cybersecurity strategies often require input and cooperation from multiple IT, legal, human resources, and finance departments. Establishing strong lines of communication and understanding between these departments is crucial for addressing security risks comprehensively and ensuring organization-wide compliance with cybersecurity policies.

Teamwork and collaboration are fundamental to the success of cybersecurity initiatives. They involve building diverse and effective teams, fostering collaborative problem-solving during incidents, engaging in cross-functional cooperation across the organization, and learning from real-world examples of successful teamwork. Cultivating these aspects of teamwork and collaboration is essential for any cybersecurity professional who is looking to make a meaningful impact in their role.

PROBLEM-SOLVING AND CRITICAL THINKING

In cybersecurity's intricate and ever-evolving landscape, problem-solving and critical thinking skills are indispensable. These abilities are central to identifying, analyzing, and mitigating cyber threats and vulnerabilities. This section delves into the multifaceted nature of cyber problem-solving, the indispensable role of critical thinking in cybersecurity analysis and decision making, the need for innovative and creative solutions in complex cyber challenges, and the importance of fostering a mindset dedicated to continuous learning and improvement.

Cyber problem-solving approaches in cybersecurity are diverse and require a blend of analytical skills, technical knowledge, and strategic thinking. Cybersecurity professionals often face complex problems that demand a comprehensive understanding of network systems, software vulnerabilities, and potential attack vectors. Effective problem-solving in this context involves identifying symptoms of security breaches and understanding the underlying causes. This process often entails thoroughly analyzing system configurations, examining logs for unusual activities, and staying informed about the latest threat intelligence. Problem-solving in cybersecurity is dynamic, requiring professionals to be agile and adaptive, ready to respond to new challenges.

Critical thinking is a cornerstone of cybersecurity analysis and decision making. It involves processing large volumes of information and critically assessing its significance and reliability. In cybersecurity, where data and information flow is immense, critical thinking enables professionals to discern between relevant and irrelevant data, identify false positives, and make judicious decisions based on the available evidence. This skill is essential in developing effective threat detection, response, and prevention strategies. It involves questioning assumptions, evaluating arguments, and synthesizing information from various sources to make informed decisions.

Creativity and innovation are often as crucial as technical expertise in addressing complex cyber challenges. The rapidly evolving nature of cyber threats demands solutions that are effective and forward-thinking. Creative solutions may involve developing unique algorithms for threat detection, designing bespoke security architectures, or implementing unconventional strategies for user education and awareness. This creativity is about new technologies and thinking outside the box regarding policies, processes, and people management to enhance cybersecurity.

Developing a mindset geared toward continuous learning and improvement is fundamental in cybersecurity. Continuous technological advancements and changes in threat landscapes characterize the field. Professionals must therefore commit to lifelong learning and staying abreast of new technologies, methodologies, and best practices. This mindset encompasses a proactive approach to skill development, embracing new challenges as opportunities for growth, and being open to new ideas and perspectives. It involves regular self-assessment, seeking feedback, and leveraging mistakes and failures as learning experiences.

Problem-solving and critical thinking are pivotal skills in cybersecurity. Effective problem-solving involves a systematic approach to understanding and mitigating cyber threats, while critical thinking is crucial in making informed and strategic decisions. Creativity and innovation are essential in developing solutions to complex challenges, and a mindset of continuous learning and improvement is crucial for staying relevant and effective in this fast-paced and dynamic field. Cultivating these skills and attitudes is essential for any cybersecurity professional who is seeking to make a significant impact and sustain a successful career in this vital sector.

STRESS MANAGEMENT AND WORK-LIFE BALANCE

Cybersecurity, known for its high stakes and fast-paced environment, can often be a source of significant stress for professionals. The critical nature of protecting information and systems from cyber threats brings a high level of responsibility and, at times, intense pressure. This section explores the crucial aspects of managing stress in high-stakes cyber roles, implementing strategies for maintaining work-life balance, understanding the importance of mental health in cybersecurity, and building resilience in this high-pressure field.

Managing stress in high-stakes cyber roles is paramount. Cybersecurity professionals often face urgent deadlines, complex problem-solving situations, and the continuous need to stay ahead of rapidly evolving cyber threats. These demands can lead to high levels of occupational stress. Effective stress management in this context involves recognizing the signs of stress, such as burnout or fatigue, and taking proactive steps to address them. This might include setting realistic goals, prioritizing tasks, and ensuring sufficient downtime. Practicing relaxation techniques like meditation, deep breathing exercises, or engaging in physical activities can also effectively manage stress.

Strategies for maintaining work-life balance are essential in the cybersecurity profession. The demanding nature of the job can sometimes blur the boundaries between professional and personal life, leading to work-life conflicts. Cybersecurity professionals should set clear boundaries between work and personal time to maintain balance. This might involve scheduling specific work hours and ensuring that they are adhered to, delegating tasks when necessary, and making time for personal activities and family. Employers can also play a role by offering flexible working arrangements and encouraging a culture that values work-life balance.

The importance of mental health in cybersecurity must not be understated. The high-pressure environment can take a toll on mental well-being, making it essential for cybersecurity professionals to be mindful of their mental health. This includes seeking support when needed, whether through professional counseling, peer support groups, or mental health resources provided by the employer. Creating an open culture where mental health is discussed and addressed can help reduce the stigma and encourage individuals to seek help when needed.

Building resilience is key to thriving in a high-pressure field like cybersecurity. Resilience involves the ability to adapt to stressful situations, recover from setbacks, and continue functioning effectively. It can be developed through various means, such as maintaining a positive outlook, building strong support networks, and continuously developing one's skills and knowledge. Resilient professionals are better equipped to handle the challenges and pressures of cybersecurity work, making it an essential quality to cultivate.

Stress management, work-life balance, mental health, and resilience are critical components for success and well-being in cybersecurity. By adopting effective stress management techniques, maintaining a healthy work-life balance, being attentive to mental health needs, and building resilience, cybersecurity professionals can navigate the challenges of their high-stakes roles while maintaining their well-being and effectiveness.

5

BUILDING A STRONG PORTFOLIO

Building a solid portfolio in cybersecurity requires a nuanced understanding of theoretical knowledge and its practical applications. This involves an in-depth exploration of how cybersecurity concepts, often learned theoretically, can be effectively applied in real-world scenarios. The essence of this process lies in recognizing that the true test of any cybersecurity strategy or model is in its application against real and evolving digital threats.

A key element in this journey is the study of real-world cyberattacks. These cases provide more than historical context; they offer critical insights into the practical implications of cybersecurity principles. Such studies reveal the complexities and challenges that arise when theoretical models are applied in real-life situations. Through these studies, learners can gain a deeper understanding of the field, moving beyond theoretical knowledge to grasp cybersecurity's subtleties and practical nuances.

Another important aspect is the hands-on application of knowledge through projects. These projects bridge the gap between theoretical concepts and practical applications, allowing learners to test and refine their skills. They enhance understanding and contribute significantly to a professional portfolio, demonstrating an individual's ability to apply theoretical knowledge in practical, real-world situations.

Staying current with the latest trends and technologies in cybersecurity is also vital. The field is dynamic, with new threats and technologies emerging regularly. Keeping abreast of these changes ensures one's skills and knowledge remain relevant and practical. This continuous learning and adaptation are crucial for maintaining a robust and up-to-date portfolio.

Critically evaluating the effectiveness of theoretical models in real scenarios is essential. This involves the testing of existing theories and models against real-world situations in order to understand their practical applications, strengths, and limitations. Such critical analysis not only deepens one's understanding of cybersecurity but also contributes to the field by identifying potential areas for improvement.

Building a solid cybersecurity portfolio requires a balanced approach that combines theoretical knowledge with practical application. It necessitates continuous learning, adaptation, and a critical evaluation of how theoretical concepts fare in the face of real-world cybersecurity challenges. This approach ensures a deep understanding of the field and the development of a portfolio that showcases one's skills and readiness to tackle the dynamic challenges of cybersecurity.

BUILDING A TRACK RECORD

Building a track record in cybersecurity is an intricate and multifaceted journey that encompasses gaining hands-on experience, contributing to collaborative endeavors, engaging in competitive environments, meticulously documenting progress, and actively participating in the cybersecurity community.

Starting with gaining experience through internships and entry-level positions, this phase is crucial for those embarking on a cybersecurity career. These roles offer a rare glimpse into the practical aspects of cybersecurity operations, allowing individuals to apply theoretical knowledge in real-world scenarios. Working in these environments exposes one to challenges and situations that textbooks cannot replicate. These early career experiences are invaluable, providing a solid foundation of practical skills and an understanding of the day-to-day realities of working in cybersecurity. Moreover, they offer the opportunity to observe and learn from seasoned professionals, understand workplace dynamics, and develop a professional work ethic.

In parallel, contributing to open-source cybersecurity projects is an excellent way to build a track record. Open-source projects offer unique platforms for aspiring cybersecurity professionals to apply their skills, learn new techniques, and contribute to meaningful projects. By engaging with these projects, individuals refine their technical abilities and demonstrate their commitment to advancing the field. Such contributions stand out in a professional portfolio, showcasing a proactive approach to learning and a willingness to contribute to the broader cybersecurity community.

Participating in cybersecurity competitions and hackathons is another critical component of building a solid track record. These events are about showcasing technical skills and developing strategic thinking, problem-solving abilities, and the capacity to work under pressure. They offer a simulated environment to confront complex cybersecurity challenges, often mirroring real-world scenarios. Excelling in these competitions can significantly enhance one's reputation and provide tangible proof of one's skills and competitive spirit.

Documenting and reflecting on personal cybersecurity projects is equally important. This involves completing projects and taking the time to analyze and understand each step of the process. It is crucial to keep a detailed record of the challenges encountered, the strategies employed to overcome them, and the outcomes achieved. Such documentation serves as a learning tool, allowing one to reflect on their progress and areas for improvement. Moreover, a well-documented portfolio of projects is a powerful asset when showcasing one's abilities to potential employers or clients because it provides a clear, tangible record of one's skills and accomplishments.

Seeking mentorship and networking within the cybersecurity community is the final puzzle. Mentorship from experienced professionals can provide invaluable guidance, insights, and support. It can accelerate learning, offer new perspectives, and provide advice on career development. On the other hand, networking is essential for building professional relationships, staying abreast of industry trends, and uncovering new opportunities. Engaging with the community through conferences, workshops, and online forums fosters a sense of belonging and provides a platform for collaboration and exchanging ideas.

Building a track record in cybersecurity is a comprehensive and dynamic process. It encompasses gaining practical experience, contributing to communal projects, participating in competitive scenarios, documenting personal learning experiences, and actively engaging with the professional community. Each of these elements plays a crucial role in developing a well-rounded professional profile, showcasing one's skills, and paving the way for a successful career in cybersecurity.

SHOWCASING PROBLEM-SOLVING SKILLS

Showcasing problem-solving skills in cybersecurity is essential to building a solid professional identity. It involves demonstrating proficiency in handling technical aspects and navigating the complexities and unpredictability inherent in cybersecurity. This multifaceted approach to problem-solving is what sets proficient cybersecurity professionals apart.

Developing a portfolio of resolved cybersecurity issues is foundational in showcasing problem-solving skills. This portfolio should include a detailed account of various cybersecurity challenges and the strategies employed to address them. Each case in the portfolio is a testament to one's ability to diagnose, strategize, and resolve complex cybersecurity problems. This portfolio becomes a tangible showcase of one's expertise, detailing the nature of the issues tackled, the solutions implemented, and the results achieved. It is a living document that demonstrates one's technical prowess and illustrates a track record of successful problem resolution.

Demonstrating skills in identifying and mitigating risks is another key element. This involves showcasing the ability to foresee potential cybersecurity threats and implementing measures to prevent them. Highlighting such proactive risk management skills is crucial, as it shows an understanding of the broader implications of cybersecurity threats and the foresight to counteract them. It is about being one step ahead, anticipating vulnerabilities, and devising robust defense mechanisms.

Highlighting experience in troubleshooting and crisis management is also vital. In the dynamic world of cybersecurity, crises are inevitable. The ability to remain calm under pressure, think critically, and rapidly devise solutions is invaluable. Showcasing this experience highlights an individual's resilience and capability to handle high-stress situations effectively. This includes technical troubleshooting and managing the crisis from a holistic perspective, which often involves communication with various stakeholders, decision making under uncertainty, and rapid response coordination.

Showcasing adaptability in diverse cybersecurity scenarios is crucial. Cybersecurity challenges come in many forms and can arise in various environments. Demonstrating the ability to adapt to different scenarios—whether a small-scale security breach in a startup or a large-scale cyberattack in a multinational corporation—is a testament to a professional's versatility. This adaptability reflects a deep understanding of the field and an ability to apply knowledge and skills in various contexts.

Finally, emphasizing creative solutions to complex cybersecurity challenges is essential. Cybersecurity is not just about following protocols; it is often about thinking outside the box to find innovative solutions to complex problems. Highlighting instances where creative thinking led to successful outcomes is important. This demonstrates technical skill and a willingness to explore uncharted territories and think creatively to devise effective solutions.

Showcasing problem-solving skills in cybersecurity involves demonstrating a blend of technical proficiency, risk management ability, crisis handling, adaptability, and creative thinking. It is about building a narrative that highlights an individual's skill set and underscores their ability to navigate and resolve the complex challenges that characterize the cybersecurity landscape. This comprehensive approach differentiates a competent cybersecurity professional and paves the way for a successful career in this dynamic field.

GAINING CONFIDENCE AND CREDIBILITY

Gaining confidence and credibility in cybersecurity is a process that involves more than just acquiring technical skills. It encompasses a broad spectrum of activities contributing to professional growth, reputation building, and establishing oneself as a trusted expert. This multifaceted approach is crucial for anyone looking to develop a strong presence in the cybersecurity community.

Earning relevant cybersecurity certifications is a significant step toward gaining confidence and credibility. These certifications formally recognize one's knowledge and skills, providing a foundation of trust with employers, clients, and peers. They often involve rigorous training and testing, ensuring that certified individuals meet a certain standard of expertise. Holding industry-recognized certifications boosts one's professional profile and instills confidence in one's abilities. It demonstrates a commitment to maintaining a high standard of professional knowledge in the ever-evolving cybersecurity landscape.

Engaging in continuous learning and professional development is another important element. Cybersecurity is dynamic, with new challenges and technologies constantly emerging. Staying updated with the latest trends, techniques, and best practices is essential. Continuous learning can take many forms, from attending workshops and conferences to enrolling in advanced courses and pursuing further qualifications. This commitment to ongoing education enhances one's skills and signals a dedication to staying at the forefront of the field.

Building a professional network in the cybersecurity field is also important for gaining credibility. Networking with other professionals opens new opportunities, insights, and collaborations. It allows for exchanging ideas, sharing experiences, and access to advice and support from peers. A solid professional network can be a valuable resource for career advancement, offering mentorship opportunities and potential collaborations. It also enhances one's visibility in the field, establishing them as an active and engaged member of the cybersecurity community.

Sharing knowledge through blogs, talks, or webinars is a powerful way to build credibility and confidence. By disseminating knowledge and insights, one helps others in the field and establishes oneself as a thought leader and expert. Writing blogs, giving talks at industry events, or hosting webinars allows one to share their expertise, opinions, and experiences. This contributes to the community and bolsters one's professional reputation, highlighting expertise and communication skills.

Finally, receiving endorsements or testimonials from peers or supervisors can enhance credibility. These endorsements testify to one's skills, work ethic, and professional contributions. Whether feedback from a successful project, recognition of a particularly challenging task, or acknowledgment of leadership and teamwork skills, these testimonials provide tangible proof of one's abilities and achievements. They are a powerful tool in building trust and credibility within the cybersecurity community.

Gaining confidence and credibility in cybersecurity involves earning relevant certifications, engaging in continuous learning, building a professional network, sharing knowledge, and receiving endorsements. These elements enhance one's professional standing, establish trust, and position oneself as a reliable and knowledgeable expert.

GETTING INVOLVED IN OPEN-SOURCE PROJECTS

Getting involved in open-source projects is a pivotal step in advancing a career in cybersecurity. This involvement enhances technical skills and offers a unique platform for collaboration, learning, and building a visible portfolio. Contributing to open-source projects can be a significant career milestone for cybersecurity professionals by showcasing their practical skills and commitment to the community.

The first step is researching and selecting relevant cybersecurity open-source projects. This involves identifying projects that align with one's interests and skills and those that offer meaningful opportunities for contribution. The selection process should consider the project's relevance to current cybersecurity challenges, its impact on the community, and the learning opportunities it presents. This research phase is crucial since it ensures that the time and effort invested in the project are rewarding and beneficial for personal and professional growth.

The next crucial step is understanding the basics of contributing to open-source communities. Open-source projects thrive on collaboration and contribution from diverse individuals. Familiarizing oneself with the community's norms, communication channels, contribution guidelines, and code of conduct is essential. This understanding helps navigate the open-source landscape effectively, make meaningful contributions, and build positive relationships with other community members.

Learning from code reviews and collaborating with experienced developers are other significant aspects of involvement in open-source projects. Open-source communities often consist of highly skilled professionals from whom one can learn much. Engaging in code reviews and collaborative development provides an opportunity to gain feedback, understand different approaches to problem-solving, and refine coding skills. This interaction is about improving technical abilities and understanding the dynamics of collaborative development and open communication.

Enhancing technical skills through hands-on involvement in these projects is a direct benefit of this engagement. Open-source projects offer real-world challenges that require practical solutions. Working on these projects allows individuals to apply their theoretical knowledge in a practical setting, tackle real-world problems, and develop new skills. This hands-on involvement is invaluable in understanding cybersecurity's complexities and developing a well-rounded skill set.

Finally, building a visible portfolio through contributions and project involvement is essential to engaging with open-source projects. Every contribution, whether writing code, fixing bugs, improving documentation, or participating in discussions, adds to an individual's portfolio. This portfolio is a tangible showcase of one's skills, involvement, and commitment to cybersecurity. It provides evidence of practical experience and highly valued skills in the cybersecurity job market.

Getting involved in open-source projects is a multifaceted approach to career development in cybersecurity. It involves carefully selecting projects, understanding community dynamics, learning through collaboration, enhancing technical skills, and building a visible portfolio. This involvement not only contributes to personal and professional growth but also demonstrates a commitment to advancing the field of cybersecurity.

INTERNSHIP SEARCH AND APPLICATION TIPS

Navigating the internship search and application process in cybersecurity requires a strategic approach that aligns with your interests and skills while effectively showcasing your potential to prospective employers. This process is crucial in gaining valuable real-world experience and can significantly impact your early career development in cybersecurity.

The first step is identifying internships that align with your cybersecurity interests and skills. This involves a thorough research process to find opportunities that match your current skill set and align with your long-term career goals. Seeking internships in areas of cybersecurity that fascinate you or where you wish to specialize can lead to a more engaging and fruitful internship experience. Consider factors such as the company's focus, the specific projects you'll be working on, and the internship's learning opportunities. This alignment ensures that the internship enhances your skills and propels you toward your desired career path.

Crafting a compelling resume and cover letter that is specific to cybersecurity is essential in standing out in the competitive internship market. Your resume should highlight relevant coursework, projects, and any prior experience that showcases your cybersecurity skills and knowledge. Tailoring your resume and cover letter to each application is essential; emphasize how your skills and experiences make you a suitable candidate for that specific role. Additionally, showcasing any involvement in cybersecurity-related activities, like hackathons or clubs, can further strengthen your application.

Another important aspect is preparing for interviews—focusing on technical and soft skills. Cybersecurity internship interviews may involve technical questions that assess your understanding of cybersecurity principles, problem-solving abilities, and practical skills. At the same time, soft skills such as communication, teamwork, and adaptability are equally important. Demonstrating a balanced skill set can make a strong impression on potential employers. Practicing common interview questions, both technical and behavioral, and preparing to discuss your past projects and experiences in detail can significantly improve your confidence and performance in interviews.

Utilizing university career services and professional networks can provide a significant advantage in your internship search. Many universities offer career services that include resume workshops, interview preparation, and internship job boards. These resources can be invaluable in preparing and connecting with potential employers. Additionally, leveraging your professional network, including professors, alums, and contacts from industry events, can open up more opportunities. Networking can often lead to learning about internships that are not widely advertised and can sometimes lead to direct referrals.

Following up post-application and networking at industry events is an often-overlooked but critical step in the internship application process. A polite follow-up email after submitting your application can demonstrate your enthusiasm and keep you on the employer's radar. Similarly, attending industry events, conferences, and seminars helps stay updated with the latest in cybersecurity and provides opportunities to network with professionals and recruiters, potentially leading to internship opportunities.

The cybersecurity internship search and application process is a multi-step journey that involves identifying suitable opportunities, tailoring your application materials, preparing thoroughly for interviews, leveraging available resources and networks, and maintaining proactive communication. By approaching this process strategically, you can significantly enhance your chances of securing an internship that will be a significant stepping-stone in your cybersecurity career.

BENEFITS OF PARTICIPATING IN HACKATHONS

Participating in hackathons offers a wealth of benefits, especially for individuals who are seeking to carve out a niche in the cybersecurity domain. These intensive, often competitive events are not just about coding; they encompass a broad spectrum of activities and learning experiences that can significantly contribute to one's professional growth and skill set.

Gaining practical experience in solving real-time cybersecurity challenges is one of the primary benefits of participating in hackathons. These events simulate real-world scenarios, requiring participants to apply their knowledge and skills to solve complex cybersecurity problems within a limited time frame. This hands-on experience is invaluable because it enhances technical skills and provides insight into the nature of real-time cybersecurity threats and the pressure of working under tight deadlines. Such experiences are crucial in developing the ability to think quickly, adapt to changing scenarios, and devise practical solutions on the fly.

Networking with industry professionals and fellow cybersecurity enthusiasts is another significant advantage of hackathon participation. These events often attract diverse individuals, including seasoned professionals, industry leaders, and aspiring cybersecurity experts. Engaging with this community can lead to meaningful connections, mentorship opportunities, and insights into the latest trends and challenges in the field. Building a professional network in such environments can open doors to future career opportunities and collaborations.

Learning and applying new technologies and methodologies is a constant feature of hackathons. As cybersecurity is continually evolving, hackathons provide a platform to explore and experiment with the latest tools, technologies, and techniques. Participants must often step out of their comfort zones and rapidly learn new skills to address the challenges. This accelerated learning environment is highly beneficial in staying current with the latest developments in cybersecurity and enhancing one's technical proficiency.

Developing teamwork and collaborative problem-solving skills is a critical aspect of hackathons. Cybersecurity challenges often require a collaborative approach to find the most effective solutions. Hackathons foster an environment where participants must work as part of a team, combining their skills and knowledge to achieve a common goal. This experience helps develop soft skills like communication, teamwork, leadership, and collaborative problem-solving, all of which are highly sought after in the professional world.

Enhancing one's resume with demonstrable hands-on experience is an essential benefit of participating in hackathons. The practical experience gained, technologies learned, and solutions developed during these events can be significant additions to a resume. Hackathon participation showcases to potential employers that you have real-world problem-solving experience, a proactive approach to learning, and the ability to work effectively in team settings. Employers often view this hands-on experience favorably because it demonstrates theoretical knowledge and the ability to apply that knowledge in practical situations.

Participating in hackathons offers multifaceted benefits for individuals in the cybersecurity field. It provides a platform for:

- Gaining practical experience
- Networking with professionals
- Learning new technologies
- Developing teamwork skills
- Enhancing one's resume with tangible, hands-on experience

These benefits collectively contribute to one's professional development and readiness to face the challenges of the cybersecurity world.

LEVERAGING EXPERIENCES FOR CAREER ADVANCEMENT

Leveraging experiences for career advancement in cybersecurity involves a strategic approach to transforming various learning and practical experiences into valuable assets for professional growth. This process is essential in navigating the competitive landscape of cybersecurity careers, where technical proficiency and practical experience are highly valued.

Translating academic and project experiences into job skills is critical to this process. Theoretical knowledge gained through academic coursework provides a solid foundation in cybersecurity principles. Still, it is the application of this knowledge in projects and practical scenarios that truly enhances one's job readiness. This involves identifying and articulating how specific academic projects, research, or coursework have helped develop skills that are relevant to the cybersecurity job market. For instance, a project involving the identification of vulnerabilities in a software system demonstrates skills in threat assessment and mitigation, which are crucial in cybersecurity.

Building a solid professional network through internships and projects is also important for career advancement. Internships provide a platform for gaining practical experience and connecting with professionals in the field.

These connections can be instrumental in learning about job opportunities, gaining insights into industry trends, and receiving career advice. Similarly, collaborative projects, whether in an academic or a professional setting, can lead to lasting professional relationships. Networking should be viewed as an ongoing process, where maintaining and nurturing these connections can open doors to future career opportunities.

Showcasing achievements and accumulated knowledge in job interviews is essential in demonstrating your value to potential employers. This involves effectively communicating the experiences you have gained, the challenges you have overcome, and the skills you have developed. Discussing specific instances where you applied your knowledge to solve real-world problems or explaining how you contributed to a specific project can make a strong impression in interviews. It is about telling a compelling story of your journey in cybersecurity—highlighting both your technical abilities and problem-solving skills.

Continuously updating skills and knowledge to stay relevant is another crucial element for career advancement. Cybersecurity is fast-paced and ever-changing, with new threats and technologies emerging constantly. Engaging in continuous learning through formal education, certifications, online courses, or self-study is vital to keeping your skills up-to-date. Staying abreast of industry developments, emerging trends, and new technologies ensures that you remain a competitive candidate in the job market.

Seeking mentorship for guidance and career development insights is highly beneficial. Experienced mentors in the field can provide invaluable advice, share their experiences, and offer perspectives that can help navigate your career path. They can assist in setting realistic career goals, provide feedback on your progress, and offer insights into industry practices and expectations. Mentorship can catalyze professional growth, offering support, motivation, and guidance as you advance in your cybersecurity career.

Leveraging experiences for career advancement in cybersecurity involves:

- Translating academic and practical experiences into job skills
- Building and utilizing a professional network
- Effectively showcasing your achievements in interviews
- Continuously updating your skills
- Seeking mentorships

Each of these elements plays a vital role in developing a well-rounded professional profile and positioning oneself for success in the dynamic and challenging field of cybersecurity.

RECOMMENDED CYBER NEWS WEBSITES

Table 5.1

Website	Description	URL
Krebs on Security	Cybersecurity journalist Brian Krebs' blog	krebsonsecurity.com
Dark Reading	Comprehensive cybersecurity coverage	darkreading.com
Threatpost	News, analysis, and insights on threats	threatpost.com
The Hacker News	Covers hacking news and cyber threats	thehackernews.com
Infosecurity Magazine	Information security news and resources	Infosecurity-magazine.com
CyberScoop	Focuses on cybersecurity news and events	cyberscoop.com
SC Magazine	Security, risk management, and compliance	scmagazine.com
SecurityWeek	In-depth cybersecurity news and analysis	securityweek.com
CSO Online	News and insights on security leadership	csoonline.com
CyberWire	Daily podcasts and cybersecurity briefings	thecyberwire.com
ZDNet Security	ZDNet's section for security news and analysis	zdnet.com/topic/security
BleepingComputer	Malware analysis, data breaches, and news	bleepingcomputer.com
Naked Security by Sophos	Security news, research, and threat intelligence	nakedsecurity.sophos.com
CISA (Cybersecurity and Infrastructure Security Agency)	Alerts, tips, and resources	cisa.gov
Security Affairs	Information on cyber threats and hacking	securityaffairs.com
Cybersecurity & Infrastructure Security News (DHS)	The official newsroom of DHS	cisa.gov/newsroom
Cybersecurity Insiders	Trends, surveys, and reports on cybersecurity	cybersecurity-insiders.com

Continued

Table 5.1 (*continued*)

Website	Description	URL
InfoSec Institute Blog	Educational articles and insights	resources.infosecinstitute.com
Security Magazine	Security news, trends, and best practices	securitymagazine.com
TrendMicro Blog	TrendMicro's blog with cybersecurity insights	blog.trendmicro.com
Help Net Security	Cybersecurity news and analysis	helpnetsecurity.com
Security Intelligence by IBM	IBM's cybersecurity blog and news	ibm.com/security/intelligence
InfoWorld	IT and cybersecurity news	infoworld.com
Security Now Podcast	Steve Gibson's podcast on security topics	twit.tv/shows/security-now
Krebs Stamos Group	Blog by Alex Stamos and Brian Krebs	krebsonsecurity.com/blog
Cyber Defense Magazine	Features articles on cyber defense	cyberdefensemagazine.com
Securelist by Kaspersky Lab	Threat research and analysis by Kaspersky	securelist.com
FireEye Blog	Insights from FireEye cybersecurity experts	fireeye.com/blog
CERT Division (Carnegie Mellon University)	Cybersecurity research and updates	cert.org
Palo Alto Networks Blog	Blog posts on cybersecurity topics	paloaltonetworks.com/blog
Fortinet Blog	Blog articles on cybersecurity by Fortinet	fortinet.com/blog
Secureworks Blog	Security insights and research by Secureworks	secureworks.com/blog
CrowdStrike Blog	Cybersecurity research and insights	crowdstrike.com/blog
Symantec Blogs	Blogs on cybersecurity by Symantec	symantec.com/blogs
Palo Alto Networks Unit 42 Blog	Threat intelligence and research blog	unit42.paloaltonetworks.com
F-Secure Blog	Cybersecurity research and insights	f-secure.com/blog
ThreatQuotient Blog	Threat intelligence and security operations	threatquotient.com/blog

Continued

Table 5.1 (*continued*)

Website	Description	URL
Recorded Future Blog	Threat intelligence and analysis	recordedfuture.com/blog
SANS Institute Blog	Educational blog by the SANS Institute	sans.org/blog
McAfee Blogs	Blogs on cybersecurity by McAfee	mcafee.com/blogs
Check Point Research Blog	Cybersecurity research and insights	research.checkpoint.com
SecureLink Blog	Blog on cybersecurity and privacy	securelink.com/blog
Microsoft Security Blog	Microsoft's blog on security	aka.ms/securityblog
Juniper Networks Blog	Security insights by Juniper Networks	blogs.juniper.net
ISACA Now Blog	Blog by ISACA (Information Systems Audit and Control Association)	isaca.org/resources/isaca-now-blog

Web Added Value™

This book has free material available for download from the Web Added Value™ resource center at *www.jrosspub.com*

6

NAVIGATING THE CYBERSECURITY JOB MARKET

CRAFTING AN EFFECTIVE RESUME

In the competitive field of cybersecurity, crafting an effective resume is a crucial step in showcasing your expertise and securing your desired role. A well-crafted resume not only highlights your relevant skills and experiences but also positions you as a strong candidate in the cybersecurity domain. This section will guide you through emphasizing skills that are specific to cybersecurity, showcasing relevant projects and experiences, including pertinent certifications and training, and demonstrating key competencies such as problem-solving and analytical abilities.

Highlighting relevant skills and experiences is the foundation of a robust cybersecurity resume. Tailoring your resume to the specific requirements of the job you are applying for is a must. This means carefully reading the job description and ensuring that your most relevant skills and experiences are prominently featured. Focus on the most in-demand skills in the cybersecurity field, such as knowledge of security protocols, experience with threat detection tools, and understanding of compliance regulations.

Identifying and emphasizing skills that are specific to cybersecurity is vital. Employers in this field seek candidates with a strong foundation in network security, ethical hacking, cryptography, and incident response. If you have experience or training in these areas, highlight them on your resume. Use specific examples to demonstrate your expertise, such as mentioning particular security tools that you are proficient with or cybersecurity challenges that you have addressed.

Showcasing relevant projects, internships, and work experiences is crucial to demonstrate your practical application of cybersecurity knowledge. Include any relevant projects you have worked on as part of your education or during your career. If you have completed internships or work experiences in cybersecurity or related fields, detail these experiences, focusing on what you learned and your contributions to the projects. This not only shows your practical experience but also demonstrates your commitment to the field.

Including your training and certifications that are relevant to cybersecurity can significantly enhance your resume. Certifications like Certified Information Systems Security Professional (CISSP), Certified Information Security Manager (CISM), or Computer Technology Industry Association Security+ are highly valued in the industry and can set you apart from other candidates. List any relevant certifications along with the date of completion. If you have undergone any specific training programs or workshops related to cybersecurity, include these as well, as they demonstrate your dedication to continuous learning and keeping your skills up-to-date.

Demonstrating problem-solving and analytical abilities is essential in a cybersecurity resume. Cybersecurity professionals must be adept at analyzing complex problems and devising effective solutions. Highlight any experiences where you have successfully identified and solved security issues. Use specific examples to illustrate how you have used your analytical skills to mitigate risks and protect against threats.

Tailoring Your Resume for the Job

In the competitive field of cybersecurity, you must customize your resume for each job application. A resume that is specifically tailored to align with the job description and the company's unique needs can significantly increase your chances of standing out from other candidates. This part of the chapter focuses on the importance of researching the job description and the company, customizing the resume to meet the specific requirements of the role, emphasizing experiences that are directly relevant to the job's needs, and avoiding a one-size-fits-all approach in your applications.

Researching the job description and the company is the first step in tailoring your resume. It involves thoroughly analyzing the job posting to understand the specific skills, experiences, and qualifications the employer seeks. Look for keywords and phrases in the job description and reflect these in your resume. Additionally, researching the company can provide valuable insights into its culture, values, and priorities. Understanding the company's mission and how the cybersecurity role contributes to it can help you tailor your resume to demonstrate how your skills and experiences align with the company's objectives.

Customizing the resume to match the specific requirements of the role is crucial. This means prioritizing and highlighting the aspects of your experience and education that are most relevant to the job. For instance, if the job requires cybersecurity technology or methodology expertise, highlight your knowledge and proficiency in that area. Tailoring your resume also involves rearranging your experiences and skills to ensure that the most relevant information catches the employer's attention first.

Your resume should not just be a list of your past roles and responsibilities but also a reflection of how those experiences make you the ideal candidate for the specific role that you are applying for. For example, if the role involves managing a cybersecurity team, highlight your leadership or team management experiences. If it requires specific technical skills, detail your experience with relevant technologies or projects.

Each job and employer is different, and your resume should reflect that. A generic resume is easy to spot and often fails to make an impact. Customizing your resume for each application shows the employer that you have put thought and effort into your application and that you are genuinely interested in the role. It demonstrates professionalism and attention to detail that can set you apart from other applicants.

Tailoring your resume for each cybersecurity job application is a critical step in your job search. It involves:

- Careful research of the job description and the company
- Customizing your resume to meet the specific requirements of the role
- Emphasizing directly relevant experiences
- Avoiding a generic approach

Personalizing your resume for each application significantly increases your chances of capturing the employer's attention and advancing in the recruitment process.

Importance of Clear and Concise Presentation

Your resume presentation is just as important as the content, especially in cybersecurity, where clarity and precision are valued. A clear and concise presentation of your resume can significantly impact its effectiveness. This chapter emphasizes the importance of organizing information in an easy-to-read format, utilizing bullet points for clarity, keeping the resume concise, and ensuring a professional layout and design.

Organize information in an easy-to-read format. Your resume should be structured to allow potential employers to grasp your essential qualifications and experiences quickly. This involves using clear headings, a logical flow of information, and a clean, uncluttered layout. The goal is to make it as easy as possible for hiring managers to find the information they are looking for without having to search through dense blocks of text.

Using bullet points is an effective way to enhance clarity and readability. Bullet points help break down information into digestible pieces, making it easier for the reader to scan and understand your qualifications and achievements. When using bullet points, start with the most impactful and relevant information, and use action verbs to describe your experiences and accomplishments. This format not only improves readability but also helps to highlight your key selling points.

Keeping the resume concise, ideally to one page, is often recommended, especially for early to mid-career professionals. A concise resume forces you to prioritize the most relevant and significant information, making your resume more focused and impactful. It shows that you can communicate your background and skills efficiently—a valuable trait in the cybersecurity field. If you have extensive experience, a two-page resume is acceptable, but ensure that every piece of information included adds value and relevance to your application.

Ensuring a professional layout and design is essential. The visual appeal of your resume can influence the first impression it makes. A professional layout means using a clean, modern design with consistent formatting, legible fonts, and appropriate colors (if any). Avoid overcomplicating the design; the focus should be on the content rather than decorative elements. Remember that your resume is a professional document, and its design should reflect the same level of professionalism.

Your resume's clear and concise presentation is vital to making a solid impact. These critical aspects include:

- Organizing information in an easy-to-read format
- Using bullet points for clarity
- Keeping the content concise
- Ensuring a professional layout and design

These elements contribute to creating a resume that is informative, engaging, and easy for potential employers to review, thereby increasing your chances of securing a cybersecurity position.

Using Keywords and Industry Terminology

Incorporating the correct keywords and industry terminology into your resume is a strategic approach that can significantly enhance its effectiveness, particularly in cybersecurity. This segment focuses on how to skillfully integrate relevant cybersecurity keywords from the job description, use industry-specific terms to demonstrate your knowledge and expertise, balance technical jargon with accessible language, and avoid the overuse of acronyms while ensuring that all terms are well-explained.

Employers often use applicant tracking systems (ATS) to screen resumes, and these systems are programmed to pick up specific keywords related to the job. Carefully read the job description and note the skills, technologies, and qualifications mentioned. Incorporating these keywords into your resume increases the chances that your resume will pass through the ATS and catch the hiring manager's attention. However, use these keywords in context and in a way that genuinely reflects your skills and experiences.

Using industry-specific terms effectively demonstrates your knowledge and expertise in the field of cybersecurity. This includes terms related to technologies, methodologies, frameworks, and best practices prevalent in cybersecurity. Using such terminology shows that you are well-versed in the field and understand the technical aspects of the role. However, it is crucial to ensure that using these terms aligns with your experience and knowledge.

Balancing technical jargon with accessible language is important, especially considering that technical and nontechnical personnel may review your resume. While it is important to demonstrate your technical expertise, it is also crucial to present your information in a way that is understandable to nonspecialists. This balance ensures that your resume is impressive—not just to a technical hiring manager, but also to HR professionals or other nontechnical reviewers who may be part of the hiring process.

Another critical aspect is avoiding the overuse of acronyms and ensuring that terms are well-explained. The cybersecurity field is rife with abbreviations and specialized language, which, while familiar to you, might not be as clear to everyone reviewing your resume. When using acronyms or less common terms, it is a good practice to spell them out and briefly explain if the context does not clarify their meaning. This approach ensures that your resume is inclusive and understandable to all potential readers.

Using keywords and industry terminology effectively in your cybersecurity resume is a delicate balance. It involves:

- Integrating relevant keywords from the job description
- Using industry-specific terms to showcase your expertise
- Balancing technical jargon with accessible language
- Carefully using acronyms

This strategic incorporation of language helps your resume pass through ATS filters. It ensures that it is understandable and impressive to a diverse range of reviewers, enhancing your chances of landing the job.

Choosing Someone to Build Your Resume versus Creating It on Your Own

In the pursuit of a career in cybersecurity, one of the initial and crucial decisions involves crafting your resume. This decision often boils down to whether to create your resume independently or seek professional help. This section explores the factors to consider in making this decision—such as assessing your skills and time availability, weighing the cost versus the benefit of professional services, and considering the investment in personal development when creating your resume.

Assessing personal skills and time availability is the first step in this decision-making process. Evaluate your ability to craft a resume that stands out effectively. This includes considering your proficiency in articulating your experiences and skills, your understanding of what employers in the cybersecurity field are looking for, and your capacity to format and design a professional and visually appealing resume. Additionally, consider your current time commitments. Creating a compelling resume can be time-consuming, and it is essential to determine whether you have the bandwidth to dedicate to this task, especially if you are currently employed or engaged in other demanding activities.

Evaluating your ability to craft a resume effectively involves an honest assessment of your writing and design skills. Are you confident in clearly and concisely describing your experiences and skills? Do you understand the cybersecurity industry's jargon and how to communicate your expertise in this area effectively? If you feel unsure about these aspects, seeking professional help might be beneficial.

Considering time constraints and the willingness to learn, resume-building is also crucial. If you are under a tight timeline to apply for jobs or prefer to focus on other aspects of your job search, such as honing your technical skills or networking, outsourcing your resume creation might be a more efficient option. On the other hand, if you have the time and are keen to develop the skill of resume writing, creating your resume could be a valuable learning experience.

Weighing the cost versus the benefit is another important consideration. Hiring a professional resume writer can be a significant investment. It is necessary to analyze the cost of these services against the potential benefits they could bring to your job search. A professionally crafted resume might give you an edge in a competitive job market, potentially leading to better job opportunities and higher salaries. However, it is important to balance this against the cost and to consider whether the investment aligns with your budget and job-search goals.

It is equally important to consider the investment in personal development when creating your resume. Crafting your resume can be a rewarding experience that improves your writing and design skills and deepens your understanding of your professional journey and goals. It encourages self-reflection and clarity about your career path, which can benefit job interviews and networking.

The decision to create your own resume or hire a professional involves carefully considering:

- Your skills
- Your time availability
- Your willingness to learn
- The cost-benefit analysis of professional services

Each option has its merits, and the right choice depends on your circumstances, career goals, and personal preferences in your journey toward a career in cybersecurity.

Seeking Professional Expertise

When considering the creation of a resume, particularly for specialized fields like cybersecurity, seeking professional expertise can be a strategic choice. This section delves into the benefits of leveraging the skills of professional resume writers, evaluating their success rate and reviews, and understanding how customization and a personal touch can make your resume stand out while still reflecting your unique professional identity.

Considering the expertise of professional resume writers is especially important in niche fields like cybersecurity. These professionals are skilled in crafting effective resumes and often have specific knowledge about the industry. They understand the jargon, they are familiar with the key skills and experiences that are valued in the field, and they know how to communicate the information to potential employers effectively. Their expertise can be particularly beneficial for those who may not be as confident in their ability to articulate their professional journey in a way that resonates with cybersecurity hiring managers.

Evaluate the success rate and reviews of professional resume-writing services before committing. Research the background and track record of the service or individual writer. Look for reviews or testimonials from previous clients, especially those in cybersecurity. This research will give you insight into their services' effectiveness and ability to deliver results. It is essential to choose a service or writer with a good reputation and a proven track record in your specific area of interest.

Customization and Personal Touch

Ensuring that your brand and voice are reflected in the resume is essential, even when using professional services. Your resume should reflect your professional persona by highlighting your unique skills, experiences, and career aspirations. A professional resume writer will work with you to effectively capture and articulate your brand. This collaboration ensures that the resume is not just a generic collection of skills and experiences but a true representation of your professional identity.

Balancing the professional polish with your unique experiences and skills is critical to a standout resume. While a professionally written resume will likely have a polished and sophisticated tone, it must not lose the essence of your professional identity. The resume should highlight the achievements, skills, and experiences that make you the ideal candidate for that specific cybersecurity role. It should blend professional expertise in resume writing with the uniqueness of your professional journey, creating a compelling and genuinely reflective document of your career path.

Seeking professional expertise in resume writing can be a valuable investment, particularly for specialized fields like cybersecurity. It involves evaluating professional writers' credentials and success rates along with ensuring that the final product is a customized representation of your personal brand and professional journey. A well-crafted resume—balancing professional polish with your unique experiences and skills—can significantly enhance your visibility and appeal to potential employers.

Learning and Development Opportunity

Treating the process of resume building as a skill development opportunity can be incredibly beneficial, especially in a field as dynamic as cybersecurity. This perspective not only aids in creating a robust resume but also contributes to your overall professional development. This section focuses on the advantages of viewing resume building as a learning experience and utilizing available resources and templates effectively if you choose to create your own resume.

Viewing resume building as a skill development opportunity allows you to gain valuable experience in personal branding and communication. A resume requires you to articulate your skills, achievements, and experiences concisely and compellingly. This process encourages you to reflect on your career journey, identify your strengths, and think critically about presenting your experiences most effectively. These skills are helpful for job applications, professional networking, and personal branding in the broader scope of your career.

If you decide to create your own resume, utilizing available resources and templates can be immensely helpful. A wealth of resources is available online, including resume templates, guides, and examples that are tailored explicitly to cybersecurity. These resources can provide a solid starting point and inspiration for structuring and formatting your resume. Templates can help ensure that your resume has a professional and organized appearance, while guides and examples can offer insights into practical ways to describe your experiences and skills.

However, it is important to remember that these resources should serve as a foundation or a guide rather than a one-size-fits-all solution. Customizing the template to fit your unique experiences and personal style is crucial. Adapt the structure and content to highlight your specific skills and achievements. The goal is to create a resume that stands out and truly represents your professional identity rather than one that blends in with countless others.

Approaching resume building as a learning and development opportunity can enhance your skills in personal branding and effective communication. When creating your resume, leverage the resources and templates that are available, but customize them to reflect your individuality and professional journey. This approach not only aids in developing a solid resume but also equips you with valuable skills that will be applicable across various aspects of your professional life in cybersecurity.

SUBMITTING RESUMES TO JOBS: TAILORING FOR EACH ROLE

In the process of applying for jobs in the field of cybersecurity, tailoring your resume for each specific role is a critical strategy. This approach ensures that your application is as relevant and impactful as possible, increasing your chances of capturing the employer's attention. This section emphasizes the importance of understanding the job description, carefully reading to discern what the employer seeks, and identifying the essential skills and experiences required for each role.

Understanding the job description is the first and most crucial step in tailoring your resume. Each job posting provides a wealth of information about what the employer is looking for in a candidate. Pay close attention to the language used in the description, the order in which requirements are listed, and any specific competencies or experiences that are emphasized. This information guides your understanding of the employer's priorities and expectations for the role.

Reading the job description carefully involves more than a cursory glance. It requires a detailed analysis to glean insights into the role and how it fits within the organization. Look for clues about the company culture, the team structure, and how the role contributes to the organization's broader goals. This deeper understanding can help you align your resume closely with the employer's needs and values.

When reading the job description, identify the key skills and experiences required for the role. Highlight the specific skills, technologies, methodologies, and experiences mentioned and compare them with your qualifications. This comparison will help you determine which aspects of your background should be emphasized in your resume for that particular application. Remember, the goal is to demonstrate how your skills and experiences make you an ideal fit for the role.

When submitting resumes for cybersecurity roles, you must tailor each resume to the job that you are applying for. This tailoring process begins with a thorough understanding of the job description, which involves carefully reading and analyzing the requirements and expectations outlined by the employer. By identifying and highlighting the essential skills and experiences that align with the role, you can create a customized resume that speaks directly to the employer's needs, thereby enhancing your chances of being noticed and considered for the position.

Customizing the Resume for Each Application

A tailored resume significantly increases your chances of standing out to potential employers and passing through the ATS. This part of the chapter will guide you through tailoring your resume to highlight the most relevant experiences and skills for each job, adapting your summary or objective statement, and incorporating relevant keywords for the most favorable ATS optimization.

Tailoring your resume to highlight the most relevant experiences and skills for each job is vital. Every cybersecurity role has its unique set of requirements and responsibilities. By customizing your resume for each application, you can ensure that your most pertinent skills and experiences are the focus, demonstrating to the employer that you are well-suited for the specific role.

This may involve rearranging sections of your resume or emphasizing different aspects of your experience depending on what the job demands. For instance, if a role heavily focuses on network security, highlighting your experience and skills in this area should take precedence.

Another crucial customization aspect is adapting your resume's summary or objective statement to align with the specific role. This statement is often the first thing an employer will read, so it should convey how your skills and goals align with the job you're applying for. Tailoring this section requires understanding what the employer is looking for and reflecting that understanding in your statement. It is about making a solid first impression and immediately establishing your relevance to the position.

Incorporating Relevant Keywords

Using keywords and phrases from the job description is important for optimizing your resume for ATS. Many employers use these systems to filter and rank resumes based on how well they match the job criteria. Incorporating keywords from the job description increases the likelihood that your resume will be flagged as a good match. However, it is essential to use these keywords naturally and contextually. Overstuffing your resume with keywords can make it difficult to read, causing it to be flagged by more sophisticated ATS as manipulative.

Ensuring that the resume language resonates with industry-specific terminology is also vital. This helps with ATS optimization and shows that you are knowledgeable about the field. Using the correct technical terms, methodologies, and tools relevant to cybersecurity demonstrates your familiarity with the industry. However, it is important to balance technical jargon with clear and comprehensible language, mainly because HR professionals may review your resume before it reaches a technical hiring manager.

Customizing your resume for each cybersecurity job application involves tailoring your content to highlight relevant skills and experiences, adapting your summary or objective statement, and incorporating keywords and industry terminology from the job description. This approach ensures that your resume is ATS-friendly and clearly demonstrates your suitability for the specific role you are applying for.

Highlighting Transferable Skills

Showcasing skills that are applicable across various roles is essential for career changers. Many skills that have been acquired in other professions—such as problem-solving, analytical thinking, project management, and effective communication—are precious in cybersecurity. When tailoring your resume, highlight these transferable skills and articulate how they are relevant to the roles you are applying for. For example, if your background is in IT or software development, emphasize how your understanding of networks and systems can be a significant asset in a cybersecurity role.

Emphasizing how your background uniquely positions you for the role involves more than just listing your past experiences; it is about drawing connections between what you have done in the past and how it can contribute to your future role in cybersecurity. This might involve illustrating how your experience in risk assessment, although in a different field, can be leveraged in cybersecurity risk management or how your skills in data analysis can be applied to cybersecurity analytics.

Proofreading and Review

Ensuring there are no errors in each customized resume is critical. A resume with typos, grammatical errors, or formatting inconsistencies can detract from the professional image you are trying to project. Thoroughly proofread each version of your resume to ensure it is error-free. Pay special attention to the details, such as dates, job titles, and technical terminologies. A well-polished resume reflects your attention to detail—an essential skill in cybersecurity.

Seeking feedback on tailored resumes from mentors or peers in the cybersecurity field can provide valuable insights. Input from experienced professionals can help you understand how your resume might be perceived by hiring managers in the field. They can advise you on aligning your resume with industry expectations and suggest improvements. This feedback can be particularly beneficial for career changers who might not yet be fully versed in the nuances of the cybersecurity field.

Highlighting transferable skills in your resume is key, especially for those who are transitioning into cybersecurity from other fields. Showcasing these skills effectively requires illustrating how they apply to cybersecurity roles and how your unique background is an asset. Additionally, meticulous proofreading and seeking feedback from professionals are essential to ensure that your tailored resume is error-free and aligned with industry standards. This approach enhances the overall impact of your resume, making it more appealing to potential employers.

IN-PERSON NETWORKING

In cybersecurity, in-person networking is invaluable for career development and staying updated with the latest industry trends. This section explores the various avenues for in-person networking, such as attending conferences and workshops and joining professional associations. It points out the importance of building a professional network and the benefits of seeking mentorship and sponsorship.

Attending conferences and workshops is one of the most effective ways to network within the cybersecurity community. These events provide insights into the latest technologies, practices, and research in the field and offer opportunities to connect with industry professionals, thought leaders, and potential employers. Conferences often feature a mix of keynote speeches, panel discussions, and training sessions, providing a rich environment for learning and networking. On the other hand, workshops offer more hands-on experience and a chance to engage more directly with peers and experts in the field.

Joining professional associations is another valuable approach to in-person networking. Associations such as the Information Systems Security Association (ISSA), the Information Systems Audit and Control Association (ISACA), the International Information System Security Certification Consortium (ISC2), and the SANS Institute offer membership to cybersecurity professionals. These associations provide a platform for networking, professional development, and staying abreast of industry standards and practices. They often host events, seminars, and local chapter meetings, providing regular opportunities for members to connect and collaborate:

- **ISSA:** ISSA is a prominent global community of cybersecurity professionals dedicated to advancing individual growth, managing technology risk, and protecting critical information and infrastructure. This organization is a hub for information security professionals, offering a platform for sharing best practices, education, and research. ISSA distinguishes itself with local chapters across various regions, providing a more localized and accessible community experience. These chapters facilitate networking, professional development, and knowledge-sharing at a regional level. Additionally, ISSA hosts international conferences, webinars, and other educational events, catering to the diverse needs of information security professionals at all stages of their careers. The association also emphasizes the importance of ethical standards and professional conduct in cybersecurity.
- **ISACA:** Originally known as the Information Systems Audit and Control Association, but now known by its acronym only, ISACA is a global professional association primarily focused on IT governance. The organization is renowned for its industry-leading certifications, such as Certified Information Systems Auditor, CISM, Certified in Risk and Information Systems Control, and Certified in the Governance

of Enterprise IT. Beyond certifications, ISACA offers its members extensive networking opportunities, a comprehensive resource library, and various professional development programs. These resources are designed to support IT audit, risk management, cybersecurity, governance, and privacy professionals. ISACA also has local chapters worldwide, providing members with opportunities to engage at a local level and fostering a community-oriented environment for professional growth and learning.

- **ISC2:** ISC2 is a highly respected nonprofit organization specializing in training and certifications for information security professionals. Known for its acclaimed certifications like the CISSP and the Certified Cloud Security Professional (CCSP), ISC2 plays a pivotal role in standardizing and promoting information security education and practices. The association offers its members a wide array of resources for professional development, including educational courses, seminars, and webinars. ISC2 is committed to helping its members stay ahead in the fast-evolving field of cybersecurity through continuous learning opportunities. Furthermore, ISC2 advocates for the profession, aiming to increase the recognition and importance of cybersecurity in the broader technology and business landscapes.

- **SANS Institute:** The SANS Institute is a globally recognized leader in cybersecurity training, research, and certification. It offers extensive training courses designed for various cybersecurity roles and skill levels, from foundational courses to advanced technical training. SANS is well-known for its intensive, hands-on approach to cybersecurity education, ensuring participants gain practical skills and knowledge. In addition to training, the SANS Institute organizes and hosts conferences, local community events, and online webinars, providing ample networking opportunities for cybersecurity professionals. These events serve as platforms for exchanging ideas, discussing the latest cybersecurity trends, and learning from leading experts in the field. SANS also contributes to the cybersecurity community through research publications, white papers, and a comprehensive library of information security resources.

Networking can lead to job opportunities, partnerships, or collaborations on projects. It is about establishing relationships with peers, mentors, and industry leaders who can provide support, guidance, and insight throughout your career.

Mentorship and sponsorship are essential aspects of professional growth. A mentor can offer advice, share experiences, and help you navigate your career path, while a sponsor can actively advocate for you and open doors to new opportunities.

In-person networking is a critical component of a successful career in cybersecurity. Strategies that can help propel your career forward in this dynamic and rapidly evolving field include:

- Attending conferences and workshops
- Joining professional associations
- Engaging in online forums and LinkedIn groups
- Building a robust professional network
- Seeking mentorships and sponsorships

INTERVIEW PREPARATION AND TECHNIQUES

Preparing for interviews in the field of cybersecurity involves more than just understanding the technical aspects of the job; it requires strategic preparation and a keen awareness of common interview questions and techniques. This section will guide you through researching and preparing for frequently asked questions in cybersecurity interviews, formulating responses to common behavioral questions, practicing responses to technical questions, and preparing examples to demonstrate essential skills like problem-solving and critical thinking.

Common Interview Questions and Answers

Researching and preparing for frequently asked questions in cybersecurity interviews is crucial. This preparation involves understanding the typical questions that employers ask during cybersecurity interviews. These questions often cover various topics, from technical knowledge and experience to problem-solving abilities and knowledge of current cybersecurity trends. Researching these questions can involve reviewing cybersecurity forums, talking to professionals in the field, or seeking advice from mentors.

Formulate thoughtful and articulate responses to common behavioral questions. Behavioral questions are designed to assess your soft skills, such as teamwork, leadership, and adaptability. Cybersecurity employers are interested in your technical abilities and how you work in a team, handle stress, and adapt to changing situations. Prepare for these questions by reflecting on past experiences where you demonstrated these qualities. Use the STAR method (situation, task, action, result) to structure your responses clearly and concisely.

Practicing responses to technical questions that are relevant to the role is an essential part of interview preparation. These questions will likely pertain to specific cybersecurity skills, tools, or methodologies pertinent to the job. Be prepared to discuss your experience with various cybersecurity technologies, your approach to securing networks and systems, and your understanding of cyber threats and defenses. Articulate your technical knowledge clearly and confidently.

Preparing examples to demonstrate problem-solving and critical thinking skills is another crucial aspect of interview preparation. Cybersecurity is a field that requires quick thinking and effective problem-solving. Employers will likely ask you to provide examples of how you have solved complex problems or dealt with challenging situations. Prepare these examples in advance, focusing on situations that showcase your analytical abilities, creativity, and resourcefulness.

Preparing for a cybersecurity interview requires a multifaceted approach. It involves researching and preparing for common technical and behavioral questions, practicing articulate responses, and preparing examples that showcase your problem-solving and critical thinking skills. A well-prepared candidate can confidently discuss their technical expertise, demonstrate their soft skills, and apply their knowledge in practical scenarios. This comprehensive preparation is critical to succeeding in cybersecurity interviews and advancing your career.

Preparing for Technical and Behavioral Interviews

Adequate preparation for both technical and behavioral interviews is crucial for candidates who are aspiring to secure cybersecurity positions. This section is a guide as to how to prepare for these two distinct but equally important aspects of the interview process. It covers reviewing critical technical concepts, tools, and methodologies in cybersecurity, understanding and applying the STAR method for behavioral questions, preparing examples of past experiences that highlight relevant skills and achievements, and studying the company's background and the specific job requirements.

Reviewing critical technical concepts, tools, and methodologies is essential for technical interviews. This preparation involves thoroughly revising the fundamental concepts of cybersecurity, including network security, encryption, threat analysis, and incident response. Familiarize yourself with the latest tools and technologies used in the field, and be prepared to discuss how you have applied these in previous roles or projects. It's also beneficial to stay updated on the latest trends and challenges in cybersecurity since this demonstrates your ongoing commitment to staying informed in your profession.

Understanding the STAR method for behavioral questions is critical to success in behavioral interviews. The STAR method helps you structure your responses in a way that clearly and concisely demonstrates your competencies. For each example you prepare, think about the *situation* you were in, the *task* that needed to be accomplished, the *actions* you took, and the *result* of those actions. This method ensures that your answers are well-organized and that you effectively communicate how your experiences align with the competencies the employer is seeking.

Prepare examples of past experiences that showcase relevant skills and achievements. Reflect on your previous work, education, or other relevant experiences to identify examples demonstrating your skills, particularly those that align with the job description. Focus on examples that showcase your problem-solving abilities, teamwork and leadership skills, and adaptability in challenging situations. These examples should not only illustrate your technical abilities but also your soft skills and how you apply your knowledge in practical situations.

Studying the company's background and the specific job requirements is an often overlooked but vital part of interview preparation. Research the company, its culture, its position in the cybersecurity industry, and any recent news or developments. Understand the specific job requirements you are applying for and consider how your skills and experiences make you a good fit for this role. Demonstrating your knowledge about the company and the role shows your interest and commitment, and it can also help you tailor your responses to align more closely with the company's needs and values.

Preparing for both technical and behavioral interviews in cybersecurity involves a comprehensive approach. It requires a solid understanding of technical concepts and tools, the ability to articulate your experiences using the STAR method, the preparation of relevant examples that demonstrate your skills and achievements, and a thorough understanding of the company and the specific job you're applying for. This well-rounded preparation will equip you to handle the various aspects of the interview process effectively and increase your chances of success.

Demonstrating Your Skills and Experiences

Effectively demonstrating your skills and experiences is a crucial aspect of the interview process, especially in a field as specialized as cybersecurity. This section focuses on how to effectively highlight your specific cybersecurity projects and accomplishments, discuss your experiences with particular technologies or challenges, explain the intricacies of complex projects or problem-solving scenarios, and demonstrate your commitment to continuous learning and professional development in the field.

Highlighting specific cybersecurity projects and accomplishments is a powerful way to demonstrate your capabilities. When preparing for an interview, identify key projects you have worked on relevant to the role you are applying for. Be ready to discuss the objectives, your role in the project, the technologies and methodologies you used, and the outcomes achieved. This approach showcases your technical skills and successfully illustrates your ability to apply them in real-world scenarios.

Discussing experiences with specific technologies or cybersecurity challenges is another vital aspect of demonstrating your expertise. Be prepared to detail your hands-on experience with various cybersecurity tools, platforms, and frameworks. Discuss how you have used these technologies to address specific security challenges or to improve security posture. This discussion can include your approach to threat detection, risk assessment, incident response, and other essential cybersecurity tasks.

Explaining the process and outcome of complex projects or problem-solving scenarios allows you to demonstrate your analytical and strategic thinking skills. Describe the challenges you faced, the steps you took to overcome them, and the results of your efforts. Be specific about your role in these projects and the impact your actions had on their success. This kind of detailed explanation helps interviewers understand your approach to problem-solving and your ability to handle complex cybersecurity tasks.

Demonstrating continuous learning and professional development in cybersecurity shows your commitment to staying updated in a rapidly evolving field. Discuss any recent certifications, courses, workshops, or conferences you have attended. Talk about how these experiences have contributed to your professional growth and how they have kept you abreast of the latest trends and best practices in cybersecurity. Highlighting your dedication to continuous learning can set you apart as a candidate committed to excellence and growth in the field.

Demonstrating your skills and experiences during a cybersecurity job interview involves a well-rounded approach. It includes:

- Highlighting your accomplishments in specific projects
- Discussing your experience with relevant technologies and challenges
- Explaining your approach to complex problem-solving scenarios
- Showcasing your commitment to continuous learning and development

This comprehensive demonstration of your abilities and achievements provides a solid foundation for a successful interview and helps position you as a strong candidate.

Post-Interview Follow-Up and Feedback

The job interview process does not end when you leave the room; following up and seeking feedback are crucial steps in the job application process, especially in the competitive field of cybersecurity. This section guides post-interview etiquette, including sending a thank-you email, inquiring about the decision timeline, seeking constructive feedback if not selected, and reflecting on the interview experience for personal growth.

Sending a thank-you email to the interviewer(s) within 24 hours of your interview is a key aspect of post-interview etiquette. This email should express your gratitude for the opportunity to interview and reiterate your interest in the position. It is an opportunity to make a lasting positive impression and to remind the interviewer(s) of your qualifications and enthusiasm for the role. Keep the email concise and professional, and if possible, personalize it with a reference to a specific part of the interview that was particularly meaningful or relevant.

Politely inquiring about the timeline for a decision or next steps is also important. Toward the end of your interview, it is appropriate to ask about the next steps in the hiring process and when you can expect to hear back. You can include a polite inquiry in your thank-you email if this information was not provided during the interview. This shows your continued interest in the position and helps you manage your expectations and timeline.

If not selected, seeking constructive feedback is a valuable practice for future improvement. If you are informed that you have not been chosen for the role, it is appropriate to ask the interviewer for feedback. This request should be made respectfully in order to learn and grow. Constructive feedback can provide insights into areas where you might improve—whether regarding technical skills, interview techniques, or other aspects of your professional presentation.

Reflecting on the interview experience to identify areas for growth is an essential self-assessment practice. After the interview, take some time to think about how it went. Consider both the positives and areas where you felt challenged. Reflect on the questions, responses, and overall interaction with the interviewers. This reflection can help you identify personal and professional development areas, making you better prepared and more confident for future interviews.

The post-interview follow-up and feedback process is integral to the job application journey. It involves:

- Sending a prompt thank-you email
- Inquiring about the hiring timeline

- Seeking and learning from feedback if not selected
- Engaging in self-reflection to identify areas for growth

These steps demonstrate professionalism and a commitment to continuous improvement—qualities that are highly valued in cybersecurity.

RESUME REVIEW CHECKLIST

Putting together a checklist is essential for cyber professionals and newcomers as a guide to crafting a compelling resume. It should outline each critical component, from contact information to technical skills, ensuring that no detail is overlooked. By leveraging a checklist, you can confidently align your resume with industry standards and expectations while enhancing your prospects. It will assist in structuring and organizing content and will emphasize the importance of tailoring the resume for specific job roles, thereby maximizing the impact and relevance of your professional presentation. The following list will help you to assemble your relevant information:

1. **Contact information accuracy:**
   - Full name
   - Professional email address
   - Phone number
   - LinkedIn profile (if applicable)
2. **Clear professional summary:**
   - A brief overview of your skills and experiences
   - Focus on cybersecurity expertise and interests
3. **Technical skills section:**
   - List relevant technical skills (e.g., network security, encryption, threat analysis)
   - Proficiency levels for each skill (if applicable)
4. **Professional experience:**
   - Chronological list of past roles (most recent first)
   - Each role should include the company name, location, dates of employment, and job title
   - Bullet points detailing responsibilities and achievements in each role
   - Emphasis on tasks related to cybersecurity
   - Quantifiable achievements (e.g., improved system security by 30%)
5. **Educational background:**
   - Degrees or certifications relevant to cybersecurity

- Name of the institution, degree, and date of graduation
- Relevant coursework or projects (for newcomers)

6. **Certifications and training:**
   - List of relevant certifications (e.g., CISSP, CCSP)
   - Dates of certification and issuing organization

7. **Projects and contributions** (especially for newcomers):
   - Personal or academic projects relevant to cybersecurity
   - Contributions to open-source projects or online communities

8. **Professional affiliations:**
   - Membership in professional organizations related to cyber-security

9. **Format and design:**
   - Clean, professional layout
   - Consistent font and formatting
   - No longer than two pages (ideally one page for newcomers)
   - Proofread for spelling and grammatical errors

10. **Tailoring for the job:**
    - Adjust the resume to align with the specific job description
    - Highlight the most relevant experiences and skills for the role

11. **Additional sections** (if applicable):
    - Volunteer work, publications, or speaking engagements related to cyber security

12. **Feedback and review:**
    - Have someone review your resume for feedback
    - Consider input from professionals in the field

7

SOCIAL NETWORKING STRATEGIES ON LINKEDIN

LinkedIn, often described as the world's largest professional network, has revolutionized how professionals connect, engage, and advance their careers. As a digital platform, it is a dynamic nexus for professional networking, career development, and industry collaboration. This chapter delves into the multifaceted world of LinkedIn, exploring its significance as a powerful tool for professionals, particularly in the cybersecurity domain. It highlights how LinkedIn facilitates connections between industry experts, job seekers, and organizations while providing a wealth of professional growth and learning resources. The platform's importance lies in providing a space for professionals to showcase their experiences, skills, and achievements, engage with relevant content, and access a vast network of opportunities and insights. LinkedIn is an invaluable resource for individuals looking to make a mark in their professional journeys, whether for job hunting, networking, professional branding, or staying updated with industry trends. This chapter aims to guide you through leveraging LinkedIn effectively, optimizing your profile, building a robust professional network, and utilizing the platform's features to advance your career in cybersecurity or any other field.

OPTIMIZING YOUR LINKEDIN PROFILE

Leveraging existing successful LinkedIn profiles as a guide is an effective strategy for optimizing your own. By examining https://www.linkedin.com/in/jasonedwardsdmist/, you can gain insights into crafting a compelling and professional LinkedIn presence. From the succinct yet informative summary section that highlights key achievements and specialties to the detailed experience section that chronicles career progress, each element of the author's profile serves a specific purpose in building a solid personal brand. You can gather valuable ideas on structuring and phrasing your content by analyzing how the author has articulated his experiences, skills, and professional journey. Furthermore, you can observe how the author engages with his network and shares industry-relevant content, which can inspire you when it comes to using LinkedIn for active networking and thought leadership. In the upcoming sections, we will explore each part of the LinkedIn profile in detail, offering tips and strategies to enhance your profile by drawing inspiration from the author's well-optimized LinkedIn presence.

Profile Photo

Creating an engaging and professional LinkedIn profile starts with selecting the right profile photo. This image is often the first impression you make on potential employers, colleagues, and industry connections, so choosing a photo that represents you in the best possible light is crucial:

- **Professional headshot and appearance:** The ideal LinkedIn profile photo should be a professional headshot that focuses on your face. This means opting for a clear, high-quality image where your face is the central point. A headshot taken from the shoulders up is usually the most effective. This photo must reflect the norms and expectations of your industry. For example, a business suit or formal attire would be appropriate if you work in a corporate environment. On the other hand, if you are in a creative field, something more casual yet professional might be suitable. The key is to look approachable and competent.
- **Recency and background:** Using a recent photo is vital for maintaining recognition, primarily if you use LinkedIn for networking or job searching. You want people to recognize you when you meet in person

or attend virtual meetings. Additionally, the background of your photo plays a significant role. A distracting background can take the focus away from you, so choosing a simple and neutral setting is advisable. A plain background or a professional setting like an office works well. The goal is to eliminate elements that could divert attention from your professional image.

- **Background photo:**

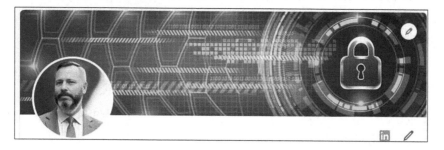

The background photo on your LinkedIn profile is a powerful tool to complement and enhance your professional brand. Unlike the profile photo, which is focused on your appearance, the background photo offers a broader canvas to express your professional identity and interests.

- **Alignment with professional brand:** When selecting a background image, consider how it reflects your professional brand and area of expertise. For instance, if you specialize in cybersecurity, you might opt for a graphic that symbolizes digital security, such as imagery of a lock, digital networks, or a more abstract representation of cyber-security concepts. The key is to choose an image that is immediately recognizable and directly related to your field. This alignment helps in reinforcing your area of expertise to viewers.

- **Simplicity and professionalism:** While the background photo is an opportunity to be creative, it is essential to maintain a balance. The image should be simple and not overly complex or busy, as this can distract from the critical information on your profile. A cluttered or overly vibrant background can detract from your profile photo and the textual content on your LinkedIn page. Therefore, a clean, professional look is advisable.

- **Dynamic updating:** Regularly updating your background photo can keep your profile looking fresh and engaging. This does not mean fre-quent changes, but occasional updates can reflect your current pro-fessional focus or any recent shifts in your career path. For example, if you have taken on a new role or are focusing on a new aspect of cybersecurity, your background photo can be a subtle way to communicate this change.

Your LinkedIn background photo should be a carefully chosen graphic that aligns with and enhances your professional brand, mainly reflecting your expertise in cybersecurity. It should be simple and not overpower any other elements of your profile, including your photo. Regular updates can help keep your profile relevant and engaging, making it a dynamic part of your online professional presence.

Headline

Dr. Jason Edwards, DMIST, CISSP, CRISC ⊘

Cybersecurity | Author | Professor | Veteran | Cheer Dad | Husband

San Antonio, Texas, United States · Contact info

Please Follow me on Amazon! ↗

69,602 followers · 500+ connections

The headline on your LinkedIn profile is more than just a job title; it is a concise statement that encapsulates your professional identity and aspirations. It is one of the first things people see when they visit your profile, so crafting an informative and attention-grabbing headline is crucial:

- **Professional title and expertise:** Start by clearly stating your current professional title or area of expertise. For example, if you are a cybersecurity expert, a headline such as *Experienced Cybersecurity Specialist* immediately tells viewers what you do. This clarity is critical, especially in cybersecurity, where expertise is highly valued. If you are in a niche area within cybersecurity, consider specifying that, such as *Cloud Security Expert* or *Cybersecurity Policy Consultant.*
- **Incorporating skills and certifications:** Your headline should also showcase your key or notable certifications. Specific certifications like Certified Information Systems Security Professional (CISSP), Certified Information Security Manager (CISM), or Computer Technology Industry Association (CompTIA) Security+ can be significant draws for employers and colleagues looking for specific expertise in cybersecurity. Including these in your headline can set you apart from others in your field. For instance, *Cybersecurity Specialist | CISSP Certified* succinctly conveys your role and professional qualifications.

- **Catchy yet professional tone:** While being clear about your role and skills is essential, there is room to make your headline engaging. Using a catchy phrase or a unique way of describing your role can make your profile memorable. However, the key is to balance creativity with professionalism. Your headline should be intriguing but still convey seriousness and competence in your field.
- **Alignment with career goals:** Tailor your headline to reflect your current position and where you aim to be in your career. If you are aspiring to move into a leadership role in cybersecurity, you might frame your headline to reflect this ambition, such as *Cybersecurity Leader in the Making* or *Aspiring Cybersecurity Director*. This shows that you are forward-thinking and career-oriented.

Your LinkedIn headline should blend clarity, conciseness, and creativity. It should clearly state your professional title or area of expertise, highlight your skills and certifications, and be engaging enough to draw attention. Most important, it should reflect where you currently are in your career and where you aspire to be, making it a vital aspect of your professional online identity.

Summary (or *About*) Section

About	🖉
(Legal Note: I do not speak on behalf of my employers, and all postings and opinions are my own.) I have over 25 years of experience in cybersecurity, risk, compliance, and technology across various industries, including finance, insurance, and energy. I hold several credentials, such as a Certified in Risk and Information Systems Control (CRISC), a Certified Information Systems Security Professional (CISSP), and a Doctorate in Management, Information Systems, and Technology, specializing in Cybersecurity Regulatory Compliance at Large Financial Institutions. Besides my professional achievements, I am passionate about sharing my knowledge and expertise. I have been an Adjunct Professor of Cybersecurity at multiple universities for over four years, teaching professional and graduate-level	

Your LinkedIn profile's Summary (or *About*) section is a critical space to provide a more detailed and personal view of your professional journey, especially in a specialized field like cybersecurity. This section should be a compelling narrative that encapsulates your experience, skills, and career aspirations:

- **Showcasing cybersecurity expertise and accomplishments:** Begin by highlighting your expertise in cybersecurity. This could involve detailing your areas of specialization, such as network security, threat analysis, or ethical hacking. Do not just list your skills; illustrate them through crucial accomplishments. For example, you could mention a cybersecurity project you led that resulted in successful threat mitigation or point out some special recognition you received for your work in the field. This approach paints a picture of your capabilities and achievements.

- **Detailing skills and experiences:** Besides broad expertise, mentioning specific skills and experiences that are relevant to cybersecurity roles is essential. This might include familiarity with specific security software, experience in cybersecurity frameworks, or knowledge of compliance regulations. If you have experiences demonstrating these skills, such as implementing a new security protocol or conducting security audits, include these to give context to your abilities.
- **Concise and engaging narrative:** While it is essential to be comprehensive, keeping your summary concise and engaging is equally important. Avoid long paragraphs and overly technical jargon that might alienate nonspecialist viewers. Instead, aim for a narrative that is accessible and exciting to a broad audience, including potential employers or collaborators who might not have a deep technical background in cybersecurity.
- **Regular updates reflecting career progress:** Your LinkedIn summary should not be static. Regularly update it to reflect your latest achievements, career shifts, or evolving goals. This keeps your profile current and shows that you are actively engaged in professional development. Whether you have gained a new certification, taken on a new challenging project, or shifted your focus within the cybersecurity field, these updates can make your profile dynamic and reflective of your professional journey.

Your LinkedIn summary should be a well-crafted narrative that highlights your cybersecurity expertise and key accomplishments. It should detail your specific skills and experiences, be concise yet engaging, and be regularly updated to reflect your professional growth. This section is your opportunity to tell your professional story in a way that resonates with your network and potential employers, making it a vital component of your LinkedIn profile.

Experience Section

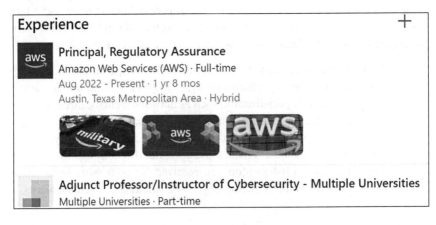

The Experience section on LinkedIn is where you can showcase your professional journey, especially highlighting your roles and contributions in cybersecurity. This section should provide a clear and concise overview of your career, focusing on how each position has contributed to your expertise and professional growth:

- **Listing relevant positions:** Start by listing the positions you have held that are relevant to cybersecurity. This includes not only positions with *cybersecurity* in the title but also roles where you had significant responsibilities or achievements related to cybersecurity. For example, if you worked as a network administrator and were responsible for implementing security protocols, this experience is highly relevant. Ensure that each listed position includes the company name, your role title, and the dates that you were in that position.

- **Detailing achievements and contributions:** For each role, go beyond just listing your job description. Highlight specific achievements and contributions you made in the context of cybersecurity. This could include successful projects you led or contributed to, significant threats you mitigated, or improvements to your organization's security posture. These specifics give viewers a better understanding of your skills and the impact of your work.

- **Using bullet points for clarity:** Structure your experiences using bullet points to enhance clarity and readability. Bullet points allow you to concisely present your responsibilities and achievements, making it easier for viewers to grasp the scope and impact of your work quickly. Each bullet point should begin with a strong action verb and, where possible, include quantifiable results or specific outcomes of your efforts.

- **Regular updates:** The Experience section should be dynamic, reflecting your current professional status. As you take on new roles, gain additional responsibilities, or achieve new accomplishments in cybersecurity, update this section. Regular updates keep your profile current and demonstrate your continued growth and active engagement in your career.

The Experience section of your LinkedIn profile is a crucial area to demonstrate your expertise and achievements in cybersecurity. It should include a clear listing of relevant positions, detailed achievements, and contributions for each role and be structured for clarity using bullet points. Keeping this section regularly updated ensures that your profile accurately reflects your professional development and expertise in the ever-evolving field of cybersecurity.

Education Section

<table>
<tr>
<td colspan="2">

Education

</td>
</tr>
<tr>
<td>

</td>
<td>

University of Phoenix
Doctor of Management in Information Systems and Technology, Cybersecurity Regulatory Testing
2015 - 2019

The University of Phoenix's Doctor of Management in Information Systems and Technology (DM/IST) program is an advanced course focused on leadershi ...see more

</td>
</tr>
<tr>
<td>

</td>
<td>

Capella University
Master of Science - MS, Information Technology
2004 - 2007

</td>
</tr>
</table>

The Education section of your LinkedIn profile is vital, especially for professionals in technical fields like cybersecurity. It is not just a place to list your degrees; it is an opportunity to showcase your academic foundation, specialized training, and ongoing commitment to learning.

- **Listing degrees and certifications:** Include all relevant educational qualifications, especially those directly related to cybersecurity and associated fields. If you hold a degree in computer science, information technology, cybersecurity, or a related discipline, make sure this is prominently listed. In addition to formal degrees, certifications play a critical role in cybersecurity. Certifications such as CISSP, CISM, Certified Ethical Hacker (CEH), or CompTIA Security+ demonstrate your specialized skills and dedication to staying current in a rapidly evolving industry. Each entry should include the institution name, degree or certification obtained, and the dates of study or attainment.
- **Highlighting honors and distinctions:** If you received any honors, awards, or distinctions during your educational journey, mention these in your profile. This could include academic awards, scholarships, or recognition for participation in cybersecurity competitions and events. These distinctions help to differentiate you and underscore your commitment and aptitude in your field of study.
- **Including relevant coursework and projects:** Beyond degrees and certifications, consider adding information about relevant coursework, projects, or research you undertook during your studies. This is particularly useful if these experiences directly relate to your cybersecurity expertise. For example, if you completed a significant project or thesis on network security, incident response, or cryptography, detailing this can add depth to your profile and give potential employers or collaborators insight into your specific areas of interest and expertise.

- **Updating with ongoing or new educational endeavors:** Cybersecurity continually evolves, so ongoing education is crucial. Update your Education section to reflect any new courses, certifications, or degrees you pursue. This could include part-time studies, online courses, or professional development programs. Keeping this section up-to-date demonstrates your commitment to continuous learning and staying abreast of the latest trends and technologies in cybersecurity.

The Education section of your LinkedIn profile is vital to outline your academic credentials, highlight your achievements, and showcase any relevant projects or coursework. Regularly updating this section with your ongoing educational pursuits conveys a strong message about your dedication to professional growth and staying at the forefront of cybersecurity.

Licenses and Certifications

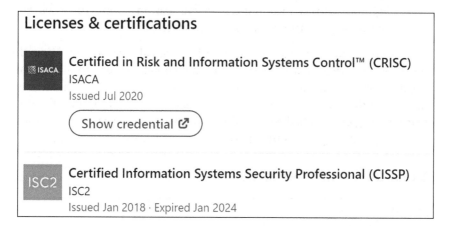

The Licenses and Certifications section of your LinkedIn profile is critical in cybersecurity, where certifications can significantly enhance your credibility and demonstrate your specialized knowledge. This section lets you showcase the qualifications you've earned that are relevant to your field:

- **Listing relevant certifications:** Begin by listing all of your certifications that are pertinent to cybersecurity. This includes both broad certifications and those specific to certain technologies or aspects of cybersecurity. Some of the most recognized certifications in the industry include CISSP, CISM, CEH, and CompTIA Security+. Ensure that each certification listed is relevant to your current role or career aspirations in cybersecurity.
- **Including certifying authority and certification date:** For each certification, include the name of the certifying authority and the date you

obtained the certification. This information adds legitimacy to your qualifications and helps viewers understand the currency of your knowledge and skills. It is essential to show that your certifications are up-to-date in cybersecurity, where technologies and threats are constantly evolving.

- **Regular updates for renewals or new certifications:** Cybersecurity is rapidly changing and maintaining current certifications is a must. Regularly update this section as you renew or obtain additional certifications. This demonstrates your commitment to staying current in your field and ensures that your profile reflects your most up-to-date qualifications.

- **Highlighting prestigious or challenging certifications:** If you have earned any certifications that are particularly prestigious or known to be challenging to obtain, make sure to highlight these. For instance, certifications like CISSP or CISM are highly regarded in the industry and indicate a significant level of expertise and commitment. Highlighting these certifications can set you apart in a competitive field and showcase your dedication to your professional development.

The Licenses and Certifications section is a critical part of your LinkedIn profile in the cybersecurity field. It should comprehensively list all relevant certifications, issuing authority, and certification dates. Keeping this section updated with new or renewed certifications and highlighting those particularly prestigious or challenging will significantly bolster your professional credibility and showcase your expertise in cybersecurity.

Skills and Endorsements

Skills

Leadership

 Endorsed by Dr. Steven Crane and 5 others who are highly skilled at this

 Endorsed by 9 colleagues at USAA

 99+ endorsements

The Skills and Endorsements section is a dynamic component to crafting a LinkedIn profile for a cybersecurity professional. It is a tangible showcase of your professional competencies and expertise, validated through peer endorsements. Here is how to optimize this section:

- **Listing relevant and updated skills:** Begin by identifying and listing essential skills that are pertinent to the field of cybersecurity. This requires staying abreast of industry trends and standards as cybersecurity rapidly evolves. Skills could range from technical ones like network security, ethical hacking, and cryptography to soft skills like problem-solving and communication. Make sure these skills are relevant not only to your current role but also to the broader cybersecurity landscape. Regular updates are vital to ensure that your profile reflects the latest developments and emerging technologies.

- **Prioritization of skills:** While it is tempting to list a vast array of skills, prioritizing the ones that are most relevant and in-demand can have a more significant impact. Focus on skills that set you apart in cybersecurity and are highly valued by employers and peers. This could include specialized competencies like cloud security, Internet of Things security, or expertise in specific cybersecurity tools and software. Prioritization helps in crafting a targeted and relevant profile, making it more appealing to potential employers or collaborators.

- **Seeking endorsements:** Endorsements from colleagues, peers, and supervisors add significant credibility to your skills. They serve as a form of social proof, validating your expertise in the eyes of profile viewers. Actively seek endorsements for your critical skills, especially from individuals with first-hand experience working with you. You can also endorse your connections' skills, which often encourages reciprocation. However, ensure that endorsements are genuine and from credible sources because they reflect on your professional reputation.

- **Regular updates and relevance evaluation:** The cybersecurity landscape continuously changes, necessitating regular reevaluation and updating of your skills. As you acquire new competencies, add them to your profile. Conversely, remove or deprioritize skills that have become less relevant. This ongoing maintenance ensures that your profile stays current and aligned with the demands of the industry. It also demonstrates your commitment to professional development and adaptability, which are highly valued cybersecurity traits.

Your LinkedIn profile's Skills and Endorsements section is a dynamic showcase of your cybersecurity expertise. It should be carefully curated to include relevant, up-to-date skills and prioritized according to industry demands. Endorsements enhance credibility, while regular updates ensure your profile remains relevant and reflects your professional growth.

Recommendations

Recommendations   + 🖉

Received   Given

 Brian Nolan · 1st
Student at University of Buffalo - Cybersecurity Professional Program.
May 29, 2023, Brian reported directly to Dr. Jason

Dr. Edwards is a world class educator. He has inspired me to go above and beyond in a field that I barely understood until I took his class. His mixture of personal experience, passion for work, and leadership qualities made him one of the most memorable professors I have had the pleasure of learning under. I would recommend everyone take at least one Cybersecurity course taught by him for the fact that

The Recommendations section of a LinkedIn profile is a powerful tool, particularly for professionals in specialized fields like cybersecurity. This section allows others to provide testimonials about your work, skills, and professional demeanor. Here is how to effectively utilize this feature:

- **Requesting recommendations:** When seeking recommendations, target individuals who can genuinely attest to your expertise and professional accomplishments. This group might include past or present colleagues, supervisors, clients, or mentors. The key is to choose individuals who are familiar with your work and who can provide specific, credible insights into your abilities and contributions. When making the request, it is helpful to personalize it by explaining why you value their endorsement and how you believe it could benefit your professional profile.
- **Providing guidance for recommendations:** To ensure that the recommendations are as practical as possible, you can guide your endorsers as to what to focus on. For instance, if you want to highlight your skills in a specific area of cybersecurity, such as threat analysis or compliance, mention this. You might also suggest they touch on projects or achievements that you have collaborated on. This guidance helps your endorsers write more focused and relevant recommendations, making them more valuable to your profile.
- **Expressing gratitude and reciprocating:** Always respond with a sincere thank you to those who take the time to write a recommendation. Acknowledging their effort is not only polite but also helps in maintaining a strong professional relationship. Additionally, consider reciprocating with a thoughtful recommendation for them, especially if you can attest to their professional skills and accomplishments. This mutual endorsement can strengthen your network and professional bonds.

- **Regular review and refresh of recommendations:** Over time, your career will evolve, and so will the recommendations on your profile. Periodically review the recommendations you have received to ensure they align with your current professional focus and goals. If you transition to a new area within cybersecurity or take on a different role, it might be time to seek new recommendations that reflect these changes. Regularly refreshing this section ensures that it remains relevant and accurately represents your professional standing.

Recommendations on LinkedIn are a vital element of your professional profile, particularly in a field as specialized as cybersecurity. They provide a personal and credible testament to your skills, work ethic, and achievements. By thoughtfully requesting, guiding, and maintaining these recommendations, you can enhance your professional credibility and showcase your expertise and accomplishments.

Accomplishments

Honors & awards $+$ $\varnothing$
Bronze Star Medal   Issued by MG Robert Caslen · Sep 2009   To all who shall see these presents, greeting: this is to certify that the President of the United States of America, authorized by executive order, 24 August 1962 has awarded the I ...see more
Defense Meritorius Service Medal   Issued by MG. Zannie O. Smith · Dec 1999   The Defense Meritorious Service Medal (DMSM) is an award bestowed upon members of the

The Accomplishments section allows you to showcase your unique contributions, achievements, and milestones that might not be fully captured in other parts of your profile. Here is how to effectively utilize this section:

- **Including projects, awards, and recognitions:** Start by listing specific projects you have worked on that significantly impacted cybersecurity. This could be anything from a successful network security implementation to a significant cybersecurity upgrade you spearheaded. Include any awards or recognitions you have received, whether from your organization, industry associations, or other professional groups. These recognitions serve as validation of your expertise and contributions to the field.

- **Highlighting publications, speaking engagements, and research:** If you have authored any articles, papers, or books related to cybersecurity, ensure that these are included in your profile. Likewise, these should also be highlighted if you have participated in speaking engagements, conferences, or panels. Such activities demonstrate your thought leadership and active participation in the broader cybersecurity community. If you have been involved in significant research projects independently or as part of a team, detailing these can further underscore your expertise and commitment to advancing the field.
- **Regular updates with new milestones:** The cybersecurity field is dynamic, and your career will likely evolve with new achievements and milestones. Regularly update this section to reflect your latest accomplishments. Whether it is a new project completion, a recently published article, or an award, keeping this section current ensures that your profile accurately represents your professional journey and keeps your network informed of your ongoing contributions to the field.
- **Showcasing unique contributions:** Use this section to differentiate yourself. Highlight accomplishments that showcase your unique cybersecurity skills, experiences, and perspective. This could include innovative solutions you have developed, cross-disciplinary work, or contributions to emerging areas within cybersecurity. Showcasing these unique aspects of your professional journey enhances your profile and demonstrates your diverse capabilities and forward-thinking approach in the field.

The Accomplishments section of your LinkedIn profile is an opportunity to spotlight your distinctive achievements and contributions in cybersecurity. By including relevant projects, awards, publications, speaking engagements, and research and by regularly updating this section with new milestones, you can effectively showcase your expertise, thought leadership, and ongoing commitment to the field. This comprehensive display of your professional accomplishments can significantly enhance your visibility and credibility.

Contact Information

The Contact Information section of your LinkedIn profile is straightforward but pivotal, particularly for cybersecurity professionals open to networking, job opportunities, or collaborations. This section should offer clear and direct ways for potential employers, recruiters, colleagues, or clients to reach you. Here is how to make the most of it:

- **Providing a professional email address:** Your email address is often the primary means of contact, so it is crucial to include one that is professional and regularly checked. Use a simple email address that ideally incorporates your name, avoiding nicknames or numbers that might seem informal or less professional. If you have a work or academic email address that you frequently use, consider including that as well, but ensure that it is appropriate for the kind of contacts you expect through LinkedIn.
- **Including links to professional websites or portfolios:** If you have a personal website, a professional blog, or an online portfolio that showcases your work in cybersecurity, include links to these sites. This is particularly important in cybersecurity, where demonstrating your skills and projects can substantively support your professional profile. Ensure these links are active and that the content on these sites is up-to-date and reflects your current professional interests and expertise.
- **Ensuring current and accessible contact information:** Regularly review your contact information to ensure that it is current. If you change your email address or phone number or move to a different organization, update this information promptly on your LinkedIn profile. Accessibility is vital; ensure that potential contacts can easily reach you without navigating through outdated or incorrect information.
- **Adding a phone number for job searches:** If you are actively seeking job opportunities or are open to being contacted for potential roles or collaborations, consider adding a phone number. This can facilitate direct and immediate communication, which is often preferred in time-sensitive situations such as job recruitment. However, be mindful of privacy considerations; if you are uncomfortable with sharing your number widely, you may opt to only provide it upon individual request or through direct messaging.

The Contact Information section is a vital yet often overlooked part of your LinkedIn profile. By providing a professional email address, linking to your professional websites or portfolios, ensuring that all information is up-to-date, and considering the inclusion of a phone number, you can make it easier for potential employers, collaborators, and others in the cybersecurity field to reach out to you directly. This can open doors to new opportunities and enable you to expand your professional network effectively.

Featured Section

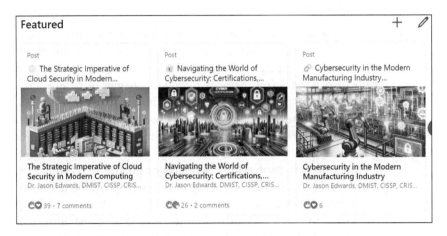

The Featured section on LinkedIn is an excellent way to visually highlight your key achievements, insights, and contributions in cybersecurity. This section is a curated portfolio of your most impactful work, allowing viewers to quickly grasp your expertise and interests. Here is how to optimize it effectively:

- **Showcasing relevant posts, articles, or documents:** Use this space to feature posts, articles, or documents that you have created or contributed to that are specifically relevant to cybersecurity. This could include thought leadership articles you have written, insightful posts or analyses on recent cybersecurity trends, or detailed case studies of projects you have worked on. By selecting content that showcases your deep understanding and experience in cybersecurity, you provide immediate value to profile viewers, whether they are potential employers, collaborators, or peers in the industry.

- **Highlighting your best work and contributions:** Choose to feature items that represent your best work or your most significant contributions to the field. This might be a groundbreaking research paper, a presentation at a significant conference, or an article that received substantial recognition from the cybersecurity community. The goal is to put forward content you are most proud of that best illustrates your skills and achievements.

- **Regular updates with new content:** The cybersecurity landscape constantly evolves, and your Featured section should reflect this dynamism. Regularly update this section with new content that aligns with your current professional focus or the latest trends in the industry. This could be a recent publication, a report on emerging cybersecurity threats, or a post reflecting your insights on new technological developments. Keeping this section current makes your profile more engaging and demonstrates your active involvement and continuous learning in the field.

- **Engaging viewers visually with your expertise:** The Featured section is a visual space, so take advantage of this to engage viewers. Include visually appealing elements such as images, infographics, or videos, especially if they add context or clarity to your content. For example, featuring a visually rich infographic that explains a complex cybersecurity concept can be both engaging and informative. The aim is to use this section to inform, captivate, and visually communicate your expertise and passion for cybersecurity.

The Featured section of your LinkedIn profile is a strategic space to showcase your expertise and achievements in cybersecurity. By carefully selecting and regularly updating content that highlights your best work, insights, and contributions and presenting it in a visually engaging way, you can make a solid and immediate impact on viewers, enhancing your professional brand and visibility in the cybersecurity community.

ENGAGING WITH INDUSTRY CONTENT ON LINKEDIN

Actively following respected industry leaders, renowned companies, and key influencers in the cybersecurity field is essential for staying informed about the latest trends, developments, and debates. Following these entities makes your LinkedIn feed a rich resource of current information, thought leadership, and industry insights. This keeps you updated and offers ideas and inspiration for your contributions. Pay attention to thought-provoking articles, innovative approaches, and strategic moves within the industry that are being shared by these leaders and organizations because they can significantly enrich your understanding and perspective.

Engage with the cybersecurity community by sharing and commenting on pertinent articles and news updates. When you share content, add your perspective or critical takeaways to make your posts more engaging and reflect your analytical skills. Commenting on posts by others, especially those made by industry leaders or peers, can increase your visibility and establish you as an active, informed participant in your field. Your comments should be insightful, adding value to the discussion and reflecting your expertise and professional demeanor.

Leverage LinkedIn as a platform to publish your articles or posts that showcase your cybersecurity knowledge and insights. This could range from in-depth articles on specific cybersecurity challenges and reflections on industry trends to commentary on recent cyber incidents. Your publications can highlight your areas of expertise, analytical skills, and ability to communicate complex ideas effectively. Regularly publishing constructive content will position you as a knowledgeable professional and can attract favorable attention from potential employers, collaborators, and peers.

Joining and actively participating in LinkedIn groups and discussions centered around cybersecurity is a great way to engage with the community. These groups are often forums for sharing information, discussing emerging trends, and debating critical issues. Participating in these discussions can enhance your network, provide learning opportunities, and allow you to contribute your expertise to collective knowledge. Engaging in these communities demonstrates your commitment to the field. It can lead to meaningful connections and professional growth.

NETWORKING AND BUILDING CONNECTIONS ON LINKEDIN

Actively seeking connections with professionals in the cybersecurity field is a fundamental aspect of leveraging LinkedIn effectively. This includes reaching out to peers, mentors, industry leaders, and potential employers. When initiating these connections, sending personalized messages that provide context for your interest is beneficial. Explain your motives, whether they are shared interests, admiration for their work, or a desire to learn from their expertise. This approach enriches your network and fosters opportunities for collaboration and knowledge sharing.

Participation in professional organizations and events is another crucial strategy. LinkedIn offers a platform to discover and engage with these groups, including virtual events, webinars, and industry discussions. Involvement in these activities expands your knowledge and skills and opens doors to meeting professionals who share your interests. This active engagement is a testament to your dedication to professional growth and helps you forge strong industry connections.

Networking also involves the exchange of knowledge and experiences. Simply by participating, you are engaging in mentorship—whether as a mentor or a mentee—and the experience is incredibly valuable. As a mentee, you gain invaluable insights and guidance, while as a mentor, you can give back to the community and hone your leadership skills. This reciprocal relationship enriches both parties and contributes to the overall health of the cybersecurity community.

Using LinkedIn's networking features can significantly enhance your professional connections. Utilize tools like the *Alumni* feature to connect with former classmates in your field, or explore the *Events* feature to find and participate in relevant industry gatherings. Consistently updating your profile, sharing your professional experiences, and interacting with your connections' content also keeps your network active and engaged. This ongoing interaction maintains your existing relationships and opens up new avenues for professional opportunities.

NETWORKING AND JOB SEARCH STRATEGIES ON LINKEDIN

One of the most effective strategies on LinkedIn for professionals in the cybersecurity industry is to build a network that includes alums from your educational institutions, current and former colleagues, and other professionals in the field. This can be done using LinkedIn's search and filter tools to find individuals with a common educational background, work experience, or interest in cybersecurity. Connecting with alumni is particularly beneficial as they often share a sense of camaraderie and are usually more open to networking. Similarly, reaching out to colleagues and professionals in your field can lead to new opportunities since they might have insights into job openings, industry trends, or valuable contacts.

LinkedIn's job search feature is a powerful tool for finding positions tailored to your skills and interests in cybersecurity. You can search for jobs based on criteria such as location, company, and job function. The platform also allows you to set up job alerts based on your preferences, ensuring that you do not miss relevant opportunities. Additionally, applying through LinkedIn can sometimes streamline the process since your profile information is readily available to employers. This feature often shows connections you might have at the hiring company, which can be an avenue for gaining more information or a referral.

Informational interviews are an underutilized strategy that can provide invaluable insights into different roles and companies in the cybersecurity sector. These are informal conversations with professionals in roles or companies that you are interested in. You can contact individuals via LinkedIn and explain your interest in learning about their career path, current role, and organization. These interviews can help you understand the skills and experiences valued in certain positions, the company culture, and potential career trajectories.

Recommendations on LinkedIn are a great way to build credibility. They provide a third-party validation of your skills, experience, and professional demeanor. You can request recommendations from colleagues, managers, or mentors who can vouch for your expertise and work ethic, especially in areas relevant to cybersecurity. Having a set of robust, genuine recommendations can make your profile stand out to potential employers, adding trust and authenticity to your online presence.

LinkedIn offers a multifaceted approach to networking and job searching, especially for those in specialized fields like cybersecurity. By strategically connecting with the right individuals, utilizing the job search features, engaging in informational interviews, and garnering recommendations, professionals can significantly enhance their chances of finding rewarding career opportunities and meaningfully expanding their network.

8

TECHNICAL ROLES IN CYBERSECURITY

Various technical roles characterize cybersecurity, each playing a critical part in protecting digital assets and infrastructures. These roles demand a profound understanding of complex technological environments and the ability to adapt to the ever-evolving landscape of cyber threats constantly. In this chapter we explore the intricate details of various technical roles within the cybersecurity domain. We focus on the specific responsibilities, the skill sets required, and the relentless need for ongoing education and skill enhancement. This exploration offers valuable insights for those aspiring to embark on or advance in their cybersecurity careers, shedding light on the multifaceted nature of these crucial roles in maintaining digital security and integrity.

APPLICATION SECURITY ENGINEER

An application security engineer is critical in safeguarding software applications against cyber threats and vulnerabilities. This specialized position focuses on the intersection of software development and cybersecurity, requiring a unique blend of skills in both domains. Application security engineers are responsible for implementing security protocols in software development, conducting rigorous security testing of applications, and managing various security tools and processes to ensure that the applications are resilient against cyberattacks. Their work is pivotal in ensuring that software applications—a crucial asset in any organization's digital infrastructure—are robust, secure, and trustworthy.

Securing applications against threats is the primary responsibility of an application security engineer. This involves identifying potential security vulnerabilities within applications and devising strategies to mitigate these risks.

These engineers work closely with software development teams to integrate security measures from the early application design and development stages. They ensure that security is not an afterthought but an integral part of the software development life cycle. This proactive approach helps build inherently secure and resilient applications to cyber threats.

Implementing security protocols in software development is crucial for application security engineers. They are responsible for establishing and enforcing security standards and best practices in the software development process. This includes integrating secure coding practices, ensuring proper data encryption, and safeguarding against common vulnerabilities like Structured Query Language injections and cross-site scripting. Their expertise ensures that security considerations are embedded in the code, making the applications robust against potential breaches.

Application security engineers perform various types of security testing, such as static application security testing, dynamic application security testing, and penetration testing, to identify and address security issues. They simulate cyberattacks on applications to test their defenses and identify any weaknesses that need to be fortified. This testing is an ongoing process, crucial for maintaining the security integrity of applications throughout their life cycles.

Managing application security tools and processes involves overseeing the tools and methodologies used to protect applications. Application security engineers select and implement security tools such as vulnerability scanners and code analyzers. They also develop and maintain processes for continuous monitoring and improvement of application security. Their management of these tools and processes ensures a comprehensive and systematic approach to application security.

For professionals who are aiming to become application security engineers, acquiring certifications such as Certified Information Systems Security Professional (CISSP), Certified Secure Software Lifecycle Professional, or Global Information Assurance Certification (GIAC) Web Application Defender can be advantageous. These certifications demonstrate a high level of expertise in application security and are recognized across the industry.

The role of an application security engineer is vital in the modern digital landscape, where cyber threats constantly target applications. Their responsibilities encompass securing applications, implementing security protocols in software development, conducting thorough security testing, and managing security tools and processes. As with each of these roles, continuous learning and professional development, including relevant certifications, are crucial for staying ahead in this dynamic and increasingly important field.

BLUE TEAM OPERATOR (DEFENDER)

In the cybersecurity arena, blue team operators, or defenders, are key players in the ongoing battle against cyber threats. These professionals are tasked with the proactive defense of computer networks and systems—focusing on robust protection, continuous monitoring, and rapid response to security incidents. Their role is pivotal in maintaining the integrity and security of an organization's digital infrastructure. The responsibilities of a blue team operator include defending against various cyber threats, diligently monitoring network security, responding effectively to security breaches, and implementing a range of protective measures to safeguard the organization's digital assets.

Defending against cyber threats is the core responsibility of a blue team operator. This involves staying vigilant against various cyberattacks, ranging from malware and phishing to more sophisticated threats like advanced persistence and ransomware. Blue team operators must be well-versed in the latest cybersecurity threats and trends in order to anticipate and prepare for potential attacks. Their defensive strategies are about thwarting attacks and creating a resilient environment that can withstand and recover from any cyber incidents.

Blue team operators employ various tools and technologies to continuously monitor the organization's networks and systems for any unusual activity that could indicate a security threat. They analyze network traffic, scrutinize system logs, and use intrusion detection systems to identify potential vulnerabilities or breaches. This continuous monitoring is crucial for early detection of threats, allowing for a prompt and effective response to protect the network.

Responding to security breaches is an essential duty of a blue team operator. In the event of a security breach, they are responsible for quickly assessing the situation, containing the breach, and mitigating its impact. This response requires a well-coordinated effort, often involving collaboration with other IT and cybersecurity teams, to isolate affected systems, eradicate the threat, and restore normal operations as swiftly as possible. Their ability to respond effectively to breaches is critical in minimizing damage and ensuring business continuity.

Implementing protective measures is a proactive part of a blue team operator's responsibilities. This involves developing and enforcing security policies, implementing firewalls, and setting up encryption protocols. They also play a crucial role in educating other employees about cybersecurity best practices and raising awareness about potential security risks. Additionally, they are often involved in designing and implementing disaster recovery and business continuity plans to ensure that the organization can quickly recover from cyber incidents.

Pursuing certifications such as CISSP, Computer Technology Industry Association (CompTIA) Security+, or Certified Ethical Hacker (CEH) can be beneficial for those aspiring to become blue team operators. These certifications not only equip professionals with the necessary skills but also validate their expertise in cybersecurity defense.

A blue team operator's role is integral to any organization's cybersecurity framework. Their duties encompass defending against cyber threats, monitoring network security, responding to breaches, and implementing protective measures.

CYBERSECURITY ENGINEER

A cybersecurity engineer's role is central to any organization's defense mechanisms in the digital age. This position demands a high level of technical expertise and a strategic approach to designing and implementing robust security solutions. Cybersecurity engineers are responsible for creating a secure computing environment that effectively shields against cyber threats and vulnerabilities. Their key responsibilities include designing and implementing security solutions, staying updated with current cybersecurity trends, conducting security audits and system improvements, and working closely with various stakeholders to understand and meet security requirements. Each of these responsibilities requires a blend of technical knowledge, innovative thinking, and collaborative skills, making the role of a cybersecurity engineer both challenging and critical.

Designing and implementing security solutions are at the forefront of any cybersecurity engineer's duties. This involves creating complex security structures and ensuring that they function effectively to protect against cyber threats. Engineers must deeply understand network architectures, software development, and the latest security technologies. They need to design solutions that are effective in thwarting attacks and that are scalable and adaptable to the evolving technological landscape. This might involve developing custom security protocols, installing firewalls, encryption tools, and antivirus software, and setting up intrusion detection systems.

Staying updated with current cybersecurity trends is crucial for a cybersecurity engineer. Cybersecurity is continuously evolving, with new threats and vulnerabilities emerging regularly. To guard against these threats effectively, engineers must keep abreast of the latest cybersecurity technologies, tactics, and strategies. This involves continuous learning and adaptation and staying connected with the broader cybersecurity community to exchange knowledge and insights.

Security audits and system improvements are another critical responsibility. Cybersecurity engineers regularly assess the organization's security posture, identify potential vulnerabilities, and recommend enhancements. They conduct rigorous testing and evaluations of existing security systems to ensure they are impenetrable and comply with all regulatory standards. This proactive approach helps identify and mitigate risks before malicious actors can exploit them.

Working closely with stakeholders on security requirements is essential for ensuring that the cybersecurity strategies align with the organization's needs and goals. Cybersecurity engineers collaborate with various organizational departments to understand their security concerns and requirements. They must be able to communicate complex security concepts using language that even nontechnical stakeholders will understand while also ensuring that security policies are effectively integrated into all aspects of the organization.

For individuals who are aspiring to become cybersecurity engineers, obtaining certifications such as CISSP, CEH, or Certified Information Security Manager (CISM) can be highly beneficial. These certifications provide a solid foundation of knowledge and skills while demonstrating a commitment to the field and a standard of professional expertise that is recognized globally.

The role of a cybersecurity engineer is pivotal in safeguarding an organization's digital assets. It requires a comprehensive skill set that includes technical proficiency, an understanding of current cybersecurity trends, the ability to conduct thorough audits and make improvements, and the capability to work effectively with various stakeholders. Continuous learning and professional development, including obtaining relevant certifications, are essential for success and growth.

FIREWALL ADMINISTRATOR

In the cybersecurity landscape, the firewall administrator holds a position of crucial importance—tasked with the essential responsibility of managing and configuring firewalls. These professionals are the guardians of network security, playing a pivotal role in protecting an organization's digital assets from external threats. The role of a firewall administrator involves a multifaceted approach to network security, including managing and configuring firewall systems, continuously monitoring network traffic, implementing and enforcing security rules and policies, and regularly conducting firewall audits to ensure optimal performance and security.

Managing and configuring firewalls is at the core of the firewall administrator's responsibilities. This involves setting up and maintaining firewall hardware and software to control the flow of inbound and outbound network traffic. Administrators must accurately configure firewall rules and settings to filter traffic, block unauthorized access, and prevent attacks. Their expertise in understanding the nuances of network protocols and security threats is crucial for tailoring firewall configurations to provide maximum protection while maintaining network efficiency and user accessibility.

Monitoring network traffic is another critical duty of a firewall administrator. They continuously scrutinize network traffic to identify abnormal patterns or potential security threats. Utilizing various network monitoring tools, the firewall administrators analyze data packets and log files to detect any signs of malicious activity or policy violations. This vigilant monitoring is key to early detection and response to potential threats, ensuring the security and integrity of the network.

Implementing security rules and policies is an essential function of the firewall administrator. They develop and enforce network security policies that dictate how the firewall manages and filters traffic. This includes creating and updating firewall rules to reflect the evolving security landscape and the organization's specific needs. Administrators must balance security requirements with business needs, ensuring that security measures do not impede organizational productivity. They also ensure compliance with regulatory standards and best practices in network security.

Conducting regular firewall audits is vital for maintaining a robust security posture. Firewall administrators regularly review and evaluate firewall configurations, rules, and policies to ensure they are effective against current threats and aligned with the organization's security objectives. These audits help identify potential vulnerabilities, ensure compliance with security standards, and adjust firewall settings. Regular audits also provide insights into network security trends, facilitating proactive measures to enhance security.

For those pursuing a career as a firewall administrator, obtaining certifications like CISSP or Cisco Certified Network Associate (CCNA) Security can be beneficial. These certifications equip professionals with a comprehensive understanding of network security and firewall management, enhancing their skills and credibility.

The role of a firewall administrator is integral to safeguarding an organization's network. It encompasses managing and configuring firewalls, monitoring network traffic, implementing security rules and policies, and conducting regular firewall audits.

FORENSIC ANALYST

The role of a forensic analyst is critical in the realm of cybersecurity, particularly in the context of investigating cybercrimes and breaches. These professionals are the detectives of the cyber world, specializing in unraveling the complexities behind cyberattacks and data breaches. Their work involves meticulous investigation, data recovery and analysis, collaboration with legal teams for evidence presentation, and staying abreast of the latest forensic analysis tools and techniques. This multifaceted role requires a unique blend of technical expertise, analytical skills, and legal knowledge, making it both challenging and essential in the fight against cybercrime.

Investigation of cybercrimes and breaches is the primary responsibility of a forensic analyst. They are tasked with delving into the details of a cyberattack to determine how the breach occurred, the extent of the damage, and who might be responsible. This process involves examining digital evidence, tracing the steps of cybercriminals, and piecing together the actions that led to the breach. Their investigations are not only crucial for understanding the specifics of an incident but also for preventing future attacks.

Data recovery and analysis from digital sources are other vital aspects of a forensic analyst's role. Critical data can be compromised, lost, or manipulated in cyber incidents. Forensic analysts use advanced techniques and tools to recover this data from various digital sources, such as hard drives, servers, and cloud storage. Once recovered, they meticulously analyze this data to glean insights and gather evidence. Their ability to recover and analyze data is essential in piecing together the timeline of events during a cyberattack.

Collaborating with legal teams for evidence presentation is an essential responsibility of forensic analysts. The evidence they collect and analyze often becomes part of the legal proceedings related to cybercrimes. Therefore, forensic analysts must work closely with legal teams to ensure the evidence is presented accurately and effectively in a legal context. This collaboration requires them to have an understanding of legal processes and the ability to communicate technical information in a way that is comprehensible in legal settings.

Staying current with forensic analysis tools and techniques is a must for forensic analysts. The field of digital forensics is constantly evolving, with new tools and methods being developed to keep up with the advancements in technology and the changing tactics of cybercriminals. Continuous learning and professional development are essential for forensic analysts to remain effective. This involves staying updated on the latest forensic software, attending workshops and training sessions, and possibly obtaining certifications such as Certified Computer Forensics Examiner or Certified Forensic Computer Examiner.

The role of a forensic analyst is indispensable in the cybersecurity landscape. It requires a detailed and methodical approach to investigating cybercrimes, expertise in data recovery and analysis, collaboration with legal teams, and a commitment to staying current with the latest tools and techniques in digital forensics. For those aspiring to this role, ongoing education and a keen interest in the technical and legal aspects of cyber forensics are critical to a successful and impactful career.

INCIDENT RESPONDER

In the high-stakes world of cybersecurity, the role of an incident responder is crucial, mainly when dealing with the immediate aftermath of security breaches. Incident responders are the first line of defense when a cyber incident occurs—tasked with rapid response, effective coordination of recovery operations, comprehensive analysis of the incident for future threat prevention, and maintaining clear communication and documentation throughout the incident management process. This role requires technical expertise, quick thinking, strong problem-solving skills, and practical communication abilities.

Rapid response to security breaches is one of the primary responsibilities of an incident responder. When a breach occurs, time is of the essence, and the ability to respond swiftly and efficiently can significantly reduce the attack's impact. Incident responders must quickly assess the situation, identify the breach's scope, and implement measures to contain and mitigate the damage. This requires a deep understanding of various cyber threats, a familiarity with the organization's IT infrastructure, and the ability to work under pressure.

Coordination of recovery operations is another critical aspect of this role. Once the immediate threat is contained, incident responders restore systems and services to normal operations. This involves coordinating with different teams within the organization, such as IT, legal, and public relations, to ensure a comprehensive recovery strategy. They must also work on identifying the incident's root cause to prevent future similar breaches.

After addressing the immediate concerns of a breach, incident responders thoroughly analyze the incident to understand how it happened and why defenses failed. This analysis is important for strengthening the organization's cybersecurity posture and preventing similar incidents in the future. It involves thoroughly examining the breach, identifying exploited vulnerabilities, and recommending improvements to security policies, procedures, and technologies.

Communication and documentation during incidents are vital for effective incident response. Incident responders must maintain clear and ongoing communication with key stakeholders throughout the incident management process. This includes providing updates on the response status, explaining the steps being taken, and outlining the potential impact. Proper documentation is also crucial since it provides a record of the incident and the response, which is essential for post-incident reviews, compliance purposes, and legal considerations.

For those interested in pursuing a career as an incident responder, certifications like EC-Council Certified Incident Handler, CISSP, and Certified Computer Security Incident Handler can provide the necessary skills and knowledge. These certifications are recognized in the industry and can help professionals demonstrate their expertise and commitment to the role.

The role of an incident responder is critical in managing and mitigating cybersecurity incidents. It requires a combination of rapid response capabilities, practical coordination skills, analytical thinking for post-incident reviews, and strong communication and documentation skills.

IDENTITY AND ACCESS MANAGEMENT (IAM) SPECIALIST

In cybersecurity, an IAM specialist is vital for ensuring the secure and efficient management of user identities and access within an organization. This role focuses on implementing and maintaining systems that control who can access specific data and resources—a crucial aspect of protecting sensitive information and maintaining operational integrity. The responsibilities of an IAM specialist include managing user identities and access privileges, implementing robust access controls, conducting thorough audits of access and authentication processes, and ensuring that these processes comply with established security policies and regulations.

Managing user identities and access forms the cornerstone of an IAM specialist's role. This involves creating, managing, and overseeing user accounts and access permissions within an organization. IAM specialists ensure that only authorized individuals can access specific systems and data based on their role and necessity. They manage the entire life cycle of user identities, from onboarding new employees and assigning access rights to offboarding departing staff and revoking their access. This task requires a deep understanding of the organization's structure and workflows to ensure that access rights align with job roles and responsibilities.

IAM specialists are responsible for setting up and managing the technology and processes restricting access to networks, systems, and data. This includes implementing authentication mechanisms, such as passwords, biometrics, multifactor authentication, and authorization protocols to ensure that users can only access the information necessary for their roles. They also work on developing and enforcing password policies and security standards to maintain the integrity of access controls.

Auditing access and authentication processes are essential for maintaining security and operational efficiency. IAM specialists regularly review and analyze these processes to ensure they function correctly and effectively. They conduct audits to identify unauthorized access attempts, assess the effectiveness of the authentication methods, and ensure that access rights are appropriately assigned and managed. These audits are critical for identifying potential security gaps and ensuring the IAM system remains robust against emerging threats.

They ensure that the organization's access management practices comply with relevant laws, regulations, and industry standards. This involves staying updated on regulatory changes, working with compliance and legal teams, and aligning IAM practices with compliance requirements. IAM specialists also play a role in educating staff about access policies and the importance of adhering to these policies to maintain security.

Obtaining certifications such as CISSP or Certified Identity and Access Manager can be advantageous for individuals interested in the IAM specialist role. These certifications provide a strong foundation in identity and access management principles and practices, enhancing the specialist's skills and credibility.

The role of an IAM specialist is integral to an organization's security infrastructure. It involves managing user identities and access, implementing and maintaining access controls, auditing these processes, and ensuring compliance with security policies. Staying informed and certified in the latest IAM practices and technologies is vital to effectively managing the complex and ever-evolving IAM challenges.

INDUSTRIAL CONTROL SYSTEMS (ICS) SECURITY SPECIALIST

An ICS security specialist is pivotal in safeguarding critical infrastructure and industrial environments from cyber threats. As industries increasingly rely on automation and intelligent technologies, the security of ICS becomes crucial for the safe and efficient operation of essential services such as power plants, water treatment facilities, and manufacturing units. ICS security specialists are tasked with securing these complex systems, assessing risks, implementing tailored security measures, and vigilantly monitoring and responding to potential threats in industrial settings.

Securing industrial control systems is the primary responsibility of an ICS security specialist. These systems, which include SCADA (Supervisory Control and Data Acquisition) systems, Distributed Control Systems, and Programmable Logic Controllers, are critical for the operational integrity of industrial processes. ICS security specialists develop and implement strategies to protect these systems from cyberattacks that could lead to disruptions, safety hazards, or operational failures. This involves understanding the unique characteristics of industrial systems, such as their real-time operational requirements and the potential impact of system downtimes.

ICS security specialists conduct thorough risk assessments to identify vulnerabilities within industrial control systems, considering digital and physical threats. This assessment includes analyzing the potential impact of various threat scenarios, identifying areas where security measures are lacking, and prioritizing risks based on their potential impact on safety and operations. Understanding the interconnectivity of networked industrial systems and their interfaces with other networks is vital for comprehensive risk assessment.

Implementing security measures in industrial settings requires a specialized approach. ICS security specialists design and implement security solutions that are tailored to the unique needs and constraints found in industrial environments. This includes securing network communications, safeguarding critical endpoints, and ensuring the integrity of control systems software. They must balance robust security measures with the requirement to maintain system performance and reliability, often working within the constraints of legacy systems and industrial protocols.

Monitoring and responding to ICS threats is an ongoing responsibility. ICS security specialists use various tools and techniques to continuously monitor industrial control systems for signs of malicious activity or security breaches. They must be prepared to respond quickly and effectively to incidents, minimizing the impact on industrial operations. This involves incident detection, analysis, and coordinated response strategies to contain and mitigate threats, as well as post-incident recovery and system hardening to prevent future attacks.

Obtaining certifications such as Global Industrial Cyber Security Professional or Certified SCADA Security Architect can be highly beneficial for those interested in a career as an ICS security specialist. These certifications provide knowledge and skills that are specific to industrial cybersecurity, demonstrating expertise in protecting critical industrial infrastructure.

The role of an ICS security specialist is essential in protecting critical industrial and infrastructure systems. Their responsibilities include securing ICS, assessing risks, implementing tailored security measures, and monitoring and responding to threats in these specialized environments. Continuous learning and staying abreast of the latest developments in industrial cybersecurity are critical to effectively addressing the complex challenges faced in securing industrial control systems.

INTERNET OF THINGS (IoT) SECURITY SPECIALIST

An IoT security specialist is critical in safeguarding the ever-growing ecosystem of interconnected devices and networks that constitute the IoT landscape. With the rapid expansion of IoT devices in various sectors, including healthcare, home automation, and industrial systems, the security of these devices becomes paramount. The responsibilities of an IoT security specialist encompass securing IoT devices and networks, assessing IoT-specific security risks, implementing robust security solutions tailored to IoT environments, and continuously monitoring these ecosystems to identify and address vulnerabilities.

Securing IoT devices and networks is the primary duty of an IoT security specialist. This task protects various devices—from simple sensors to complex, intelligent machines—against potential cyber threats. Given the diversity and volume of IoT devices, this requires a deep understanding of different hardware and software configurations, network protocols, and the unique security challenges they present. IoT security specialists must ensure that these devices are not only secure individually but also when they interact within the more extensive network, thereby safeguarding the entire IoT ecosystem.

IoT security specialists conduct comprehensive risk assessments to identify vulnerabilities within IoT devices and networks. This includes evaluating the potential for unauthorized access, data breaches, and other cyberattacks. Given the often-limited computing capabilities and unique operational contexts of IoT devices, this risk assessment requires a specialized approach to gauge the threat landscape and prioritize security measures accurately.

Implementing IoT security solutions involves developing and deploying strategies to protect IoT devices and networks from cyber threats. IoT security specialists design security architectures that are scalable and adaptable to the diverse nature of IoT devices. This might involve implementing robust authentication mechanisms, encryption protocols, and network segmentation strategies. They also ensure that firmware and software within IoT devices are regularly updated and patched to protect against known vulnerabilities.

Monitoring IoT ecosystems for vulnerabilities is an ongoing responsibility. IoT security specialists use various tools and techniques to continuously scan and analyze IoT networks, identifying anomalies or signs of malicious activity. This proactive monitoring is essential to detect and respond to threats in real time, minimizing potential damage. They must also stay updated with the latest trends and developments in IoT security to anticipate new threats and refine their monitoring strategies accordingly.

For professionals aiming to specialize in IoT security, acquiring certifications such as Certified Internet of Things Practitioner can be highly advantageous. These certifications provide a comprehensive understanding of IoT security concepts and best practices, equipping specialists with the skills needed to address the unique challenges in this field.

An IoT security specialist's role is critical in the digital connectivity age. Their responsibilities include securing IoT devices and networks, assessing risks, implementing tailored security solutions, and monitoring IoT ecosystems for vulnerabilities. As the IoT landscape evolves, staying abreast of the latest security trends and technologies is crucial for effectively protecting the vast and varied world of interconnected devices.

MALWARE ANALYST

A malware analyst plays a pivotal role in the cybersecurity ecosystem, focusing on identifying, analyzing, and mitigating malware—one of the most prevalent cyber threats. This specialized role demands a deep understanding of various types of malware, the skills to develop effective protection strategies, and expertise in reverse engineering. Malware analysts are integral in understanding the nature of malicious software and devising ways to defend against it, working in close collaboration with broader cybersecurity teams to ensure comprehensive threat mitigation.

Identifying and analyzing malware involves detecting and dissecting malware to understand its functionalities, mechanisms, and potential impact. Malware analysts use various tools and techniques to scrutinize malware samples, determining how they infiltrate systems, the type of data they target, and how they propagate. Their detailed analysis helps to understand the attacker's motives and methodologies, providing crucial insights into defending against similar threats in the future.

Developing protection strategies against malware is a critical task for malware analysts. Based on their analysis, they formulate strategies to protect computer systems and networks from potential malware attacks. This involves designing and implementing security measures to detect and neutralize malware before it is damaged. These strategies include developing antivirus software, creating intrusion detection systems, and implementing security protocols that minimize vulnerabilities exploited by malware.

Reverse engineering of malicious software is another critical area of expertise for malware analysts. This complex process involves dissecting malware to understand its source code, functionality, and communication mechanisms. Reverse engineering is crucial, not only in understanding how the malware operates but also in developing effective countermeasures. It allows analysts to anticipate potential updates or variations of the malware and strengthens the overall cybersecurity defense mechanism.

Collaboration with cybersecurity teams for threat mitigation is essential in the role of a malware analyst. Their specialized knowledge of malware is critical to a broader cybersecurity strategy. Malware analysts work with other cybersecurity professionals to implement comprehensive security measures. This collaboration ensures a unified and practical approach to managing and mitigating cyber threats, thereby enhancing the organization's security posture.

For individuals aspiring to a career as a malware analyst, gaining certifications such as Certified Reverse Engineering Analyst or GIAC Reverse Engineering Malware can be highly beneficial. These certifications validate the individual's skills in malware analysis and reverse engineering and signify a commitment to specialized expertise in this challenging field.

The role of a malware analyst is vital in combating one of the most significant threats in the cyber world. It requires technical expertise in identifying and analyzing malware, developing protective strategies, reverse engineering, and collaborating with cybersecurity teams.

MOBILE SECURITY ENGINEER

A mobile security engineer is vital to cybersecurity, focusing on protecting mobile applications and devices, which have become integral to personal and business realms. As mobile technology continues to evolve rapidly, encompassing everything from smartphones to tablets, the need for robust security measures to protect these devices and their applications from cyber threats is more pressing than ever. The role of a mobile security engineer includes securing mobile applications and devices, implementing mobile security protocols, conducting thorough security assessments of mobile devices, and managing mobile security operations.

Securing mobile applications and devices is the primary responsibility of a mobile security engineer. This task involves developing strategies to protect mobile apps from cyber threats like malware, phishing attacks, and unauthorized data access. Engineers must have a profound understanding of iOS and Android operating systems and the security challenges that are unique to each platform. They must ensure that mobile applications are built and maintained with security as a priority, incorporating features like secure authentication, data encryption, and intrusion detection systems.

Mobile security engineers develop and enforce policies and guidelines to maintain the security integrity of mobile devices within an organization. This includes managing the configuration of security settings on mobile devices, ensuring compliance with corporate security policies, and protecting against unauthorized access. They often work with development teams to integrate security measures into the app development life cycle, ensuring that security is considered at every app creation and deployment stage.

Conducting mobile device security assessments is essential to identify and mitigate potential vulnerabilities. Mobile security engineers perform regular security audits and assessments to evaluate the effectiveness of existing security measures. They analyze mobile applications and devices for vulnerabilities, assess the risk levels, and recommend necessary enhancements or updates. These assessments are vital in staying ahead of potential security breaches and ensuring the ongoing protection of mobile ecosystems.

Managing mobile security operations involves overseeing daily security tasks related to mobile devices and applications. This includes monitoring for security breaches, responding to security incidents, and maintaining up-to-date knowledge of the latest mobile security threats and trends. Mobile security engineers collaborate with other cybersecurity teams to develop comprehensive security strategies encompassing mobile and traditional IT environments.

For those pursuing a career as a mobile security engineer, obtaining certifications such as the CISSP or the GIAC Mobile Device Security Analyst can be beneficial. These certifications provide in-depth knowledge and skills specific to mobile security and are recognized in the cybersecurity industry.

The role of a mobile security engineer is critical in today's technology-driven world, where mobile devices and applications are ubiquitous. Their responsibilities encompass securing mobile apps and devices, implementing and managing security protocols, conducting thorough security assessments, and overseeing mobile security operations. Staying updated with the latest mobile security technologies and trends is essential for effectively protecting mobile ecosystems from evolving cyber threats.

NETWORK SECURITY ENGINEER

A network security engineer holds a pivotal position in the cybersecurity infrastructure of any organization and is dedicated to protecting network infrastructure from cyber threats. This role is increasingly vital as businesses rely heavily on networked systems for daily operations, making network security a cornerstone of overall digital security. The responsibilities of a network security engineer include safeguarding the network infrastructure, implementing a variety of network security measures, continuously monitoring the network for security incidents, and managing network security tools and processes to ensure a robust defense against cyber threats.

Protecting network infrastructure involves securing the organization's internal networks and connections to the external internet. The task encompasses safeguarding against unauthorized access, data breaches, and other cyberattacks that could compromise network integrity. Network security engineers must understand the network architecture thoroughly, including its vulnerabilities and potential threat entry points. Their work includes fortifying network perimeters, securing network components, and ensuring the entire network is resilient against attacks.

Network security engineers are responsible for designing and applying various security strategies to protect the network. This might include installing and configuring firewalls, intrusion detection systems, and antivirus software. They also implement security protocols and policies, such as virtual private networks for secure remote access and encryption standards to protect data in transit. Developing and enforcing these measures requires a deep understanding of network security principles and the latest cybersecurity technologies.

Monitoring the network for security incidents is a continuous responsibility. Network security engineers use advanced monitoring tools and techniques to constantly oversee the network for signs of suspicious activity or potential breaches. They analyze network traffic, monitor security logs, and utilize threat intelligence to identify and respond to real-time security incidents. This proactive monitoring is crucial for the early detection of threats and minimizing the impact of security breaches.

Managing network security tools and processes involves overseeing the security infrastructure and ensuring that all security measures are effective and current. Network security engineers are responsible for maintaining and updating security software, conducting regular security audits, and refining security protocols as needed. They also manage the deployment of security patches and updates, ensuring the network is protected against known vulnerabilities.

For those interested in becoming network security engineers, certifications such as CISSP, CCNA Security, or Certified Network Security Engineer can be highly advantageous. These certifications equip professionals with essential knowledge and skills in network security and validate their expertise in the field.

The role of a network security engineer is crucial in maintaining the security and integrity of an organization's network infrastructure. Their responsibilities include protecting the network, implementing various security measures, continuously monitoring for incidents, and managing security tools and processes.

PENETRATION TESTER

Penetration testers, often ethical hackers, play a pivotal role in cybersecurity by identifying and assessing network and application vulnerabilities. Their expertise lies in simulating cyberattacks in order to uncover weaknesses in computer systems, networks, and applications—akin to a hacker but intending to strengthen rather than exploit. This proactive defense strategy is essential in preempting real cyberattacks because it brings to light potential vulnerabilities that malicious entities could exploit. Penetration testers must be adept in various hacking techniques and tools, ranging from automated vulnerability scanners to manual testing processes, and they must be able to think like attackers to anticipate unconventional security breaches.

In addition to vulnerability assessment, developing and executing comprehensive test plans is a cornerstone of a penetration tester's role. These plans are meticulously crafted roadmaps that detail the methodologies and tactics for conducting thorough security assessments. They require an in-depth understanding of the latest cybersecurity threats, the specific system or application architecture under review, and the most effective testing tools. Executing these plans is a delicate balance of thoroughness and efficiency, ensuring comprehensive coverage without compromising system integrity.

The role extends beyond testing to include reporting and recommending robust security enhancements. After conducting tests, penetration testers must compile their findings into comprehensive reports that provide a clear over-view of vulnerabilities and potential impact. These reports are critical in or-der for stakeholders to understand the risks and for IT teams to prioritize and implement security measures. The recommendations made by penetra-tion testers often lead the way in fortifying an organization's cybersecurity infrastructure.

Continuous learning and skill development are nonnegotiable aspects of being a successful penetration tester. With the cybersecurity landscape constantly shifting, professionals in this role must stay abreast of emerging threats, new hacking techniques, and advancements in security technology. This pursuit of knowledge can be bolstered through certifications such as CEH, Offensive Security Certified Professional, and Licensed Penetration Tester, which are highly regarded in the industry. These certifications vali-date a penetration tester's skills and ensure they are equipped with the latest knowledge and best practices in the field.

The role of a penetration tester is integral to the cybersecurity ecosystem, requiring a blend of technical expertise, strategic planning, and continuous professional development. The responsibilities extend from identifying vul-nerabilities to actively shaping organizations' cybersecurity strategies.

SECURITY ANALYST

A security analyst plays a crucial role in the cybersecurity framework of an organization by focusing on safeguarding information systems from potential threats and vulnerabilities. This position requires a keen eye for detail and a deep understanding of network architecture and cybersecurity principles. The primary responsibilities of a security analyst include monitoring network traffic for anomalies, conducting comprehensive threat and risk assessments, implementing robust security measures and protocols, and collaborating effectively with IT and cybersecurity teams. This in-depth exploration will delve into these critical areas, highlighting the skills and competencies needed to excel in this role and the recommended certifications that can enhance a security analyst's professional standing in the cybersecurity community.

Monitoring network traffic for anomalies is a fundamental task for a security analyst. This involves continuous vigilance over the network to detect any unusual activity that could signify a security breach or an attempted attack. Security analysts use various tools and software to monitor real-time data and logs, analyze traffic patterns, and identify deviations from the norm. Their expertise lies in quickly recognizing potential threats and immediately investigating and mitigating any risks.

Conducting threat and risk assessments involves evaluating the organization's cybersecurity posture, identifying vulnerabilities in the system, and assessing the potential risks that are associated with these vulnerabilities. Security analysts must stay updated with the latest cybersecurity trends and threat intelligence in order to anticipate and prepare for emerging threats. They develop and update risk management strategies to protect the organization's digital assets against current and future cyber threats.

Security analysts are involved in designing and establishing security frameworks and policies that safeguard the organization's IT infrastructure. This includes implementing firewalls, intrusion detection systems, and encryption tools. They also play a crucial role in developing incident response plans and ensuring that security protocols are followed across the organization.

Collaboration with IT and cybersecurity teams is crucial for the effective functioning of a security analyst. They work closely with other IT professionals to ensure cybersecurity strategies are integrated into the broader IT infrastructure. Collaboration and communication with different departments are essential to ensure security policies are understood and implemented effectively throughout the organization.

For those aspiring to become security analysts, acquiring specific certifications can significantly enhance their expertise and employability. Certifications such as the CISSP, CISM, and CompTIA Security+ are highly valued in the industry. These certifications validate the analyst's skills and knowledge in various aspects of cybersecurity and demonstrate their commitment to professional growth and adherence to industry standards.

The role of a security analyst is integral to maintaining the cybersecurity integrity of an organization. It demands technical proficiency, analytical skills, risk management capabilities, and collaborative abilities. Pursuing relevant certifications and staying abreast of the latest developments in the field are essential for anyone looking to build a successful career.

SECURITY INFORMATION AND EVENT MANAGEMENT (SIEM) SPECIALIST

SIEM specialists are critical in an organization's cybersecurity framework. They are responsible for managing SIEM solutions—essential tools for real-time analysis of security alerts generated by applications and network hardware. The role of an SIEM specialist is multifaceted, involving monitoring and analyzing security events, implementing and fine-tuning SIEM configurations, and responding promptly and effectively to security alerts. These professionals ensure that potential security incidents are quickly identified, assessed, and addressed.

Managing SIEM solutions is a core responsibility of a SIEM specialist. This task involves overseeing the SIEM platform, which aggregates and correlates data from various sources within the IT infrastructure, including network devices, servers, and databases. The specialist ensures that the SIEM system is effectively collecting, managing, and analyzing this data to provide a comprehensive view of the organization's security state. They must also maintain the SIEM software, ensuring it is up-to-date and functioning optimally.

SIEM specialists are tasked with continuously monitoring the organization's network and systems for unusual activity that could indicate a security threat. They analyze the security logs and event data collected by the SIEM system in order to identify patterns or anomalies that might signify a potential security breach. Their ability to discern between false positives and genuine threats is essential in maintaining adequate security monitoring.

Implementing SIEM configurations is another critical responsibility. SIEM specialists customize the SIEM tool's configurations to meet their organization's specific security needs. This involves setting up rules, alerts, and dashboards to ensure that the SIEM system effectively identifies and reports critical security events. The specialist tailors these configurations to minimize noise—unnecessary or irrelevant alerts—and to highlight the most critical security information that requires attention.

When the SIEM system identifies a potential security incident, the specialist is responsible for assessing the alert, determining its severity, and initiating an appropriate response. This might involve conducting further investigation to confirm the nature of the threat, collaborating with other cybersecurity team members to address the incident, and ensuring that the appropriate remedial actions are taken.

For professionals who are interested in becoming SIEM specialists, certifications such as CISSP, GIAC Security Essentials, or CISM can be beneficial.

These certifications provide a solid foundation in information security principles and practices, including using and managing SIEM systems.

The role of a SIEM specialist is pivotal in the continuous monitoring and analysis of security events within an organization. Their responsibilities include managing SIEM solutions, monitoring and analyzing security events, implementing SIEM configurations, and responding to security alerts. Staying current with the latest developments in SIEM technologies and practices and obtaining relevant certifications are critical to effectively performing in this vital cybersecurity role.

THREAT HUNTING

In the ever-evolving landscape of cybersecurity, the role of a threat hunter is increasingly recognized as essential for a proactive defense. Unlike traditional security measures focusing on reactive responses to threats, threat hunting involves a proactive approach to search for, identify, and mitigate cyber threats before they manifest into actual security incidents. This dynamic role encompasses proactively searching for cyber threats, analyzing network and system behaviors to uncover subtle signs of compromise, identifying potential security incidents early on, and implementing effective threat mitigation strategies.

Proactively searching for cyber threats involves going beyond automated alerts and standard security protocols to seek out sophisticated threats that might evade traditional detection methods. Threat hunters use advanced analytical skills, an understanding of attacker tactics, and deep knowledge of their IT environment to hunt for signs of malicious activity. They often utilize threat intelligence and hypothesis-driven approaches to anticipate potential attack methods and uncover hidden threats.

Analyzing network and system behaviors is critical to the threat-hunting process. Threat hunters can detect anomalies and patterns that are indicative of malicious activities by thoroughly examining network traffic, logs, and system behaviors. This analysis requires a keen eye for detail and a deep understanding of normal behavior in their specific environment. Sophisticated tools and technologies are often employed to aid in sifting through vast amounts of data to identify subtle signs of compromise.

By recognizing the signs of an attack in its early stages, threat hunters can take swift action to mitigate the threat before it escalates into a full-blown breach. This early identification is crucial for limiting the potential damage of cyberattacks and maintaining the overall security and integrity of the organization's IT infrastructure.

Implementing threat mitigation strategies is the final step in the threat-hunting process. Once a potential threat is identified, threat hunters contain and neutralize it. This might involve isolating affected systems, removing malicious files, and strengthening security controls to prevent similar attacks in the future. They also collaborate with other cybersecurity team members to improve the overall security posture and to develop more effective defense strategies based on their findings.

For those pursuing a career in threat hunting, obtaining certifications such as CEH, GIAC Certified Incident Handler, or CISSP can be highly beneficial. These certifications provide the skills and knowledge to hunt and mitigate cyber threats effectively.

The role of a threat hunter is proactive and exploratory, crucial for identifying and mitigating cyber threats before they result in significant harm. It involves a relentless search for threats, detailed analysis of network and system behaviors, early identification of potential incidents, and the implementation of effective mitigation strategies. Continuous learning and staying abreast of the latest threats, intelligence, and cybersecurity practice developments are crucial to excelling in this critical and challenging role.

WIRELESS SECURITY SPECIALIST

In the contemporary digital landscape, where wireless networks are ubiquitous, the role of a wireless security specialist has become increasingly crucial. These professionals specialize in securing wireless networking systems that are inherently vulnerable to a unique set of security challenges due to the nature of their transmission. The responsibilities of a wireless security specialist encompass securing wireless networks, implementing robust wireless security protocols, conducting comprehensive wireless network audits, and managing various wireless security measures to safeguard against unauthorized access and cyber threats.

Securing wireless networks is a primary responsibility of a wireless security specialist. Given the susceptibility of wireless networks to threats like eavesdropping, unauthorized access, and data interception, it is essential to implement strong security measures. Specialists in this field work to protect the integrity, confidentiality, and availability of data transmitted over wireless networks. They are responsible for setting up secure wireless infrastructures, which include configuring wireless access points, routers, and other related devices to prevent unauthorized access and data breaches.

Wireless security specialists select and deploy the most appropriate security protocols, such as Wi-Fi Protected Access 3, Wired Equivalent Privacy, and others, depending on the network's requirements. They ensure these security protocols are correctly configured and updated to defend against emerging threats. This role also involves securing authentication and encryption methods to protect data as it travels across wireless networks.

Conducting wireless network audits is an essential function to assess and enhance the security posture of wireless networks. Wireless security specialists regularly evaluate the wireless network setup, inspecting for any vulnerabilities or security gaps. These audits involve testing the network's defenses, identifying potential weaknesses, and assessing the effectiveness of existing security measures. The findings from these audits are crucial in understanding the network's security status and formulating strategies to address identified vulnerabilities.

Managing wireless security measures includes maintaining and optimizing security tools and strategies to protect wireless networks. This involves regularly updating firmware and software, monitoring network traffic for unusual patterns that may indicate a security threat, and responding to security incidents. Wireless security specialists also play a crucial role in developing and enforcing wireless security policies and training users on safe wireless practices.

For professionals interested in specializing as wireless security specialists, obtaining certifications such as Certified Wireless Security Professional or CISSP can be advantageous. These certifications provide in-depth knowledge of wireless security principles and best practices, equipping specialists with the necessary skills to secure complex wireless networks effectively.

The role of a wireless security specialist is integral to protecting wireless networks from a myriad of cyber threats. Their responsibilities include securing wireless networks, implementing appropriate security protocols, conducting thorough network audits, and managing wireless security measures.

9

MANAGEMENT ROLES IN CYBERSECURITY

In cybersecurity, management roles orchestrate and oversee the strategic and operational aspects of an organization's cybersecurity efforts. These roles demand a blend of technical knowledge, leadership skills, and strategic thinking, making them fundamental for integrating cybersecurity strategies effectively into the organization's broader goals. The various management roles within cybersecurity come with distinct responsibilities, necessary skill sets, and a significant impact on the organization's security posture. These roles are instrumental in shaping cybersecurity policies, managing teams and resources, and coordinating with key organizational stakeholders, ensuring a comprehensive and cohesive approach to cybersecurity.

CHIEF INFORMATION SECURITY OFFICER (CISO)

The CISO is a senior-level executive who is responsible for the overall direction and management of an organization's cybersecurity endeavors. As a key figure in the management structure, the CISO plays a critical role in strategic planning and policy development, leadership and management of the cybersecurity team, budgeting and resource allocation for security initiatives, and communicating with executive management and other stakeholders.

Strategic planning and policy development are at the core of the CISO's responsibilities. The CISO is responsible for developing and implementing a comprehensive cybersecurity strategy that aligns with the organization's objectives and risk appetite. This involves assessing current and future security risks, setting security goals and objectives, and formulating policies and procedures to mitigate risks. The CISO ensures that cybersecurity policies are integrated into the organization's operations and business processes.

This role involves leading and managing a team of cybersecurity professionals, fostering a culture of security awareness, and ensuring the team is equipped with the necessary skills and resources to protect the organization from cyber threats. The CISO also plays a crucial role in talent development, mentoring team members, and building a cohesive and effective cybersecurity team.

Budgeting and resource allocation for security initiatives is another critical area of responsibility. The CISO is tasked with determining the budgetary needs for cybersecurity initiatives and ensuring that resources are allocated effectively to meet security objectives. This includes investing in the right technologies, tools, and training programs to enhance the organization's security posture and resilience against cyber threats.

Interacting with executive management and stakeholders is vital to the CISO's role. The CISO bridges the cybersecurity team and other departments, executive management, and external stakeholders. This involves communicating the importance of cybersecurity, reporting on security status and incidents, and advising on security best practices. The CISO ensures that cybersecurity is critical in organizational decision making and that stakeholders are informed and engaged in cybersecurity matters.

A CISO typically holds a bachelor's degree in computer science, information technology, cybersecurity, or a related field. However, given the strategic nature of the role, a master's degree in information security, business administration, or a related discipline can be highly beneficial. Advanced degrees offer deeper insights into cybersecurity's technical aspects and the business acumen that is required for strategic planning and management.

Several professional certifications can significantly enhance a CISO's qualifications. Certifications such as Certified Information Systems Security Professional (CISSP), Certified Information Security Manager (CISM), and Certified Chief Information Security Officer are highly regarded in the industry. These certifications demonstrate high expertise in information security management and strategy. Additionally, certifications like CISSP-Information Systems Security Management Professional specifically focus on the management aspects of information security, which is crucial for a CISO's role.

Ongoing professional development is vital for CISOs to stay abreast of the latest cybersecurity trends, threats, and technologies. Attending industry conferences, participating in professional networks, and continuous learning through courses and seminars are essential for keeping their knowledge and skills up-to-date.

A CISO's role is central to an organization's cybersecurity management structure. The responsibilities encompass strategic planning, team leadership, budgeting for security initiatives, and effective communication with stakeholders. The CISO's leadership and strategic insight are essential for ensuring its cybersecurity measures are robust, effective, and aligned with its overall goals and objectives.

SECURITY ARCHITECT

A security architect holds a vital position in the cybersecurity domain—responsibility for the intricate task of designing and building secure IT systems. This role demands a deep understanding of technical and security principles and a strategic insight into the organization's needs. Security architects are entrusted with creating robust IT architectures that effectively safeguard against cyber threats while aligning with the organization's operational and business objectives. They navigate complex challenges, considering various factors such as network security, data protection, and user access control to develop comprehensive security solutions.

The role extends beyond design to encompass the development and analysis of security blueprints. These blueprints serve as detailed guides for implementing security measures across the IT infrastructure. Security architects meticulously analyze potential risks and strategize to mitigate them, thereby ensuring that security is integral to the IT systems from the ground up. Their expertise transforms technical requirements and business goals into secure, efficient IT solutions.

Another critical aspect of a security architect's role is ensuring compliance with security policies and regulations. They must constantly update their knowledge of the changing landscape of cybersecurity laws and industry standards. This involves staying abreast of regulatory changes, conducting compliance audits, and adapting the security architecture as needed. Their work ensures that the organization's IT systems adhere to cybersecurity norms and regulations, thus maintaining legal and ethical standards.

Collaboration with IT departments is essential for integrating security into the broader IT infrastructure. Security architects work closely with IT teams to ensure that security measures are woven into all facets of IT operations. This partnership is crucial for creating a unified approach to cybersecurity, aligning security strategies with the organization's overall IT strategy, and fostering a secure yet operational IT environment.

A combination of advanced education and professional certifications is recommended for those aspiring to become security architects. Typically, a bachelor's degree in computer science, information technology, or cybersecurity is required, with a master's degree in a related discipline offering an added advantage. Professional certifications such as CISSP, CISM, and Certified Cloud Security Professional are highly valued. These certifications validate expertise in information security architecture and keep professionals updated with the latest trends and best practices in the field.

A security architect's role encompasses various responsibilities, from designing secure IT systems to ensuring compliance with security standards and collaborating with IT departments. Advanced education, along with relevant certifications, is essential for mastering the complexities of this role and staying current in the ever-evolving field of cybersecurity.

SECURITY CONSULTANT

In the multifaceted world of cybersecurity, a security consultant plays a crucial role in advising organizations on effective security strategies. This position demands a profound understanding of cybersecurity principles and practices and the ability to tailor this knowledge to meet the specific needs of different organizations. Security consultants are experts in conducting thorough risk assessments and audits, which are crucial for identifying vulnerabilities and recommending appropriate countermeasures. Their responsibilities also extend to developing and delivering training and awareness programs, which are essential for fostering a security culture within organizations.

Advising organizations on security strategies involves working closely with clients to understand their unique security needs and challenges. Consultants analyze the organization's security posture, identify areas for improvement, and develop comprehensive strategies to enhance their cybersecurity defenses. This strategic advisory role requires staying up-to-date with the latest cybersecurity trends and technologies to provide the most effective and current recommendations.

Conducting risk assessments and audits forms a critical part of their duties. Security consultants meticulously evaluate an organization's IT infrastructure, policies, and procedures to identify potential vulnerabilities and risks. They assess the likelihood and potential impact of cyber threats, thereby helping organizations prioritize their security efforts. These assessments and audits are pivotal in creating a roadmap for strengthening cybersecurity measures and mitigating risks.

Providing training and awareness programs is another important aspect of a security consultant's role. They develop educational programs and workshops to enhance cybersecurity knowledge and awareness for all staff members of the organization. These programs are designed to inform employees about common cyber threats, safe online practices, and how to respond to security incidents. By empowering employees with this knowledge, security consultants play a vital role in strengthening the organization's human defense line against cyber threats.

The cybersecurity landscape continually changes, with new threats and vulnerabilities emerging regularly. Security consultants must stay informed about these developments in order to provide their clients with the most current and practical advice. This involves continuous learning, research, and engagement with the cybersecurity community.

A combination of specialized education and certifications is highly beneficial for those looking to become security consultants. A degree in cybersecurity, information technology, or a related field provides a strong foundation. Certifications such as CISSP, CISM, or Certified Ethical Hacker are valuable for demonstrating expertise in the field.

The role of a security consultant is integral in guiding organizations to strengthen their cybersecurity posture. Their expertise in advising on security strategies, conducting risk assessments and audits, providing training, and staying updated on cybersecurity threats is crucial. A blend of formal education and professional certifications is essential to excel in this role.

SECURITY DIRECTOR

A security director holds a pivotal leadership position in cybersecurity and is responsible for shaping and guiding an organization's long-term security strategy and vision. This role demands a comprehensive understanding of cybersecurity challenges and solutions and strong leadership and strategic planning abilities. The security director's responsibilities include developing a cohesive security strategy and coordinating cross-functional security initiatives, leading large cybersecurity teams, and playing a pivotal role in cultivating an organization-wide culture of security awareness and compliance.

Developing a long-term security strategy and vision involves setting the direction for the organization's cybersecurity efforts, ensuring they align with the overall business objectives and risk management strategy. The security director assesses current and future security risks, trends, and technological advancements to formulate a strategy that is both proactive and adaptable to changing cyber landscapes. This strategic planning is essential for ensuring the organization's resilience against evolving cyber threats.

Coordination of cross-functional security initiatives is another critical aspect of the role. Security directors oversee and integrate cybersecurity efforts across various departments within the organization. This involves working collaboratively with IT, legal, human resources, and other departments to ensure a unified and comprehensive approach to cybersecurity. They ensure that cybersecurity initiatives are not siloed but integral to the organization's broader operational and strategic plans.

Leading large cybersecurity teams is a crucial responsibility. Security directors manage and mentor a team of cybersecurity professionals. They are responsible for guiding the team in implementing the cybersecurity strategy, overseeing day-to-day operations, and ensuring the team has the necessary skills and resources. Effective leadership involves fostering a collaborative and innovative work environment, encouraging professional development, and ensuring that the team is equipped to meet the organization's cybersecurity needs.

Security directors play a significant role in promoting a culture of security awareness throughout the organization. This includes advocating for regular employee training, developing policies emphasizing the importance of cybersecurity, and leading by example to instill a sense of responsibility for security at all levels of the organization. By influencing the security culture, security directors ensure that cybersecurity is a shared responsibility and an integral part of the organizational ethos.

For professionals aspiring to become security directors, a combination of higher education in cybersecurity or related fields and professional certifications is beneficial. Advanced cybersecurity, information technology, or business administration degrees can provide the necessary knowledge and skills. CISSP or CISM are valuable for demonstrating cybersecurity management and strategy expertise.

The role of a security director is crucial in shaping and executing an organization's cybersecurity strategy. Their responsibilities span strategic planning, leading cybersecurity teams, coordinating cross-functional initiatives, and fostering a strong security culture. Advanced education and professional certifications are crucial to excelling in this role and effectively navigating the complexities of cybersecurity leadership.

COMPLIANCE DIRECTOR

In the increasingly regulated landscape of cybersecurity, a compliance director's role is paramount. This position focuses on ensuring that an organization adheres to the myriad cybersecurity laws and regulations governing its operations. The responsibilities of a compliance director include developing and maintaining comprehensive compliance programs, conducting regular compliance audits to ensure adherence, and playing a pivotal role in training and educating staff on various compliance issues. This role is essential for mitigating legal and regulatory risks and maintaining the trust of customers and stakeholders.

A compliance director's core responsibility is ensuring adherence to cybersecurity laws and regulations. They are tasked with understanding and interpreting various national and international cybersecurity regulations that impact the organization. This includes laws like the General Data Protection Regulation, the Health Insurance Portability and Accountability Act, and others, depending on the industry and geography of the organization. Compliance directors must ensure that the organization's policies, procedures, and practices align with these legal requirements to avoid potential legal repercussions and fines.

Compliance directors design and implement programs that address and integrate the legal requirements into the organization's day-to-day operations. These programs often include policies and procedures for data protection, incident response, and risk management. The aim is to create a framework that meets legal standards and supports the organization's cybersecurity strategy and objectives.

Conducting regular compliance audits assess the organization's compliance programs' effectiveness and identify any areas of noncompliance or potential risk. Compliance directors systematically review the organization's cybersecurity practices, procedures, and documentation. These audits help preemptively identify issues and implement corrective actions to ensure ongoing compliance.

Training and educating staff on compliance issues is another important aspect of their responsibilities. Compliance directors develop and deliver training programs to educate employees about cybersecurity laws, regulations, and compliance policies. These training programs are vital for fostering a culture of compliance and ensuring that employees understand their role in maintaining compliance. This education helps minimize risks associated with noncompliance and empowers employees to identify and address potential compliance issues.

For individuals aiming to become compliance directors, a blend of education in law, cybersecurity or related fields, along with professional certifications, is recommended. Certifications such as Certified Information Systems

Auditor, Certified Compliance and Ethics Professional, or Certified Information Privacy Professional can be advantageous. These certifications provide the necessary knowledge and skills related to compliance in the cybersecurity context.

The role of a compliance director is integral to ensuring that an organization adheres to the necessary cybersecurity laws and regulations. Their responsibilities include developing compliance programs, conducting audits, and educating staff about compliance. A combination of relevant education and professional certifications is vital to excelling in this role.

10

RESEARCH AND DEVELOPMENT IN CYBERSECURITY

The field of research and development in cybersecurity is vital for advancing the technologies and methodologies that protect digital assets and information. This domain is characterized by continuous innovation that requires deep technical knowledge, creative problem-solving, and forward-thinking approaches. Research and development professionals in cybersecurity are on the front lines of creating new solutions to emerging threats, enhancing existing security systems, and exploring future-proof technologies. Their work is instrumental in staying ahead of sophisticated cyber attackers and shaping the future of cybersecurity practices.

CRYPTOGRAPHER

A cryptographer is a specialized professional in cybersecurity, primarily focused on developing and analyzing encryption algorithms and security protocols. Cryptographers are crucial in securing digital communications and data by creating systems that protect against unauthorized access and cyber threats. Their responsibilities include not only the development of new cryptographic methods but also the analysis and enhancement of existing security systems.

Developing encryption algorithms and security protocols is a primary task for cryptographers. They design and create complex algorithms that encode data, ensuring that sensitive information remains secure during transmission and storage. These algorithms are fundamental to various aspects of cybersecurity, including secure communications, digital signatures, and data encryption. Cryptographers must fully understand mathematics and algorithmic theory to develop effective and efficient cryptographic techniques.

Cryptographers continually assess the strength and efficacy of existing cryptographic methods against emerging threats and vulnerabilities. This involves rigorous testing and evaluation to ensure that the encryption algorithms and protocols can withstand new cyberattacks and hacking strategies. Cryptographers also work on optimizing cryptographic systems for performance, scalability, and adaptability.

Researching quantum-resistant cryptography is an emerging and increasingly important area of focus. With the advent of quantum computing, many traditional cryptographic methods are at risk of becoming obsolete. Cryptographers are at the forefront of developing new cryptographic techniques that are resistant to quantum computing threats. This cutting-edge research is essential for ensuring the long-term security of digital systems in a post-quantum world.

Providing data protection and privacy expertise is an integral part of a cryptographer's responsibilities. They offer guidance and advice on implementing cryptographic techniques to safeguard data privacy and integrity. Cryptographers work closely with other cybersecurity professionals to integrate robust encryption methods into broader security strategies, ensuring comprehensive protection against data breaches and unauthorized access.

For those aspiring to become a cryptographer in cybersecurity, specialized training and certification are essential in order to gain the necessary skills and expertise. The training for a cryptographer should focus primarily on developing and analyzing encryption algorithms and security protocols. This requires a deep understanding of mathematics and algorithmic theory since cryptographers design and create complex algorithms that encode data, ensuring the security of sensitive information during transmission and storage. Training should cover various aspects of cybersecurity, including secure communications, digital signatures, and data encryption, equipping aspiring cryptographers with the knowledge to develop effective cryptographic techniques.

Cryptographers must continually assess and enhance the strength and efficacy of current cryptographic methods against emerging threats and vulnerabilities. Training should include rigorous testing and evaluation methodologies to ensure encryption algorithms and protocols are resilient against new cyberattacks and hacking strategies. Training in optimizing cryptographic systems for performance, scalability, and adaptability is also essential.

Training and providing data protection and privacy expertise are also integral for cryptographers. They must understand how to implement cryptographic techniques to safeguard data privacy and integrity and work closely with other cybersecurity professionals to integrate robust encryption methods into broader security strategies.

While there are no specific certifications for cryptographers, certifications that provide foundational knowledge in cybersecurity and advanced mathematics can be beneficial. Certified Information Systems Security Professional (CISSP) or Certified Information Security Manager can provide a solid foundation in cybersecurity principles. Additionally, advanced degrees or coursework in mathematics, computer science, or related fields are often essential for those pursuing a career in cryptography.

Overall, a combination of specialized training in cryptography and relevant certifications or educational qualifications is crucial for those looking to excel as cryptographers. This educational path equips them with the necessary skills to develop and analyze encryption algorithms, enhance existing security systems, research quantum-resistant cryptography, and provide data protection and privacy expertise.

The role of a cryptographer is central to the research and development efforts in cybersecurity. Their work in developing, analyzing, and improving encryption algorithms and protocols is crucial for protecting data and ensuring privacy. Continuous learning and staying abreast of cryptographic technologies and quantum computing advancements are essential for cryptographers to remain effective in their vital role in cybersecurity.

SECURITY SOFTWARE DEVELOPER

A security software developer plays an essential role in the cybersecurity landscape by focusing on designing and developing software solutions that enhance digital security. Their work is pivotal in creating applications and systems that are inherently secure, protecting against a wide range of cyber threats. The responsibilities of a security software developer include not only the development of security-centric software but also the integration of security principles into general application development, conducting thorough security testing and code reviews, and staying current with the latest trends and best practices in software development.

A security software developer's primary responsibility is designing and developing security software solutions. This involves creating software to protect against cyber threats, such as antivirus programs, firewalls, and intrusion detection systems. These developers must fully understand cybersecurity threats and software engineering principles in order to build effective and efficient security solutions. Their work often involves coding, system design, and cryptographic techniques to ensure data confidentiality, integrity, and availability.

Integrating security into application development is a crucial aspect of their role. Security software developers work to ensure that security is a foundational element of all software development projects, not just those explicitly focused on cybersecurity. This involves embedding security measures into the development life cycle, from initial design to deployment. They collaborate with other developers to incorporate security best practices, such as secure coding techniques and vulnerability assessments, into all software applications.

Conducting security testing and code reviews is essential for maintaining the integrity of software. Security software developers rigorously test software for vulnerabilities and potential security flaws. This includes performing code reviews, running static and dynamic analysis, and implementing penetration testing. These processes help identify and rectify security weaknesses before the software is deployed, thereby reducing the risk of exploitation by cyber attackers.

Software development constantly evolves, with new technologies, programming languages, and methodologies emerging regularly. Staying current with these trends is essential for developing innovative security solutions and ensuring existing software remains effective against the latest cyber threats. Continuous learning and professional development are crucial to staying at the forefront of software development and cybersecurity.

For an individual who aspires to become a security software developer, specialized training and certifications are critical for acquiring the skills to design and develop robust security software solutions. The training for a security software developer should emphasize cybersecurity threats and software engineering principles. This includes learning to create software to protect against cyber threats, such as antivirus programs, firewalls, and intrusion detection systems. Training should cover the aspects of coding, system design, and the application of cryptographic techniques to ensure data confidentiality, integrity, and availability.

Security software developers must learn how to embed security measures into the entire development life cycle, from initial design to deployment. This involves collaborating with other developers to incorporate security best practices, such as secure coding techniques and vulnerability assessments, into all software applications, not just those explicitly focused on cybersecurity.

Conducting security testing and code reviews is crucial for maintaining software integrity. Training should focus on rigorously teaching developers how to test software for vulnerabilities and potential security flaws. This includes learning to perform code reviews, run static and dynamic analysis, and implement penetration testing to identify and rectify security weaknesses before software deployment.

Staying updated with the latest trends in software development is vital. Software development is dynamic, with new technologies, programming languages, and methodologies emerging regularly. Training should include methods for continuous learning and professional development to stay at the forefront of software development and cybersecurity.

In terms of certifications, several can be beneficial for security software developers. Certifications like CISSP or Certified Secure Software Lifecycle Professional provide foundational knowledge in cybersecurity and secure software development. Additionally, certifications in specific programming languages or methodologies can enhance a developer's technical skills and adaptability to various software projects.

Overall, targeted cybersecurity and software engineering training, along with relevant certifications, is critical for those who are looking to excel as security software developers. This educational path equips them with the necessary skills to develop secure software solutions, integrate security principles into general application development, conduct thorough security testing and code reviews, and stay current with the latest software development and cybersecurity trends.

The role of a security software developer is important in building secure software applications and integrating security into all aspects of software development. Their responsibilities span from designing security-focused solutions to ensuring the overall security of software applications. Keeping updated with the latest software development trends and obtaining relevant certifications are essential for this type of professional to contribute to an organization's cybersecurity resilience effectively.

SECURITY RESEARCHER

A security researcher plays a pivotal role in advancing the field of cybersecurity through cutting-edge research. These professionals are at the forefront of identifying and analyzing emerging threats, contributing significantly to the collective understanding of the cybersecurity landscape. Their work delves deep into the latest cyber threats, vulnerabilities, and attack methodologies. The responsibilities of a security researcher include conducting comprehensive research and publishing their findings, providing insights on threat mitigation, and collaborating with peers in academic and industry circles.

Security researchers engage in in-depth analysis and an exploration of new and evolving cyber threats, techniques used by hackers, and the vulnerabilities of current systems and software. This research is vital in uncovering potential security weaknesses before malicious actors can exploit them. Security researchers use various methods, including reverse engineering, code analysis, and threat modeling, in order to better understand cyber threats and develop new ways to protect against them.

Identifying and analyzing emerging threats is crucial in the dynamic cybersecurity field. Security researchers constantly monitor the digital landscape to spot new cyberattack trends and patterns. They analyze malware, study cybercrime tactics, and evaluate security breaches to understand how and why they occur. This ongoing analysis is essential for staying ahead of attackers and providing timely insights into the latest threats facing individuals and organizations.

Security researchers share their knowledge and discoveries through academic journals, industry publications, and conference presentations. By disseminating their findings, they contribute to the broader cybersecurity knowledge base and help develop more effective defense strategies. Their expertise is also sought after for advising organizations on mitigating and defending against identified threats, thereby enhancing overall cybersecurity resilience.

Collaborating with academic and industry partners is critical to the success of a security researcher. By working with universities, research institutions, cybersecurity firms, and other industry entities, they can exchange ideas, share resources, and contribute to joint research initiatives. These collaborations often lead to breakthroughs in cybersecurity technologies and methodologies, benefiting the wider community and advancing the field.

For those aspiring to become a security researcher in cybersecurity, a combination of advanced training and certifications is essential to develop the expertise needed for this role. The training for a security researcher should focus on conducting comprehensive research into cybersecurity. This includes an in-depth analysis of new and evolving cyber threats, techniques used by hackers, and the vulnerabilities of current systems and software. Training should cover a range of methods, such as reverse engineering, code analysis, and threat modeling, to gain a deeper understanding of cyber threats and develop new protective strategies.

Identifying and analyzing emerging threats involves constantly monitoring the digital landscape to spot new cyberattack trends and patterns. Training should include methods for analyzing malware, studying cybercrime tactics, and evaluating security breaches to understand their occurrences and impacts. This ongoing analysis is vital for staying ahead of attackers and providing timely insights into the latest threats.

Security researchers must learn to effectively communicate their research findings through academic journals, industry publications, and conference presentations. Training should include developing skills to advise organizations on mitigating and defending against identified threats. It should also include developing skills for working in joint research initiatives, exchanging ideas, and sharing resources with universities, research institutions, cybersecurity firms, and other industry entities.

While there are no specific certifications for security researchers, certifications that provide a deep understanding of cybersecurity can be beneficial. Certifications such as CISSP or Certified Ethical Hacker (CEH) can provide foundational knowledge in cybersecurity. Additionally, advanced degrees in cybersecurity, computer science, or related fields often play a crucial role in preparing individuals for a career in security research.

A combination of specialized training in cybersecurity research and relevant certifications or academic qualifications is vital for those looking to excel as security researchers. This educational path equips them with the necessary skills to conduct advanced research, identify and analyze emerging threats, publish their findings, advise on threat mitigation, and collaborate effectively with academic and industry partners.

The role of a security researcher is integral to understanding and combating cyber threats. Their responsibilities include conducting comprehensive research, identifying emerging threats, publishing findings, and collaborating with various partners. Continuous learning and staying abreast of the latest developments in cybersecurity are crucial for security researchers to remain effective in their roles and contribute significantly to the field.

SECURITY SYSTEMS ADMINISTRATOR

Security systems administrators are responsible for managing and maintaining an organization's security systems. This role is crucial for ensuring the continuous protection of information systems against cyber threats. A security systems administrator's duties include effective management of security infrastructure, implementation of network security policies, regular monitoring of system performance and security, and swift response to and resolution of security incidents.

Managing and maintaining security systems is the foremost responsibility of a security systems administrator. They oversee the operation of security solutions such as firewalls, antivirus software, intrusion detection systems, and other security management tools. Their job involves ensuring these systems are functioning correctly—updating and patching them regularly and configuring them to meet the organization's specific security needs. This management is critical for maintaining the integrity and effectiveness of the security infrastructure.

They are responsible for implementing policies and procedures that govern the use and security of the organization's network and systems. This includes defining user access controls, managing network security settings, and ensuring compliance with internal and external security standards and regulations. Implementing these policies is essential for safeguarding the network from potential security breaches and maintaining organizational cybersecurity standards.

Monitoring system performance and security is an ongoing duty. Security systems administrators constantly supervise the network and systems to detect unusual activities or potential security threats. They utilize various monitoring tools to track system performance, identify vulnerabilities, and ensure that security measures work as intended. Continuous monitoring allows for the early detection of issues, thereby enabling proactive measures to prevent security incidents.

In the event of a security breach or suspicious activity, security systems administrators are tasked with promptly addressing the issue. This involves investigating the incident, containing the threat, and implementing measures to prevent future occurrences. Their response is crucial in minimizing the impact of security incidents and restoring normal operations as quickly as possible.

The role of a security systems administrator is essential in the upkeep and defense of an organization's cybersecurity infrastructure. Their responsibilities encompass managing security systems, implementing security policies, monitoring system security, and responding to security incidents. A combination of formal education and professional certifications is critical to excelling in this role and effectively safeguarding an organization's information systems against cyber threats.

VULNERABILITY ANALYST

A vulnerability analyst plays a critical role in cybersecurity, focusing on identifying and evaluating system vulnerabilities. This position is central to the proactive defense strategy of an organization, involving a deep dive into the IT infrastructure to uncover weaknesses that cyber attackers could potentially exploit. The duties of a vulnerability analyst encompass not only detecting vulnerabilities but also developing strategies to mitigate them, conducting regular security audits, collaborating with security teams, and maintaining detailed documentation and reports on their findings.

Vulnerability analysts use various tools and techniques to scan and assess networks, systems, and applications for weaknesses. This process involves analyzing the results of vulnerability scans, understanding the nature of each vulnerability, and evaluating the potential risks associated with these weaknesses. The ability to accurately identify and assess vulnerabilities is crucial for the organization's overall security posture.

Once vulnerabilities are identified, the vulnerability analyst will formulate strategies and recommendations to address these security gaps. This might involve patching vulnerabilities, implementing additional security controls, or making configuration changes to enhance security. Their recommendations are essential for preventing potential cyberattacks and strengthening the organization's defense mechanisms.

Conducting regular security audits is an essential part of their role. Vulnerability analysts systematically review the organization's cybersecurity practices and systems to ensure that security measures are effective and that vulnerabilities are adequately addressed. These audits help identify new or unresolved vulnerabilities and assess the effectiveness of current security measures.

They work closely with other cybersecurity professionals, including security engineers, incident responders, and IT staff, to ensure a coordinated approach to cybersecurity. Their collaboration ensures that vulnerability management is integrated into the broader cybersecurity strategy of the organization.

Maintaining detailed documentation and reports is vital for tracking and communicating vulnerabilities and the actions taken to address them. Vulnerability analysts create comprehensive reports that outline their findings, the risks associated with identified vulnerabilities, and their recommendations for mitigation. This documentation is essential for keeping track of the organization's vulnerability management efforts and for reporting to senior management and other stakeholders.

In terms of certifications, several are beneficial for vulnerability analysts. Certifications such as CISSP or CEH provide foundational knowledge in cybersecurity. Additionally, certifications specific to vulnerability assessment and penetration testing, such as Offensive Security Certified Professional or Global Information Assurance Certification Certified Vulnerability Analyst, can be particularly relevant.

Overall, a combination of targeted training in identifying and evaluating vulnerabilities, developing mitigation strategies, conducting security audits, collaborating with security teams, and maintaining detailed documentation—along with relevant certifications—is critical for those looking to excel as vulnerability analysts. This educational path equips them with the necessary skills to effectively detect vulnerabilities, formulate and implement mitigation strategies, and contribute to the overall cybersecurity posture of an organization.

11

POLICY AND TRAINING ROLES IN CYBERSECURITY

In the comprehensive field of cybersecurity, policy and training roles are critical for cultivating a security-conscious culture within organizations. These roles are focused on developing, implementing, and overseeing cybersecurity policies and educational programs. Professionals in these roles ensure that employees are well-informed about cybersecurity risks and know how to protect themselves and the organization from cyber threats. They are responsible for bridging the gap between complex cybersecurity concepts and practical, everyday applications. Their work is pivotal in reinforcing the human element of cybersecurity, which is often considered the first line of defense against cyber threats.

AWARENESS PROGRAM COORDINATOR

An awareness program coordinator is integral to promoting cybersecurity within an organization. This role involves creating and managing cybersecurity awareness campaigns, engaging employees in understanding and adopting cybersecurity best practices, organizing educational events and workshops, and monitoring and reporting on the effectiveness of these programs.

Awareness program coordinators design and implement comprehensive awareness campaigns to educate employees about cybersecurity threats, such as phishing, malware, and social engineering attacks. These campaigns are tailored to resonate with the audience, making complex cybersecurity concepts accessible and relevant to their daily work. The coordinator ensures that the content is engaging and informative, often using a mix of media such as videos, posters, emails, and intranet articles.

Engaging employees in cybersecurity best practices is crucial for the success of these awareness programs. The coordinator actively works to promote a culture of security within the organization. This involves disseminating information and encouraging active participation and feedback from employees. They may organize interactive sessions, quizzes, and challenges that foster employee engagement and reinforce learning.

The awareness program coordinator plans and executes various educational events such as seminars, workshops, and training sessions. These events are designed to provide deeper insights into specific cybersecurity topics and offer hands-on experiences. They often bring in external experts or utilize in-house talent to deliver these sessions, ensuring that the content is up-to-date and relevant.

Monitoring and reporting on program effectiveness is vital for measuring the impact of the awareness initiatives. The coordinator tracks various metrics such as employee participation rates, feedback scores, and behavioral changes post-campaign. They analyze this data to assess the awareness program's effectiveness and identify improvement areas. Regular reporting to management ensures that the organization is informed about the progress and impact of these cybersecurity awareness efforts.

For those aspiring to become an awareness program coordinator in cybersecurity, targeted training and certifications play a crucial role in developing the necessary skills and knowledge. The training for an awareness program coordinator should focus on creating and managing effective cybersecurity awareness campaigns. The training should also cover methods to make complex cybersecurity concepts accessible and engaging for employees, using a mix of media like videos, posters, emails, and intranet articles.

In terms of certifications, while there are no specific certifications for awareness program coordinators, certifications in broader areas of cybersecurity and communication can be beneficial. For example, certifications such as Certified Information Systems Security Professional (CISSP) can provide foundational cybersecurity knowledge, while certifications in communication or education can enhance program design and delivery skills.

A combination of targeted training and relevant certifications is critical for those looking to become successful awareness program coordinators in cybersecurity. This educational path equips them with the necessary skills to create fruitful awareness campaigns, engage employees in cybersecurity best practices, organize educational events, and monitor and report on program effectiveness.

The role of an awareness program coordinator is essential in fostering a cybersecurity-aware culture within organizations. Their responsibilities include creating and managing awareness campaigns, engaging employees in best practices, organizing educational events, and monitoring program effectiveness. The success of their role significantly contributes to strengthening the organization's overall cybersecurity posture by empowering employees with the knowledge and tools to protect against cyber threats.

CYBERSECURITY POLICYMAKER

A cybersecurity policymaker shapes the framework within which an organization secures its digital assets and information. This position demands a thorough understanding of cybersecurity principles and the ability to foresee potential threats and vulnerabilities. The responsibilities of a cybersecurity policymaker include developing and implementing comprehensive cybersecurity policies, collaborating with various stakeholders to establish practical and effective guidelines, staying current with legal and regulatory changes, and continuously assessing the effectiveness of implemented policies to make necessary adjustments.

Cybersecurity policymakers are tasked with crafting policies that provide clear guidelines on protecting the organization's IT systems and data. This involves identifying the specific security needs of the organization and translating these needs into formal policies. These policies cover many areas, including access control, data encryption, incident response, etc. The policymaker ensures that these policies are comprehensive, clear, and actionable, providing a solid foundation for the organization's cybersecurity practices.

Coordinating with stakeholders to establish guidelines is crucial for ensuring the policies are practical and align with the organization's objectives. Cybersecurity policymakers work closely with various departments within the organization, including IT, legal, human resources, and executive management, to ensure a holistic approach to cybersecurity. This collaboration is vital for ensuring that the policies are well-integrated into the organization's operations and that they address the concerns and requirements of all stakeholders.

Staying informed about legal and regulatory changes is essential in the rapidly evolving field of cybersecurity. Cybersecurity policymakers must keep abreast of new laws, regulations, and industry standards that could impact the organization's cybersecurity practices. This knowledge is crucial for ensuring that the organization's policies remain compliant with legal requirements and industry best practices, thereby mitigating the risk of legal issues and enhancing the organization's cybersecurity posture.

Assessing policy effectiveness and making adjustments are ongoing responsibilities of a cybersecurity policymaker. Regularly reviewing and evaluating the implemented policies helps identify areas where they may fall short or new threats have emerged. This assessment involves soliciting feedback, analyzing security incidents, and monitoring the overall security landscape. Based on these assessments, the policymaker makes necessary adjustments to the policies, ensuring they remain practical and relevant in protecting the organization against current and future cyber threats.

The role of a cybersecurity policymaker is critical in establishing and maintaining an organization's cybersecurity framework. Their responsibilities encompass developing cybersecurity policies, coordinating with stakeholders, staying updated on legal and regulatory changes, and continuously assessing policy effectiveness. Their work ensures that the organization remains protected against cyber threats and adheres to legal standards and best practices in cybersecurity.

In terms of certifications, several are beneficial for cybersecurity policymakers. Certifications such as CISSP or Certified Information Security Manager provide a solid foundation in cybersecurity management and practices. Additionally, certifications focused on policy development and governance, such as Certified in Governance of Enterprise IT, can be particularly relevant.

A combination of specialized training and relevant certifications is crucial for those looking to excel as cybersecurity policymakers. This educational path equips them with the necessary skills to develop and implement effective cybersecurity policies, collaborate with various stakeholders, stay updated with legal and regulatory changes, and continuously assess and adjust policies to safeguard the organization effectively.

CYBERSECURITY TRAINER

A cybersecurity trainer occupies a pivotal role in enhancing an organization's cybersecurity posture through education and awareness. This position requires a deep understanding of cybersecurity concepts and practices and the ability to communicate this knowledge to others effectively. The responsibilities of a cybersecurity trainer include designing and delivering comprehensive cybersecurity training programs, developing educational materials and courses, ensuring that training content remains relevant to current cybersecurity trends, and evaluating the effectiveness of these training programs in content delivery and learner engagement.

Cybersecurity trainers create training modules that are tailored to the needs of the organization and its employees—ranging from essential cybersecurity awareness for all staff to more advanced training for IT personnel. These training programs are essential for equipping employees with the knowledge and skills to effectively recognize and respond to cyber threats. The trainer ensures that the training is engaging and accessible, using various teaching methods and tools to cater to different learning styles.

Developing educational materials and courses involves creating comprehensive and up-to-date content that covers a wide range of cybersecurity topics. This includes the latest trends in cyber threats, best practices in digital security, and guidelines for responding to incidents. The educational materials might encompass various formats, such as presentations, handouts, interactive modules, and online courses. A cybersecurity trainer ensures that these materials are informative while also being easy to understand and apply in practical scenarios.

Cybersecurity trainers must continuously update their knowledge and skills to include the latest threats, technologies, and mitigation strategies. This ensures that the training programs provide the most current and relevant information, thereby enabling employees to stay ahead of emerging threats and adapt to new cybersecurity challenges.

Evaluating training effectiveness and learner engagement is essential for continuously improving training programs. Cybersecurity trainers assess the impact of their training through feedback surveys, quizzes, and practical exercises. They analyze this feedback to gauge how well the training has been received and how much of the content has been retained by the employees and staff. This evaluation helps identify areas for improvement, modify training approaches, and enhance the overall effectiveness of cybersecurity training programs.

The role of a cybersecurity trainer is crucial in fostering a culture of cybersecurity awareness and preparedness within an organization. Their responsibilities include designing and delivering training programs, developing educational materials, keeping training aligned with current trends, and assessing the effectiveness of these programs. Their work ensures that employees are well-informed and equipped to contribute to the organization's cybersecurity defense.

SECURITY CURRICULUM DEVELOPER

A security curriculum developer plays a vital role in shaping the educational landscape of cybersecurity. They specialize in creating comprehensive and relevant cybersecurity curricula for educational institutions, ensuring that the next generation of cybersecurity professionals is well-equipped to meet the challenges of the digital world. This role involves collaborating with academic and industry experts, aligning curricula with current industry certifications and standards, and incorporating practical, hands-on learning experiences into the curriculum.

Developing cybersecurity curricula for educational institutions is the core duty of a security curriculum developer. They are responsible for designing educational programs that provide a thorough grounding in cybersecurity principles, practices, and technologies. This involves creating a structured curriculum that covers essential topics such as network security, ethical hacking, digital forensics, and information assurance. The curriculum developer ensures that the content is academically rigorous and reflective of the real-world scenarios that students will encounter in their professional lives.

Security curriculum developers work closely with cybersecurity professionals, industry leaders, and academic scholars to gather insights and stay updated on the latest trends and challenges in the field. This collaboration helps ensure that the curriculum is aligned with the cybersecurity industry's current needs and expectations, thereby enhancing employability and preparedness for their graduates.

Along those same lines, aligning curricula with industry certifications and standards is essential in a field that is heavily influenced by professional certifications. Security curriculum developers integrate elements of well-recognized certifications such as CISSP, Certified Ethical Hacker, or Computer Technology Industry Association Security+ into the curriculum. This alignment ensures that students are academically prepared for the certification exams that are often crucial for their career advancement in cybersecurity.

Incorporating hands-on and practical learning experiences is a crucial aspect of curriculum development. Security curriculum developers recognize the importance of practical skills in cybersecurity education. They design lab exercises, simulations, and real-world project work that allow students to apply theoretical knowledge in practical settings. This experiential learning is fundamental in developing the skills and confidence required to navigate the cybersecurity landscape effectively.

The role of a security curriculum developer is instrumental in preparing future cybersecurity professionals. Their responsibilities encompass developing comprehensive curricula, collaborating with experts, aligning educational content with industry standards, and incorporating practical learning experiences. Their work ensures that cybersecurity education is dynamic, relevant, and aligned with the evolving demands of the cybersecurity field.

12

RISK AND COMPLIANCE
ROLES IN CYBERSECURITY

Risk and compliance roles in cybersecurity safeguard organizations against potential threats and ensure adherence to regulatory requirements. These roles focus on identifying, assessing, and managing risks and ensuring organizations comply with cybersecurity laws and standards. Professionals in these positions are crucial in developing strategies and frameworks that protect organizations from cyber risks while maintaining regulatory compliance. Their work involves a deep understanding of cybersecurity's technical aspects and the legal and regulatory environment in which organizations operate.

BUSINESS CONTINUITY PLANNER

A business continuity planner is essential in preparing organizations for potential disruptions caused by cyber incidents and other emergencies. This role involves developing and maintaining business continuity plans, which is crucial for ensuring an organization can continue operating and recover swiftly from unforeseen events. The responsibilities of a business continuity planner include not only creating these plans but also coordinating business continuity exercises, updating plans to reflect current threats, and training staff in business continuity procedures.

Developing and maintaining business continuity plans is a primary responsibility. Business continuity planners assess an organization's critical functions and the risks that could impact these areas. They develop comprehensive plans detailing the procedures to be followed during a disruption—whether a cyberattack, natural disaster, or other crises. These plans encompass strategies for maintaining essential functions and services, data backup and recovery, and resource allocation during an emergency.

The business continuity planner organizes regular drills and simulations to test the effectiveness of the continuity plans in real-life scenarios. These exercises help identify any weaknesses or gaps in the plans and familiarize staff with emergency procedures. By regularly testing and updating these plans, the planner ensures that they are practical and actionable in the event of an actual emergency.

As cyber threats evolve and business operations change, continuity plans must be regularly reviewed and revised. The business continuity planner stays informed about the latest cybersecurity trends, threats, and organizational structure and operations changes. This ongoing assessment ensures that the business continuity plans align with the current risk landscape and organizational needs.

Training staff in business continuity procedures is a vital part of this role. Business continuity planners develop and deliver training programs to ensure all employees know the continuity plans and their roles and responsibilities in an emergency. This training ensures a coordinated and efficient response to disruptions, minimizing the impact on the organization's operations.

For aspiring business continuity planners, engaging in specialized training is essential to build a solid foundation in the field. Training should ideally cover various topics, starting with risk management and assessment. This encompasses learning to identify and evaluate potential threats to an organization's operations. Additionally, gaining expertise in disaster recovery and emergency management is crucial, focusing on strategies to respond effectively to various crises, including natural disasters and cyber incidents. Cybersecurity awareness is another critical training area, given the increasing prevalence of cyber threats. This includes understanding how to protect sensitive data and incorporate cybersecurity measures into comprehensive business continuity plans. Beyond technical knowledge, training in communication and leadership skills is also invaluable. A planner will need to communicate effectively with different stakeholders and lead teams during emergencies, making these skills crucial for success.

Alongside training, obtaining relevant certifications can significantly enhance a business continuity planner's qualifications. One prominent certification is the Certified Business Continuity Professional, offered by DRI International. This certification is recognized globally and is suitable for those with some experience in the field, as it validates an individual's expertise in developing and implementing business continuity plans. The Associate Business Continuity Professional certification, also from DRI International, is a great starting point for those who are newer to the field. It provides foundational knowledge and skills in business continuity planning. These certifications affirm a planner's competence and commitment to the field and keep them updated with the latest best practices and trends in business continuity.

The role of a business continuity planner is crucial in ensuring that organizations are prepared and resilient in the face of disruptions. Their responsibilities include developing business continuity plans, coordinating exercises, keeping these plans updated with current threats, and training staff. Their work ensures organizations can quickly recover from incidents and continue their critical operations with minimal impact.

COMPLIANCE DIRECTOR

A compliance director's role in the crucial cybersecurity arena ensures that an organization adheres to various cybersecurity regulations and standards. This position demands a comprehensive understanding of the legal and regulatory landscape and the ability to implement effective compliance strategies within the organization. The responsibilities of a compliance director include overseeing compliance with cybersecurity regulations, developing and enforcing compliance policies, leading compliance audits and investigations, and providing expert advice to organizational leadership on compliance matters.

Compliance directors ensure that the organization's practices, policies, and procedures meet cybersecurity standards and legal obligations. This involves staying current with the evolving landscape of cybersecurity laws, guidelines, and best practices. The compliance director ensures that the organization remains compliant with regulations such as the General Data Protection Regulation (GDPR), the Health Insurance Portability and Accountability Act (HIPAA), and others, depending on the nature of the business and the geographical regions in which it operates.

Developing and enforcing compliance policies is another critical aspect of the role. The compliance director creates comprehensive policies addressing various cybersecurity compliance aspects. These policies serve as a guideline for the organization in maintaining compliance and mitigating cybersecurity risks. The director develops these policies and ensures effective implementation across the organization, often working with different departments to integrate compliance practices into their operations.

The compliance director oversees regular internal audits to assess the effectiveness of the organization's compliance measures. They also lead investigations in response to any compliance breaches or irregularities. These audits and investigations are vital for identifying potential areas of noncompliance and implementing corrective measures to mitigate any risks identified.

Advising leadership on compliance matters is a vital function of a compliance director. They act as the primary advisor to the organization's senior management and board on all matters related to cybersecurity compliance. This includes providing insights into regulatory changes, potential risks, and the impact of compliance strategies on the organization's operations and reputation. Their expertise is crucial in guiding the strategic decision-making process and ensuring that the organization's leadership is well-informed about compliance issues.

A combination of targeted training and specialized certifications is highly recommended for those aiming to excel as a compliance director in cybersecurity. The training for a compliance director should encompass a deep dive into the legal and regulatory frameworks relevant to cybersecurity. This includes understanding laws like GDPR, HIPAA, and other region-specific regulations. The training should also cover the evolving landscape of cybersecurity laws and best practices, equipping the individual with the skills to keep the organization updated and compliant. Furthermore, training in the development and enforcement of compliance policies is essential. This involves learning how to create comprehensive policies that address various aspects of cybersecurity compliance and understanding how to implement these policies effectively across different departments of an organization.

Another critical area of training involves learning how to lead compliance audits and investigations. This training should focus on methodologies for conducting thorough internal audits, assessing the effectiveness of compliance measures, and leading investigations in response to compliance breaches. Additionally, training in advisory skills is crucial because a compliance director needs to provide expert advice to organizational leadership on compliance matters. This includes understanding how to communicate complex regulatory information and its implications for the organization's operations and reputation.

Regarding certifications, there are several that can significantly bolster a compliance director's credentials. Certifications such as Certified Information Systems Security Professional (CISSP) and Certified Information Security Manager (CISM) are highly regarded in the field and demonstrate a deep understanding of information security management and practices. Additionally, certifications specific to compliance, such as the Certified Compliance & Ethics Professional (CCEP) or Certified in Healthcare Compliance, can be invaluable, especially for those working in sectors with stringent regulatory requirements. These certifications validate the individual's expertise in compliance and cybersecurity and ensure they are well-versed in the latest trends and best practices.

The role of a compliance director is critical in ensuring that an organization meets its cybersecurity regulatory and legal obligations. Their responsibilities encompass overseeing compliance, developing and enforcing policies, leading audits and investigations, and advising leadership on compliance matters. Their work is essential in protecting the organization from legal and regulatory risks, thereby maintaining its integrity and reputation in the digital world.

DATA PROTECTION OFFICER

A data protection officer (DPO) is crucial in an organization's cybersecurity and data privacy landscape. This role is increasingly important in a world where data protection and privacy are paramount, particularly in enforcing stringent data protection laws such as the GDPR. The DPO oversees data protection strategies, ensures compliance with data protection laws, manages data breaches and their subsequent notifications, and acts as the primary liaison with data protection authorities.

DPOs are tasked with developing, implementing, and maintaining policies and practices that safeguard personal data that is being processed by the organization. This involves ensuring that the data protection policies align with legal requirements and best practices and address all aspects of data privacy—from collection and processing to storage and disposal. The DPO ensures that these policies are effectively communicated and embedded into the organizational culture.

With laws like GDPR setting the benchmark for data protection standards globally, the DPO must ensure that the organization's data handling practices are fully compliant with these regulations. This includes staying updated on the latest legal developments in data protection, assessing the organization's data processing activities, and implementing necessary changes to maintain compliance. The DPO's expertise is vital in navigating the complex regulatory landscape and avoiding potential legal penalties and reputational damage.

Managing data breaches and notifications is an essential duty. In a data breach, the DPO oversees the response and mitigation process. This includes assessing the scope and impact of the breach, coordinating the response efforts to contain and rectify the situation, and ensuring proper notification procedures are followed. The DPO works closely with other teams, such as IT security and legal, to manage the breach effectively and minimize any adverse impacts.

Another key responsibility is acting as a point of contact for data protection authorities. The DPO is the primary liaison between the organization and regulatory bodies concerning data protection matters. They handle all communications, including reporting breaches and responding to queries or investigations by the authorities. The DPO plays a crucial role in maintaining a positive and compliant relationship with these regulatory bodies, ensuring that the organization is represented accurately and professionally.

For those aspiring to become a DPO, a well-rounded approach to training and certification is critical to mastering the complexities of this role. Training for a DPO should be comprehensive, covering areas such as developing, implementing, and maintaining data protection and privacy policies. This includes understanding how to align these policies with legal requirements and best practices, covering all aspects of data privacy from collection to disposal. An emphasis should be placed on ensuring these policies are effectively communicated and ingrained in the organizational culture.

Another critical area of training is ensuring compliance with data protection laws, particularly with regulations like the GDPR, which have set global benchmarks for data protection standards. DPOs must be well-versed in the latest legal developments in data protection, capable of assessing the organization's data processing activities, and adept at implementing necessary changes to maintain compliance. This training is vital for navigating the complex regulatory landscape and avoiding potential legal penalties and reputational damage.

Training in managing data breaches and notifications is equally essential. DPOs need to be trained in overseeing the response to data breaches, which includes assessing the breach's scope and impact, coordinating containment and rectification efforts, and ensuring adherence to proper notification procedures. Collaboration skills are also important, as DPOs work closely with IT security, legal, and other teams in managing breaches effectively.

Regarding certifications, DPOs can benefit from a range of relevant qualifications. Certifications such as the Certified Information Privacy Professional and the Certified Data Protection Officer offer specialized knowledge in data protection and privacy laws and practices. These certifications demonstrate a DPO's expertise in the field and keep them updated with the latest trends and best practices in data protection and privacy.

Additionally, acting as a point of contact for data protection authorities is a significant responsibility. Training should, therefore, include skills in communication and as a liaison, equipping DPOs to handle communications with regulatory bodies efficiently, including reporting breaches and responding to queries or investigations. The DPO's role in maintaining a compliant and positive relationship with these authorities is crucial, necessitating professional knowledge and excellent communication skills.

The role of a DPO is integral to ensuring an organization's compliance with data protection laws and safeguarding personal data. Their responsibilities include overseeing data protection policies, ensuring legal compliance, managing data breaches, and coordinating with data protection authorities. The DPO's role is critical in navigating the complexities of data privacy and protection, thereby maintaining the trust and confidence of customers, stakeholders, and regulatory bodies.

INFORMATION SECURITY AUDITOR

An information security auditor is vital in assessing and enhancing an organization's cybersecurity posture. This position requires a deep understanding of various security standards and practices and the ability to evaluate security controls and processes critically. An information security auditor's responsibilities include conducting internal and external security audits, evaluating the effectiveness of security measures, reporting on audit findings, recommending improvements, and staying current with evolving auditing standards and techniques.

An information security auditor's primary duty is to conduct internal and external security audits. They thoroughly examine an organization's security infrastructure, policies, and procedures. Internal audits focus on reviewing the organization's security measures to ensure they are compliant with internal standards and effective in protecting against cyber threats. External audits may involve evaluating the security posture of third-party vendors or partners to ensure they meet the organization's security requirements. These audits are crucial for identifying vulnerabilities and ensuring that all cybersecurity aspects are adequately managed.

Information security auditors assess the security measures to determine their effectiveness in safeguarding the organization's digital assets. This includes evaluating firewalls, intrusion detection systems, encryption protocols, access controls, and other security tools. They also review data protection, incident response, and user access management processes. This evaluation helps in understanding the strengths and weaknesses of the current security setup.

Reporting audit findings and recommending improvements is essential for enhancing an organization's cybersecurity. The information security auditor compiles a detailed report outlining their findings after an audit. This report includes any identified vulnerabilities, areas of noncompliance, and potential security risks. Based on these findings, the auditor recommends strengthening the organization's security posture. These recommendations are vital for guiding the organization in making informed decisions about enhancing its cybersecurity measures.

To excel as an information security auditor, one must pursue specific training and certifications that cater to the unique demands of this role. The training for an information security auditor should focus on a deep understanding of various security standards and practices, along with the development of skills necessary to evaluate security controls and processes critically. This includes learning how to conduct both internal and external security audits effectively. Training should emphasize the methodologies for performing thorough examinations of an organization's security infrastructure, policies, and procedures, ensuring they comply with internal standards and are effective against cyber threats. Additionally, auditors must be trained to evaluate third-party vendors or partners to ensure they meet the organization's security requirements.

Another critical aspect of training involves evaluating security controls and processes. Information security auditors must assess existing security measures, including firewalls, intrusion detection systems, encryption protocols, access controls, and other security tools. Training should also cover reviewing data protection, incident response, and user access management processes. This is essential for understanding the strengths and weaknesses of the current security setup and making informed recommendations. Training in reporting audit findings and recommending improvements is also crucial.

Several certifications are highly beneficial for information security auditors, each validating an auditor's expertise in the field with a specific focus on audit processes, management practices, and compliance standards critical to safeguarding sensitive information. The Certified Information Systems Auditor (CISA) and CISSP certifications are particularly relevant. These certifications demonstrate a comprehensive understanding of information security audit processes and management practices.

In addition to CISA and CISSP, certifications related to the Qualified Security Assessor (QSA) and Payment Card Industry Data Security Standard

(PCI DSS) compliance are invaluable for auditors and inspectors working within the payment card industry. The QSA certification is designed for professionals who assess and validate an entity's adherence to PCI DSS, ensuring that merchants and service providers maintain the highest payment card information security standards.

Staying updated with evolving auditing standards and techniques is a continuous process for information security auditors. Cybersecurity is dynamic, with new threats and technologies emerging regularly. Therefore, ongoing learning and professional development are necessary to ensure that auditing methods remain effective and that auditors can provide current and comprehensive advice on cybersecurity matters. This includes keeping abreast of the latest developments in cybersecurity, auditing standards, and best practices, a crucial aspect of maintaining excellence in this role.

The role of an information security auditor is critical in ensuring that an organization's cybersecurity measures are effective and compliant with relevant standards. Their responsibilities encompass conducting security audits, evaluating security controls, reporting findings, recommending improvements, and staying current with auditing practices. Their expertise is crucial for identifying vulnerabilities and guiding organizations in strengthening their cybersecurity defenses.

REGULATORY COMPLIANCE ANALYST

A regulatory compliance analyst manages and ensures an organization's adherence to the ever-evolving landscape of cybersecurity regulations and standards. This role requires a comprehensive understanding of cybersecurity principles and their legal framework. The primary responsibilities of a regulatory compliance analyst include monitoring and analyzing cybersecurity regulations, ensuring that the organization complies with these laws and standards, advising on regulatory changes and updates, and preparing detailed reports and documentation for compliance audits.

A regulatory compliance analyst is responsible for staying abreast of new and existing laws, regulations, and industry standards that affect the organization's cybersecurity posture. This continuous monitoring is crucial as it allows the organization to address changes in the regulatory environment proactively. The analyst must understand the implications of these regulations and how they apply to the organization's specific context.

The regulatory compliance analyst evaluates the organization's cybersecurity practices and policies to ensure that they align with legal and regulatory requirements. This involves working closely with various departments to implement compliance measures and integrate these requirements into everyday business processes. Their role is pivotal in mitigating the risk of legal penalties, reputational damage, and other consequences of noncompliance.

The compliance analyst interprets the regulations and guides management and relevant departments on how these changes impact the organization. They play a critical advisory role in developing strategies and action plans to address gaps in compliance and adapt to new regulatory requirements.

Regulatory compliance analysts must also compile comprehensive documentation that details the organization's compliance with relevant cybersecurity regulations. This documentation is critical during internal and external audits, demonstrating the organization's commitment to regulatory compliance. The analyst ensures that these reports are thorough, accurate, and prepared in a manner that meets auditing standards.

For individuals aspiring to become a regulatory compliance analyst, specialized training and certification are essential to navigate the complex interplay of cybersecurity and regulatory compliance. Training for a regulatory compliance analyst should focus on developing a deep understanding of cybersecurity principles and the legal frameworks and regulations surrounding them. This involves comprehensive knowledge of various laws, regulations, and industry standards affecting an organization's cybersecurity posture. Such training should enable the analyst to keep up with new and existing cybersecurity regulations and understand their implications for the organization's specific context. Another critical training area is ensuring organizational compliance with these laws and standards.

Training in advising on regulatory changes and updates is also important. Regulatory compliance analysts must understand how to interpret regulations and provide actionable guidance to management and relevant departments. This includes developing strategies and action plans to address compliance gaps and adapt to new regulatory requirements.

Preparing reports and documentation for compliance audits is another essential training aspect. Analysts must learn to compile thorough and accurate documentation demonstrating the organization's compliance with relevant cybersecurity regulations. This documentation is crucial during audits, showcasing the organization's commitment to regulatory compliance.

In terms of certifications, several are particularly beneficial for regulatory compliance analysts. Certifications such as CISSP or CISM can provide foundational knowledge in cybersecurity. Additionally, certifications specifically focused on compliance such as CCEP, can offer more specialized insights into regulatory compliance. These certifications validate the analyst's expertise and ensure they are updated with the latest trends and best practices in cybersecurity and regulatory compliance.

A combination of targeted training and relevant certifications is critical for those looking to excel as a regulatory compliance analyst. This educational path equips them with the necessary skills to monitor and analyze regulations, ensure organizational compliance, advise on regulatory changes, and prepare comprehensive compliance documentation.

The role of a regulatory compliance analyst is integral to an organization's ability to navigate and comply with the complex regulatory environment of cybersecurity.

RISK ANALYST

A risk analyst focuses on identifying and assessing potential cybersecurity risks. Their work is essential for understanding and mitigating threats that could compromise the organization's information systems and data. The responsibilities of a risk analyst include identifying and assessing cybersecurity risks, developing strategies to mitigate these risks, conducting regular assessments and reviews, and collaborating with various departments to ensure comprehensive risk management throughout the organization.

A risk analyst details the organization's network, systems, and processes to identify potential vulnerabilities and threats. This involves understanding the organization's technology landscape, the data it handles, and how cyber threats could impact various business processes. Risk analysts use various tools and techniques to evaluate the likelihood and potential impact of different cyber threats, helping the organization prioritize its security efforts.

Developing risk mitigation strategies is a crucial responsibility. Once risks are identified and assessed, the risk analyst works on formulating strategies to address these risks effectively. This may involve recommending security measures such as implementing new technologies, enhancing existing security controls, or changing business processes. The aim is to reduce the organization's exposure to cyber threats and minimize the potential impact of security incidents.

Regular risk assessments and reviews are essential for maintaining an up-to-date understanding of the organization's risk profile. Cybersecurity is a rapidly evolving field, with new threats emerging regularly. Risk analysts continuously monitor the threat landscape and reassess the organization's vulnerabilities in light of these developments. Regular reviews ensure that the risk mitigation strategies remain practical and relevant.

Collaborating with different departments on risk management is vital for a holistic approach to cybersecurity. Risk analysts work with IT, legal, finance, operations, and other departments to integrate risk management into the organization's operations. This collaboration ensures that cybersecurity risk management is not siloed but is considered a part of the organization's broader risk management framework. By working with different departments, risk analysts help create a culture of risk awareness and ensure that cybersecurity considerations are embedded in all organizational processes.

Specialized training and certifications are essential for those aspiring to excel as a risk analyst in cybersecurity. The training for a risk analyst should encompass a comprehensive understanding of the cybersecurity landscape, focusing on identifying and assessing potential risks. This includes learning to analyze an organization's network, systems, and processes to identify vulnerabilities and threats. Training should cover the various tools and techniques used to evaluate the likelihood and potential impact of different cyber threats, enabling the risk analyst to help the organization prioritize its security efforts.

Developing risk mitigation strategies is another critical area of training. Risk analysts must learn how to formulate effective strategies to address identified risks. Training should equip analysts with the skills to reduce the organization's exposure to cyber threats and minimize the potential impact of security incidents.

Regular risk assessments and reviews are crucial in the rapidly evolving field of cybersecurity. Training should include methodologies for continuously monitoring the threat landscape and reassessing the organization's vulnerabilities in light of new developments. This ensures that risk mitigation strategies remain effective and relevant.

Training should also emphasize the importance of integrating risk management into all aspects of an organization's operations, working with IT, legal, finance, operations, and other departments. This collaborative approach is vital for ensuring that cybersecurity risk management is part of the broader risk management framework and for fostering a culture of risk awareness within the organization.

In terms of certifications, several are highly beneficial for risk analysts. Certifications such as CISSP and CISM offer foundational knowledge in cybersecurity. Additionally, certifications focused on risk management, such as the Certified in Risk and Information Systems Control or the Certification in Risk Management Assurance, are particularly relevant. These certifications validate the analyst's expertise in cybersecurity risk management and ensure they are up-to-date with the latest trends and best practices in the field.

Overall, targeted training and relevant certifications are vital for those looking to become successful risk analysts in cybersecurity. This educational path equips them with the necessary skills to identify and assess risks, develop mitigation strategies, conduct regular assessments, and collaborate effectively across the organization for comprehensive risk management.

13

THREAT INTELLIGENCE ROLES IN CYBERSECURITY

Threat intelligence roles in cybersecurity are crucial for proactively identifying, analyzing, and countering sophisticated cyber threats. These roles require technical expertise, analytical skills, and strategic thinking. Professionals in threat intelligence are tasked with understanding the ever-changing landscape of cyber threats, including the tactics, techniques, and procedures of potential attackers. They are vital in providing actionable intelligence to inform and enhance an organization's cybersecurity strategies. Their work is pivotal in reacting to threats and anticipating and mitigating them before they impact the organization.

CYBER COUNTERINTELLIGENCE SPECIALIST

A cyber counterintelligence specialist operates at the forefront of cybersecurity, identifying and neutralizing threats from foreign intelligence entities. Their role is crucial in safeguarding national and organizational security interests in the cyberspace arena. The responsibilities of a cyber counterintelligence specialist include identifying threats from foreign intelligence entities, conducting counter-surveillance and deception operations, protecting sensitive information from espionage activities, and collaborating with law enforcement and intelligence agencies.

Cyber counterintelligence specialists monitor and analyze cyber activities to identify espionage attempts and threats from foreign governments or organizations. This involves understanding the modus operandi of these entities and staying ahead of their strategies. The specialist uses their expertise to detect signs of espionage and to develop countermeasures to protect sensitive information and critical infrastructure.

Conducting counter-surveillance and deception operations is another key aspect of their role. Cyber counterintelligence specialists deploy a range of techniques to mislead and confuse adversaries. This might include setting up honeypots, disseminating false information, and using other deceptive tactics to protect against intelligence-gathering activities. These operations are designed to thwart espionage efforts and gather intelligence about their adversaries.

Protecting sensitive information from espionage involves implementing robust security measures and strategies to safeguard critical data. The specialist assesses the organization's vulnerabilities and develops plans to enhance the protection of sensitive information. They ensure the necessary physical and digital security measures are in place to prevent unauthorized access and data breaches.

Collaborating with law enforcement and intelligence agencies is vital for a comprehensive approach to counterintelligence. Cyber counterintelligence specialists work closely with various governmental agencies to share information, coordinate responses, and develop joint strategies to address national security threats. This collaboration enhances the overall effectiveness of counterintelligence operations and contributes to the broader effort to protect against foreign cyber threats.

For individuals pursuing a career as a cyber counterintelligence specialist, acquiring a blend of specialized certifications and training is essential to develop the necessary skill set for this role. Training in information security, ethical hacking, computer forensics, threat intelligence, counterintelligence tactics, and intelligence analysis is crucial. Certifications like the Certified Information Systems Security Professional (CISSP) offer a broad understanding of cybersecurity principles, while the Certified Ethical Hacker (CEH) provides insight into the techniques used by hackers, which is crucial for counterintelligence work. Specialized training in computer forensics, such as the Certified Forensic Computer Examiner or Certified Computer Forensics Examiner (CCFE), equips professionals with the skills to analyze cyber intrusions and gather digital evidence. Additionally, certifications like the Global Information Assurance Certification (GIAC) Cyber Threat Intelligence (GCTI) are tailored specifically for threat intelligence, focusing on advanced cyber threats. Formal training in counterintelligence tactics—often provided by government or military institutions—is invaluable in understanding espionage activities and national security protocols. Furthermore, courses in digital forensics and intelligence analysis enhance the ability to interpret data and intelligence effectively, a key component in counterintelligence work. This combination of certifications and specialized training is fundamental in preparing individuals for the complex and dynamic field of cyber counterintelligence.

The role of a cyber counterintelligence specialist is crucial in threat intelligence and cybersecurity. Their responsibilities include identifying and countering foreign intelligence threats, conducting counter-surveillance operations, protecting sensitive information, and collaborating with law enforcement and intelligence agencies. Their expertise is vital to defending against sophisticated espionage activities and ensuring the security of critical information and infrastructure.

CYBER INTELLIGENCE RESEARCHER

A cyber intelligence researcher is a critical professional in the field of cybersecurity, playing a crucial role in understanding and anticipating emerging cyber threats. This role demands a high level of expertise in cyber threat analysis, including conducting in-depth research, tracking and profiling threat actors, and disseminating findings to aid in cybersecurity defense. The responsibilities of a cyber intelligence researcher include conducting deep-dive research into new and evolving cyber threats, tracking the tactics, techniques, and procedures (TTPs) of threat actors, developing detailed profiles of these actors and their methodologies, and publishing research findings and advisories to inform the cybersecurity community and stakeholders.

Cyber intelligence researchers delve into the intricacies of new and emerging threats in the cyber landscape, exploring their origins, mechanisms, and potential impact. This research is vital for uncovering unknown or poorly understood threats that could pose significant risks to organizations and individuals. Cyber intelligence researchers contribute to the broader understanding of the cybersecurity threat environment through their investigations.

Tracking threat actor TTPs is crucial for preventing potential cyberattacks. Cyber intelligence researchers analyze the behavior of threat actors, studying their patterns, methods, and strategies. By understanding how these actors operate, researchers can predict potential targets and attack methods, which is essential for developing effective cybersecurity measures. This tracking also aids in identifying common and evolving trends in cybercriminal activities.

Developing profiles on threat actors and their methodologies involves creating comprehensive reports on various cybercriminal groups or individuals.

These profiles provide insights into the motivations, targets, and techniques of threat actors, thereby offering valuable intelligence for cybersecurity professionals and organizations. By profiling these actors, cyber intelligence researchers help understand the broader context of cyber threats, enabling more targeted and effective cybersecurity strategies.

Publishing research findings and advisories is a crucial aspect of the role of a cyber intelligence researcher. They share their insights and discoveries with the cybersecurity community, law enforcement, and other relevant stakeholders. This dissemination of information includes publishing reports, advisories, and articles that detail their findings on emerging threats and threat actors. They contribute to the collective effort to enhance cybersecurity awareness and preparedness by sharing their research.

A combination of specialized training and certifications is key for a cyber intelligence researcher to develop the expertise required for this complex role. These professionals benefit from training in cyber threat analysis, digital forensics, and intelligence gathering. Particularly valuable certifications include the CISSP, which offers a broad understanding of cybersecurity principles, and the CEH, which provides insight into the tactics used by cybercriminals. Advanced certifications such as the GCTI are specifically tailored for threat intelligence and are ideal for those who are focusing on advanced cyber threats. Additionally, training in intelligence analysis techniques through formal courses or workshops enhances the ability to interpret and analyze complex data effectively. Training in digital forensics can also be beneficial by providing the technical skills needed to understand the intricacies of cyber threats at a deeper level. These certifications and training programs equip cyber intelligence researchers with the necessary skills and validate their expertise in the field, making them invaluable assets in the fight against cyber threats.

The role of a cyber intelligence researcher is integral in the battle against cyber threats. Their responsibilities include conducting in-depth research on emerging threats, tracking and profiling threat actors, and disseminating their findings to the broader community. Their work is essential in providing actionable intelligence that informs and improves cybersecurity strategies and defenses.

INTELLIGENCE OPERATIONS MANAGER

An intelligence operations manager holds a strategic position in cybersecurity and is primarily responsible for overseeing threat intelligence operations and teams. This role requires leadership skills, strategic planning, and a deep knowledge of cybersecurity threats and intelligence gathering. The key responsibilities of an intelligence operations manager include managing and guiding intelligence teams; developing and implementing intelligence strategies; ensuring effective coordination between intelligence, analysis, and response teams; and overseeing the resources and tools necessary for effective intelligence gathering.

Overseeing threat intelligence operations and teams is a primary responsibility. An intelligence operations manager directs teams that are responsible for gathering and analyzing information about cyber threats. This involves leading a group of analysts and researchers who are dedicated to identifying, assessing, and understanding the cyber threats that the organization faces. The manager ensures that these teams operate efficiently and effectively, providing guidance, direction, and support to help them achieve their objectives.

The intelligence operations manager devises comprehensive strategies for threat intelligence gathering and analysis. These strategies are designed to proactively anticipate and identify potential cyber threats, enabling the organization to prepare and respond effectively. The manager ensures that the intelligence strategy aligns with the organization's cybersecurity goals and objectives.

Coordinating intelligence, analysis, and response teams is essential for a cohesive cybersecurity approach. The intelligence operations manager facilitates collaboration and communication among various teams within the cybersecurity department. This includes ensuring that the intelligence team's findings are effectively communicated to the analysis team for in-depth evaluation and to the response team for timely action. This coordination is vital for ensuring that insights gained from intelligence gathering are translated into actionable security measures.

Managing resources and tools for intelligence gathering involves overseeing the technological and human resources required for effective intelligence operations. The intelligence operations manager ensures that the teams have access to the latest tools and technologies for monitoring, gathering, and analyzing cyber threat information. They are also responsible for allocating the necessary budget and resources, ensuring that the intelligence operations are well-equipped to handle the complex and evolving nature of cyber threats.

For an intelligence operations manager, acquiring a comprehensive set of certifications and undergoing specialized training is crucial to effectively leading and managing threat intelligence operations. This role demands a deep understanding of cybersecurity threats, intelligence processes, and team management. Valuable certifications for this position include the CISSP, which provides a broad foundation in cybersecurity, and the Certified Information Security Manager (CISM), which focuses on the management and strategy aspects of information security. In addition, the GIAC Certified Incident Handler certification is beneficial by offering insights into handling and responding to security incidents—an essential aspect of intelligence operations.

Specialized training in intelligence analysis and cybersecurity management is also essential. Training programs that focus on strategic analysis, threat assessment, and intelligence-gathering techniques are essential for developing the skills to manage complex intelligence operations. Leadership and management courses that are tailored explicitly for cybersecurity professionals can also be advantageous because they help hone the skills needed for effectively leading a team of analysts.

Furthermore, staying updated with the latest cybersecurity and threat intelligence developments is vital. Participating in cybersecurity and intelligence workshops, seminars, and continuing education courses can provide the intelligence operations manager with the latest knowledge and best practices in the field. This continuous learning is important for ensuring that the intelligence strategies being developed are proactive and effective in countering the evolving cyber threats.

The role of an intelligence operations manager is central to the effectiveness of an organization's threat intelligence efforts. Their responsibilities encompass overseeing intelligence operations, developing strategies, coordinating with different cybersecurity teams, and managing resources and tools. Their leadership and strategic vision are crucial in equipping the organization with the intelligence to identify and respond to cyber threats proactively.

OPEN SOURCE INTELLIGENCE (OSINT) ANALYST

An open source intelligence (OSINT) analyst specializes in collecting and analyzing publicly available information to identify potential cybersecurity threats. This role is increasingly important in the digital age, where vast information is accessible through public channels. The responsibilities of an OSINT analyst include gathering data from open sources such as social media, public records, and various online platforms; identifying potential security threats from this information; utilizing these open sources for intelligence gathering; and integrating OSINT findings with other intelligence sources for a comprehensive security overview.

OSINT analysts use various tools and techniques to scour the internet and other public domains for information that could indicate potential cybersecurity threats or vulnerabilities. This involves sifting through a large amount of data, identifying relevant information, and analyzing it for insights into potential security issues. The ability to effectively gather and interpret open-source information is crucial to the success of an OSINT analyst.

Identifying potential threats from open sources involves a keen eye for detail and a deep understanding of cybersecurity threats. OSINT analysts look for indications of emerging threats, such as new malware, phishing campaigns, or emerging hacker tactics being discussed in public forums or on social media. They also monitor for any leaked information or data breaches that could impact their organization. This proactive approach to threat identification enables organizations to anticipate and prepare for potential security incidents.

Social media platforms, online forums, and other public data sources can be rich mines of information for cybersecurity intelligence. OSINT analysts adeptly navigate these platforms to collect valuable intelligence that can inform the organization's security strategies. They are skilled in differentiating between credible information and noise, ensuring the intelligence gathered is accurate and relevant.

Integrating OSINT with other intelligence sources is crucial for a holistic understanding of the cybersecurity landscape. An OSINT analyst does not work in isolation but collaborates with other intelligence and cybersecurity teams within the organization. By combining open source intelligence with information from other sources, such as internal threat intelligence, network monitoring, and external cybersecurity reports, OSINT analysts contribute to a more comprehensive and multidimensional view of the organization's security posture.

For an OSINT analyst, specialized certifications and training are essential in honing the skills required to analyze and leverage publicly available information for cybersecurity purposes. Given the unique nature of this role, which involves gathering intelligence from open sources like social media, public records, and online forums, a combination of technical and analytical skills is crucial.

Certifications such as the CISSP can provide a strong foundation in cybersecurity principles. Additionally, more specialized certifications, like the Open Source Intelligence Certified Professional or the Certified Open Source Intelligence Specialist, focus explicitly on the skills needed for effective open-source intelligence gathering and analysis. These certifications teach methodologies for efficiently collecting and analyzing vast amounts of open-source data and converting them into actionable intelligence.

Training in data analysis, digital forensics, and cybersecurity analysis also benefits an OSINT role. These training programs can help develop the analytical skills to sift through large datasets in order to identify relevant information. Courses or workshops on advanced search techniques, social media intelligence, and cyber threat intelligence can provide specific insights into the tools and methods used in open source intelligence gathering.

Moreover, given the rapidly evolving nature of the cybersecurity landscape and the tools available for intelligence gathering, continuous learning and staying up-to-date with the latest developments in open source intelligence techniques are critical. Participation in industry conferences, webinars, and online communities dedicated to OSINT can provide valuable ongoing learning opportunities and insights into current best practices.

The role of an open source intelligence analyst leverages publicly available information to enhance an organization's cybersecurity efforts. Their responsibilities include collecting and analyzing open-source data, identifying potential threats, utilizing social media and public platforms for intelligence gathering, and integrating their findings with other intelligence sources. Their expertise enables organizations to proactively identify and respond to emerging cybersecurity threats in the vast landscape of publicly available information.

SECURITY OPERATIONS CENTER (SOC) ANALYST

An SOC analyst plays a pivotal role in an organization's cybersecurity team, specializing in real-time monitoring and analysis of security events to safeguard against potential cyber threats. These professionals are integral in the early detection, assessment, and response to cybersecurity incidents, providing a crucial line of defense for the organization.

An SOC analyst's primary responsibility is continuously monitoring and analyzing security events in real time. This involves vigilantly overseeing the organization's networks and systems using sophisticated security tools and technologies. SOC analysts can detect signs of potential cybersecurity threats by constantly scanning for anomalies or unusual activities. Their expertise lies in accurately interpreting complex data from security systems, identifying potential threats, and assessing the severity and potential impact of these events.

In addition to monitoring, SOC analysts play a critical role in identifying and escalating potential security incidents. Once a threat is detected, they are responsible for quickly analyzing the situation to determine the most appropriate response. This includes an in-depth analysis of the nature of the incident, its potential impact on the organization, and the urgency of the required response. SOC analysts must be adept at escalating significant security incidents to higher-level security personnel or specialized teams for further investigation and response, ensuring that potential threats are addressed promptly and effectively.

As the first responders to cyber threats, their immediate actions can be pivotal in preventing or minimizing damage from a security incident. They implement predetermined security protocols, such as blocking malicious traffic or isolating compromised systems, to contain incidents and prevent further spread. Their ability to act swiftly and decisively is crucial in mitigating the impact of security breaches.

Utilizing threat intelligence is an essential component of effective SOC operations. SOC analysts integrate intelligence from various sources, including external threat feeds, internal analysis, and historical incident data, into their monitoring and response strategies. This integration of threat intelligence is vital for providing insights into the latest cyber threats, attacker tactics, and system vulnerabilities, enabling SOC analysts to anticipate and prepare for potential attacks more effectively.

A solid educational background in cybersecurity, IT, or a related field is typically required for those interested in pursuing a career as an SOC analyst. This is often achieved through a bachelor's degree in these disciplines. Additionally, obtaining professional certifications can significantly enhance an SOC analyst's qualifications and expertise. Certifications such as CISSP, CISM, Computer Technology Industry Association Security+, or GIAC Certified Intrusion Analyst are highly valued in the industry. These certifications provide comprehensive knowledge and skills in cybersecurity and information security while demonstrating a commitment to the field and a readiness to handle the complexities of an SOC environment.

The role of an SOC analyst is vital in the early detection, assessment, and mitigation of cybersecurity threats. Their responsibilities include continuously monitoring security events, identifying and escalating potential incidents, acting as the first line of defense, and utilizing threat intelligence. A combination of formal education and professional certifications is essential for excelling in this role and effectively protecting an organization from emerging cyber threats.

THREAT INTELLIGENCE ANALYST

A threat intelligence analyst focuses on gathering, analyzing, and interpreting data to identify potential cyber threats and vulnerabilities. This role requires a blend of technical skills, analytical acumen, and the ability to provide actionable intelligence for risk mitigation. The responsibilities of a threat intelligence analyst include collecting data on potential threats, providing actionable insights to guide cybersecurity strategies, utilizing various tools for threat monitoring and analysis, and collaborating with both internal security teams and external agencies.

Gathering and analyzing data on potential threats is a core function of a threat intelligence analyst. They use a range of sources, including cyber threat feeds, hacker forums, and industry reports, to collect information on emerging threats and trends in the cybersecurity landscape. This process involves sifting through vast amounts of data to identify relevant information and analyzing it to understand the nature of the threats, their potential impact, and the methods used by attackers.

Threat intelligence analysts synthesize their findings into concise, informative reports that inform decision makers within the organization. They highlight potential vulnerabilities, recommend security enhancements, and advise on best practices to counter identified threats. Their insights help organizations prioritize security efforts and allocate resources more effectively to protect against cyberattacks.

These analysts use advanced cybersecurity tools to monitor networks and systems continuously. These tools help in detecting unusual activities that could signal a security breach. Analysts also use data analysis software to process and analyze large datasets, which enables them to draw meaningful conclusions from the information.

Collaborating with internal security teams and external agencies is vital for comprehensive threat intelligence efforts. Threat intelligence analysts work closely with other cybersecurity professionals, such as SOC analysts and incident responders, to share intelligence and coordinate security measures. They may also collaborate with external agencies, such as law enforcement or other cybersecurity organizations, to exchange information and stay updated on global cybersecurity trends and incidents.

Obtaining specialized certifications and training is highly beneficial for those who are aspiring to become a threat intelligence analyst. Certifications such as the CISSP provide a broad understanding of cybersecurity principles. More specialized certifications, like the GIAC GCTI, focus on skills specific to threat intelligence, including analysis and reporting. Additionally, training in data analysis, cybersecurity tools and technologies, and intelligence-gathering methods is crucial for developing the necessary expertise for this role.

In summary, a threat intelligence analyst requires a unique set of skills to effectively gather and analyze data on cyber threats and provide actionable intelligence. Their responsibilities are critical in guiding an organization's cybersecurity strategy and response to emerging threats. Achieving relevant certifications and targeted training is critical to excelling in this role and contributing effectively to cybersecurity threat intelligence.

14

CLOUD SECURITY ROLES
IN CYBERSECURITY

In the evolving cybersecurity landscape, cloud security roles have become increasingly vital due to the widespread adoption of cloud computing. Professionals in these roles specialize in safeguarding cloud environments against cyber threats and ensuring compliance with data protection regulations. Their expertise lies in understanding the unique challenges associated with cloud security and implementing strategies to protect cloud-based systems and data.

CLOUD ACCESS SECURITY BROKER (CASB) SPECIALIST

A CASB specialist manages and secures cloud environments. Their primary responsibilities include implementing and managing CASB solutions, monitoring and controlling cloud access and activities, integrating CASB systems with existing security infrastructure, and analyzing cloud usage to ensure secure and compliant data sharing.

Implementing and managing CASB solutions involves setting up and maintaining systems that help regulate access to cloud services and protect sensitive data in the cloud. CASB specialists are responsible for configuring these solutions to align with the organization's security policies and cloud usage requirements. They ensure that CASB tools effectively provide visibility into cloud services, detect and mitigate threats, and control user access.

The CASB specialist oversees who is accessing cloud services and their activities. This involves monitoring for unauthorized access, potential security breaches, and abnormal user activities. They play a crucial role in identifying potential security incidents and responding promptly to mitigate risks.

Integrating a CASB with existing security infrastructure is essential for a cohesive security strategy. CASB specialists ensure that the CASB solutions are seamlessly integrated with the organization's security tools and infrastructure. This integration is crucial for a unified approach to security management, providing comprehensive protection across all environments, whether on-site or in the cloud.

Analyzing cloud usage to ensure secure and compliant data sharing involves regularly reviewing how cloud services are used within the organization. The CASB specialist assesses cloud applications and services for compliance with security policies and regulatory standards. They ensure that data shared and stored in the cloud is done securely, adhering to data protection laws and best practices.

To excel as a CASB specialist, professionals should consider pursuing specific certifications and training. Certifications such as the Certified Cloud Security Professional (CCSP) or the Computer Technology Industry Association Cloud+ offer comprehensive knowledge of cloud security. Additionally, vendor-specific certifications, such as those offered by cloud service providers like Amazon Web Services (AWS), Azure, or Google Cloud, can provide specialized knowledge in implementing and managing security in specific cloud environments. Training programs focused on CASB technology, cloud computing security, and data protection regulations are also beneficial for developing the necessary skills and knowledge for this role.

A CASB specialist is integral to securing cloud environments. Their role encompasses implementing and managing CASB solutions, monitoring cloud activities, integrating a CASB with existing security infrastructure, and ensuring compliant data sharing in the cloud. Achieving relevant certifications and targeted training is essential for professionals looking to succeed in this crucial cloud security role.

CLOUD COMPLIANCE MANAGER

In cloud security, a cloud compliance manager is essential for ensuring that cloud-based operations adhere to various data security standards and regulations. This role is particularly crucial in the context of compliance with laws such as the General Data Protection Regulation (GDPR) and the Health Insurance Portability and Accountability Act (HIPAA). The responsibilities of a cloud compliance manager include ensuring regulatory compliance in cloud environments, conducting compliance audits and reviews, advising on the compliance implications of cloud migrations, and developing and maintaining comprehensive cloud compliance documentation.

Cloud compliance managers are tasked with understanding the specific requirements of regulations like GDPR and HIPAA and ensuring that the organization's cloud infrastructure and operations meet these standards. This involves implementing and enforcing policies and controls that protect sensitive data and ensure privacy in cloud-based systems.

Conducting compliance audits and reviews in cloud settings is crucial for maintaining ongoing compliance. The cloud compliance manager regularly evaluates the organization's cloud operations to identify areas where compliance may be lacking. These audits help proactively address potential issues, avoiding regulatory penalties and reputational damage. The manager also reviews the effectiveness of existing compliance measures and recommends enhancements where necessary.

Advising on compliance implications during cloud migrations is essential, especially as more organizations move their operations to the cloud. The cloud compliance manager plays an important role in ensuring that cloud migrations are conducted in a manner that maintains compliance with necessary regulations. They provide expert guidance on the transfer of data, implementation of security controls, and management of cloud services to ensure regulatory compliance throughout the migration process.

The cloud compliance manager creates detailed documentation outlining the organization's cloud compliance policies, procedures, and practices. This documentation is a reference for internal stakeholders and regulatory bodies, demonstrating the organization's commitment to maintaining compliance in its cloud operations.

Professionals aspiring to be cloud compliance managers should pursue specialized training and certifications in cloud security and compliance. Certifications such as the Certified Information Systems Security Professional and the CCSP offer a comprehensive understanding of cloud security and compliance issues. Additionally, certifications and courses specific to regulatory standards (e.g., GDPR Compliance Certification, HIPAA Compliance Training) are beneficial in understanding the intricacies of these regulations. Training in cloud computing platforms (e.g., AWS, Azure, Google Cloud) and focusing on their compliance and security features is also advantageous. These certifications and training programs equip cloud compliance managers with the knowledge and skills to manage compliance in complex cloud environments effectively.

The role of a cloud compliance manager is critical in ensuring that cloud-based operations comply with relevant data security standards and regulations. Their responsibilities encompass ensuring regulatory compliance, conducting audits, advising on cloud migrations, and maintaining compliance documentation. Achieving targeted certifications and undergoing specialized training is critical for professionals to excel in this vital cloud security role.

CLOUD SECURITY ARCHITECT

A cloud security architect is a critical figure in cloud computing who specializes in designing and implementing secure cloud architectures and solutions. This role ensures that cloud environments are robustly secured against cyber threats while supporting the organization's technological and business needs. The responsibilities of a cloud security architect include designing secure cloud infrastructure, implementing security controls in cloud environments, assessing and mitigating risks associated with cloud deployments, and collaborating with IT and development teams for seamless and secure cloud integration.

Designing secure cloud architecture and solutions involves creating efficient, scalable frameworks embedded with solid security measures. Cloud security architects must fully understand cloud services and models, such as infrastructure as a service, platform as a service, and software as a service, and the unique security challenges each presents. Their designs should protect data, comply with regulatory standards, and integrate security best practices like encryption and access control.

Cloud security architects are responsible for practically applying security strategies in the cloud. This includes configuring cloud services and infrastructure for optimal security, setting up firewalls, identity and access management systems, and intrusion detection systems, along with ensuring that all cloud deployments adhere to established security policies and standards.

Assessing and mitigating risks in cloud deployments requires the architect to evaluate the security posture of cloud environments continually. They identify potential vulnerabilities and risks associated with cloud services and infrastructure and develop mitigation strategies. This proactive approach to risk management safeguards sensitive data and maintains the integrity of cloud-based systems.

Collaborating with IT and development teams ensures that cloud solutions are securely integrated into the organization's broader IT environment. Cloud security architects work closely with these teams to guarantee that security considerations are incorporated from the early stages of cloud project development and throughout the system life cycle. This collaboration is vital to aligning security practices with IT and business objectives and ensuring that cloud deployments support the organization's overall technology strategy.

Professionals should pursue specialized training and certifications in order to excel as cloud security architects. Certifications such as the CCSP and the AWS Certified Solutions Architect offer comprehensive cloud security and architecture knowledge. Additionally, vendor-specific certifications, such as the Microsoft Certified: Azure Security Engineer Associate or the Google Cloud Certified-Professional Cloud Architect, provide in-depth expertise in the security features and best practices of specific cloud platforms. Training in cloud risk management, secure software development, and enterprise security architecture can further enhance a cloud security architect's skills. These certifications and training programs equip them with the knowledge and expertise to effectively design and implement secure and compliant cloud solutions.

The role of a cloud security architect is vital in the planning and execution of secure cloud strategies. Their responsibilities include designing secure cloud architectures, implementing security controls, managing cloud risks, and collaborating with IT and development teams. Achieving targeted certifications and undergoing specialized training are essential for professionals aspiring to succeed in this role.

CLOUD SECURITY ANALYST

A cloud security analyst plays a pivotal role in monitoring and securing cloud environments by ensuring they are protected against cyber threats. This position is essential in today's increasingly cloud-centric IT landscapes, where the security of cloud-based systems and data is paramount. The responsibilities of a cloud security analyst include monitoring cloud environments for security threats, analyzing incidents and breaches that occur within the cloud, implementing security policies and best practices, and reporting on the cloud security posture and compliance of the organization.

Cloud security analysts are responsible for continuously overseeing cloud-based applications and infrastructure to detect potential security risks or malicious activities. This involves using various monitoring tools and technologies to identify unusual patterns or anomalies that could indicate a security breach or vulnerability within the cloud environment.

In the event of a security incident, cloud security analysts conduct thorough investigations to understand the nature and impact of the breach. They analyze how the breach occurred, what data or systems were affected, and the potential implications of the incident. Their analysis is crucial in developing effective response strategies and preventing similar incidents in the future.

Implementing security policies and best practices for cloud usage involves ensuring that cloud services are used securely and that they comply with organizational policies and standards. Cloud security analysts develop and enforce guidelines on secure cloud usage, covering data encryption, access controls, and user authentication. They ensure that these policies are aligned with best practices in cloud security and are adhered to by all users of the organization's cloud services.

Reporting on cloud security posture and compliance is essential for maintaining visibility into the security status of cloud environments. Cloud security analysts prepare regular reports detailing the security health of the cloud infrastructure, including any identified incidents or vulnerabilities. These reports inform management and relevant stakeholders about the organization's cloud security status and ensure compliance with regulatory requirements.

Specific training and certifications are highly beneficial for those who are aiming to become cloud security analysts. Certifications such as the CCSP provide a comprehensive understanding of cloud security concepts and practices. Additionally, vendor-specific certifications, like the AWS Certified Security-Specialty or the Microsoft Certified: Azure Security Engineer Associate, offer specialized knowledge in securing cloud platforms from significant providers. Training in cloud computing, cybersecurity, and data privacy regulations enhances an analyst's ability to secure cloud environments effectively. These certifications and training programs help develop the technical expertise and analytical skills required for this crucial role in cloud security.

The role of a cloud security analyst is crucial in ensuring the security and compliance of cloud environments. Their responsibilities encompass monitoring for threats, analyzing security incidents, implementing security policies, and reporting on cloud security. Pursuing relevant certifications and specialized training is critical for those looking to excel in this role and effectively protect cloud-based systems and data.

CLOUD SECURITY CONSULTANT

A cloud security consultant is a key asset in the cybersecurity landscape, offering organizations expertise in cloud security strategies. Their role is increasingly important as more businesses transition to cloud platforms, requiring specialized knowledge to navigate the unique security challenges of the cloud. The responsibilities of a cloud security consultant include providing expert advice on cloud security strategies, assisting organizations in securely transitioning to cloud platforms, conducting cloud security training and awareness programs, and keeping abreast of evolving cloud technologies and threats.

Cloud security consultants assess an organization's current security posture and cloud usage to develop tailored security strategies. They advise on best practices and security policies and implement cloud security solutions to ensure robust protection against potential cyber threats in the cloud environment.

Assisting organizations in transitioning to secure cloud platforms involves guiding them through the complexities of migrating to the cloud while maintaining security. Cloud security consultants play a crucial role in this process, ensuring that the migration is smooth and secure. They help identify the most suitable cloud services and configurations, considering the organization's security requirements and compliance obligations.

Conducting cloud security training and awareness programs ensures that the organization's staff understands cloud security risks and best practices. Cloud security consultants develop and deliver training programs tailored to various organizational levels, from technical teams to executive management. These programs are designed to raise awareness about cloud security and empower employees to contribute to a secure cloud environment.

A cloud security consultant must stay updated on evolving cloud technologies and threats. The cloud computing landscape continuously evolves, with new technologies, services, and security threats emerging regularly. Consultants must keep pace with these developments to provide current and practical security advice. Continuous learning is critical to understanding the latest cloud technologies and the associated security challenges and opportunities.

Pursuing specialized training and certifications is highly beneficial for professionals aspiring to be cloud security consultants. Certifications such as the CCSP and the AWS Certified Solutions Architect offer comprehensive cloud security and architecture knowledge. Vendor-specific certifications like the Microsoft Certified: Azure Security Engineer Associate or the Google Cloud

Certified-Professional Cloud Architect provide insights into specific cloud platforms. Training in cloud risk management, cybersecurity frameworks, and data protection regulations is also advantageous for a holistic understanding of cloud security. These certifications and training programs equip cloud security consultants with the expertise needed to advise organizations effectively on securing their cloud environments.

The role of a cloud security consultant is integral in guiding organizations through the complexities of cloud security. Their responsibilities include advising on security strategies, assisting with secure cloud transitions, conducting training programs, and staying updated on cloud advancements.

CLOUD SECURITY ENGINEER

A cloud security engineer focuses on developing, maintaining, and enhancing the security of cloud-based systems and infrastructure. This role is pivotal as organizations increasingly rely on cloud services for critical operations. The responsibilities of a cloud security engineer include developing and maintaining cloud security systems, performing vulnerability assessments and penetration testing in cloud environments, automating security processes for efficient cloud operations, and troubleshooting and resolving cloud security issues.

Cloud security engineers are responsible for designing and implementing robust security measures to protect cloud-based systems and data. This involves configuring cloud services and infrastructure with appropriate security settings and implementing firewalls, intrusion detection systems, and other security controls. Ensuring these security systems are regularly updated and maintained is critical to defending against evolving cyber threats.

Performing vulnerability assessments and penetration testing in cloud environments help identify and address potential security weaknesses. Cloud security engineers thoroughly evaluate cloud infrastructure to detect vulnerabilities that cyber attackers could exploit. They use penetration testing techniques to simulate cyberattacks on cloud systems, thereby helping to identify and remediate security gaps before they can be exploited in real-world scenarios.

Automating security processes for cloud operations is essential for efficient and effective security management. Cloud security engineers leverage automation tools to streamline various security tasks, such as monitoring, alerting, and responding to incidents. Automation helps reduce the response time to security incidents and ensures consistent application of security policies across cloud environments.

When security incidents occur, cloud security engineers are tasked with quickly identifying the root cause and implementing solutions to resolve the issues. Their ability to effectively troubleshoot and mitigate security problems is vital in minimizing the impact of security breaches and maintaining the integrity of cloud-based operations.

Pursuing targeted training and certifications is highly recommended for professionals who are aiming to excel as cloud security engineers. Certifications such as the CCSP and the AWS Certified Security-Specialty provide a strong foundation in cloud security principles and practices. Vendor-specific certifications, such as the Microsoft Certified: Azure Security Engineer Associate or the Google Cloud Certified-Professional Cloud Security Engineer, offer specialized knowledge in securing specific cloud platforms. Training in cloud computing, ethical hacking, and automation can further enhance a cloud security engineer's skills. These certifications and training programs equip them with the technical expertise and practical skills to secure cloud environments and respond effectively to security challenges.

15

ARTIFICIAL INTELLIGENCE (AI) ROLES IN CYBERSECURITY

In the rapidly evolving landscape of technology, AI and machine learning (ML) stand out as pivotal areas driving innovation and transformation across industries. As we delve into these fields' career opportunities, we must first delineate the distinction between AI and ML, understanding their scope, approaches, objectives, and how they interrelate.

Artificial intelligence encompasses a broad spectrum of computer science focused on creating systems capable of tasks that traditionally require human intelligence. These tasks include, but are not limited to, reasoning, learning, perception, problem solving, and natural language understanding. The ambition of AI is profound—to mimic or even surpass human cognitive functions through machines that can operate autonomously, adapt to new situations, and perform complex tasks without explicit instructions. AI's breadth includes various approaches, from rule-based systems and optimization to the more dynamic methods found in machine learning, showcasing the diverse methodologies that underpin intelligent systems.

Machine learning, a critical subset of AI, emphasizes the capacity of algorithms to learn from and make decisions based on data. Unlike the broader AI field, which may utilize hard-coded rules, ML is exclusively dedicated to models that improve task performance through data exposure. This learning process can take multiple forms, including supervised, unsupervised, semi-supervised, and reinforcement learning, each offering a unique mechanism for how machines interpret and learn from information. ML represents a paradigm shift towards data-driven intelligence, focusing on deriving actionable insights and patterns directly from data rather than through manual programming.

AI DATA SCIENTIST

An AI data scientist in cybersecurity analyzes large datasets to extract security insights and develops predictive models to anticipate cybersecurity incidents. They play a crucial role in ensuring AI's ethical use and governance in security settings and often collaborate on cross-functional projects that integrate big data and AI technologies.

Analyzing large datasets for security insights involves using advanced analytical techniques to identify patterns and anomalies that may indicate potential security threats. AI data scientists apply ML algorithms to sift through vast amounts of data, enabling the detection of sophisticated cyber threats that might be undetectable through traditional methods.

These professionals use AI and ML expertise to build models that predict how and when cybersecurity incidents might occur. This predictive capability is crucial for proactive threat detection and response, allowing organizations to mitigate risks before they materialize into actual breaches.

Ensuring AI's ethical use and governance in security is a critical aspect of their work. AI data scientists must navigate the complex ethical considerations of using AI, particularly in handling sensitive data and making automated decisions. They ensure that AI applications in cybersecurity adhere to ethical standards and regulatory requirements, safeguarding against biases and maintaining user privacy.

Collaborating on cross-functional projects involving big data and AI requires that AI data scientists work alongside other professionals in IT and cybersecurity. They contribute their specialized knowledge to broader team efforts, ensuring that AI and data analytics are effectively integrated into cybersecurity strategies.

A comprehensive approach to training and certification is essential for individuals who are aspiring to become AI data scientists in cybersecurity. Foundational certifications such as the Certified Information Systems Security Professional (CISSP) provide a broad understanding of cybersecurity principles. Specialized certifications, like the Certified Data Privacy Solutions Engineer, focus on data privacy and the ethical use of technology, which are crucial in AI applications.

In-depth AI and ML knowledge can be gained through certifications like the NVIDIA Certified AI Data Scientist, which offers expertise in AI algorithms and their practical applications. Additionally, pursuing advanced data science, ML, or cybersecurity degrees can provide a solid theoretical and practical foundation.

Training programs and courses in big data analytics, ethical AI, and advanced ML techniques are also highly beneficial. These programs help develop the skills to analyze complex datasets, create predictive models, and ensure responsibility.

AI ETHICAL HACKER

An AI ethical hacker represents a cutting-edge role in cybersecurity, blending the sophisticated capabilities of AI with the skilled practices of ethical hacking. This role is crucial in identifying system vulnerabilities and enhancing security measures through AI-driven techniques. AI ethical hackers utilize advanced AI tools to probe systems and networks while uncovering weaknesses that conventional methods might overlook. Their work is pivotal in fortifying cybersecurity defenses against increasingly complex cyber threats.

Using AI to identify vulnerabilities in systems and networks is a core function of an AI ethical hacker. They leverage AI algorithms to analyze network structures, detect anomalies, and identify potential security weaknesses. By employing ML and AI, they can uncover hidden patterns and vulnerabilities that might elude traditional security assessments. This innovative approach allows for a more thorough and proactive identification of security gaps in an organization's infrastructure.

AI ethical hackers design and execute sophisticated penetration testing strategies, utilizing AI to simulate cyberattacks and assess the resilience of systems and networks against such threats. These AI-driven tests provide insights into how an organization's defenses would fare in the face of real-world cyberattacks, thereby enabling the development of more robust security measures.

Developing AI techniques for ethical hacking practices involves innovating and refining AI applications in cybersecurity. AI ethical hackers are at the forefront of creating new methodologies that integrate AI into ethical hacking. Their work includes customizing AI models to simulate various cyberattack scenarios and using AI to automate and enhance ethical-hacking processes. This continuous development is crucial for staying ahead in a field where attackers use sophisticated techniques.

Keeping updated with the latest AI advancements in cybersecurity is essential for AI ethical hackers. The field of AI is rapidly evolving, with new technologies and methodologies emerging regularly. Staying abreast of these advancements enables AI ethical hackers to continually refine their skills and apply the latest AI innovations to ethical hacking practices. This ongoing learning is critical to maintaining a cutting-edge approach to cybersecurity.

For those aspiring to become AI ethical hackers, specialized training and certifications are crucial for developing skills and staying competitive. Foundational certifications like Certified Ethical Hacker provide a comprehensive understanding of ethical hacking techniques and practices. Advanced certifications such as Offensive Security Certified Professional or CISSP offer deeper insights into cybersecurity and ethical hacking.

Training in AI and ML is also vital, with certifications like the NVIDIA Certified AI Data Scientist focusing on practical AI applications. Additional courses in AI for cybersecurity, ML for ethical hacking, and advanced AI algorithms can enhance an AI ethical hacker's proficiency in integrating AI into security practices.

Moreover, continuous professional development through workshops, seminars, and courses in the latest AI and cybersecurity trends is essential. This ensures that AI ethical hackers remain knowledgeable about the latest technological advancements and innovative practices in AI and cybersecurity fields.

The role of an AI ethical hacker leverages AI to enhance cybersecurity measures. Their responsibilities include using AI for vulnerability assessments, conducting AI-driven penetration tests, developing AI ethical-hacking techniques, and staying updated with AI advancements. Like all of the roles in this chapter, achieving relevant certifications and undergoing specialized training is critical for professionals who are aiming to excel in this innovative and crucial role in the cybersecurity ecosystem.

AI SECURITY ANALYST

An AI security analyst is a pivotal figure in modern cybersecurity, harnessing the power of AI to enhance the monitoring and analysis of cyber threats. This role is central to developing cybersecurity strategies, integrating advanced AI tools to provide deeper insights, achieving more efficient threat detection, and implementing swift response mechanisms. AI security analysts augment traditional security systems with AI capabilities, thereby ensuring that organizations can effectively counter the sophisticated cyber threats of the digital age.

Utilizing AI tools for monitoring and analyzing cybersecurity threats is a vital responsibility of an AI security analyst. They employ advanced AI-driven systems to scan and analyze network traffic continuously, identify unusual patterns, and detect potential security breaches. By leveraging ML and AI algorithms, these analysts can process vast amounts of data more efficiently than traditional methods, enabling quicker identification of emerging threats.

Enhancing threat detection and response with AI technologies involves developing and implementing AI-based solutions that can rapidly identify and react to potential cyber threats. AI security analysts work on integrating AI tools that automate the detection process and provide real-time alerts, thereby reducing the time between threat identification and response. This proactive approach is crucial in mitigating the impact of cyber incidents.

AI security analysts ensure that AI technologies are seamlessly incorporated into the organization's cybersecurity infrastructure. This integration involves aligning AI tools with the organization's security policies and protocols, ensuring that all systems work cohesively to strengthen the overall security posture.

Staying abreast of emerging AI trends in cybersecurity is vital for AI security analysts. The field of AI is rapidly advancing, with new technologies, techniques, and applications emerging regularly. Keeping up-to-date with these developments allows analysts to continuously refine their strategies and leverage the latest AI innovations to bolster cybersecurity defenses.

For professionals who are aiming to become AI security analysts, specialized training and certifications are instrumental in acquiring the necessary expertise. Foundational cybersecurity certifications like CISSP provide a broad understanding of cybersecurity principles. Certifications that are focused on AI, such as the Certified Artificial Intelligence Professional or the NVIDIA Certified AI Data Scientist, offer specific insights into applying AI in cybersecurity.

Additional ML, data analytics, and AI programming training can further enhance an AI security analyst's skill set. Courses that specialize in AI applications for cybersecurity, ethical AI, and advanced data analysis techniques are particularly beneficial. Regular participation in workshops, webinars, and conferences on the latest AI and cybersecurity trends is important for continuous learning and staying current.

The role of an AI security analyst is integral to the modern cybersecurity landscape, merging AI technologies with traditional security practices to enhance threat monitoring, detection, and response. Their responsibilities include utilizing AI tools for threat analysis, improving threat response with AI, integrating AI into cybersecurity frameworks, and keeping updated with AI advancements in cybersecurity.

AI SECURITY PRODUCT MANAGER

An AI security product manager occupies a strategic role in the intersection of cybersecurity, AI, and product development. This position is essential for spearheading the creation of AI-driven cybersecurity products, balancing technical possibilities with business needs, and ensuring products align with market demands. The responsibilities of an AI security product manager include leading the development of AI-driven cybersecurity solutions, acting as a liaison between technical teams and business units, managing the product life cycle from conception through deployment, and incorporating market needs and customer feedback into product design.

Leading the development of AI-driven cybersecurity products involves overseeing the entire process of creating sophisticated security solutions that leverage AI technology. An AI security product manager coordinates with engineers, data scientists, and cybersecurity experts to conceptualize and develop products that effectively address current and emerging security threats. This role requires a deep understanding of the technical aspects of AI and cybersecurity and the practical applications of these technologies in product development.

AI security product managers ensure that product development aligns with the broader goals and strategies of the organization. They translate complex technical concepts into tangible business benefits, facilitating communication and understanding between technical teams and stakeholders. This includes aligning product development with business models, market positioning, and profitability goals.

Managing the product life cycle from conception to deployment involves overseeing all stages of product development. This includes initial concept generation, design, development, testing, and final deployment. An AI security product manager ensures that each stage of the product life cycle is executed efficiently, meets quality standards, and adheres to timelines and budget constraints. They also address any challenges during product development, ensuring a smooth progression toward the final product release.

Understanding market needs and customer feedback is essential for guiding product features and ensuring the product's relevance and appeal in the market. AI security product managers conduct market research, gather customer feedback, and analyze industry trends for product development. This customer-centric approach ensures that the products meet the actual needs of users and address specific security challenges faced by customers in various sectors.

For those who are aspiring to be AI security product managers, targeted training and certifications are crucial. Foundational certifications in project management, such as Project Management Professional or Agile Certified Practitioner, provide essential skills in managing complex projects. Cybersecurity certifications like CISSP or Certified Information Security Manager (CISM) offer insights into the security landscape.

Specialized training in AI and product management is also beneficial. Courses in AI, ML, and data science can provide the technical understanding necessary for overseeing AI product development. Additionally, certifications or courses in product management, such as Certified Product Manager or Professional Scrum Product Owner, can enhance product life-cycle management and market analysis skills.

The role of an AI security product manager is crucial in developing and successfully deploying AI-driven cybersecurity products. Their responsibilities encompass leading product development, bridging the technical-business divide, managing product life cycles, and understanding market dynamics.

AI SECURITY RESEARCHER

An AI security researcher focuses on the innovative intersection of AI and security. Their expertise is instrumental in pushing the boundaries of how AI can be leveraged to enhance cybersecurity measures. Responsibilities include developing new AI algorithms for cybersecurity applications, researching AI vulnerabilities and threat vectors, publishing their findings to contribute to the broader academic and industry knowledge base, and collaborating with fellow cybersecurity researchers and AI specialists.

Developing new AI algorithms for cybersecurity applications is a core task for an AI security researcher. They work on creating advanced algorithms that can predict, detect, and respond to cyber threats more effectively than traditional methods. This involves a deep understanding of AI and ML principles and a keen insight into cybersecurity challenges and how AI can address them. The goal is to design AI solutions that are robust, efficient, and capable of evolving with the changing landscape of cyber threats.

AI security researchers examine the potential weaknesses in AI systems that cyberattackers could exploit. They investigate how AI algorithms can be manipulated or misled (such as through adversarial ML techniques) and work on developing strategies to mitigate these vulnerabilities. This research is essential in ensuring the security and integrity of AI applications in cybersecurity.

Publishing findings and contributing to academic and industry knowledge is crucial for advancing the field of AI in cybersecurity. AI security researchers share their research through academic journals, conferences, and industry publications. By disseminating their findings, they contribute to the collective understanding of AI's role in cybersecurity, influencing future research and application directions.

Collaborating with other cybersecurity researchers and AI specialists fosters innovation and comprehensive research. AI security researchers often work in multidisciplinary teams, combining their expertise with other cybersecurity and AI professionals. This collaboration enables the exchange of ideas, techniques, and knowledge, leading to more holistic and practical cybersecurity solutions.

Specialized training and certifications are important for professionals aiming to become AI security researchers. Foundational cybersecurity certifications such as CISSP provide a broad understanding of cybersecurity principles. Advanced AI certifications, like the NVIDIA Certified AI Data Scientist, offer in-depth AI and ML knowledge.

Courses in ethical hacking, data science, and AI development are beneficial for understanding cybersecurity's offensive and defensive aspects. Additionally, ML and AI ethics certifications are essential for comprehending AI's potential risks and ethical considerations in security.

The role of an AI security researcher is critical in exploring and developing AI-driven solutions for cybersecurity challenges. Their responsibilities include creating new AI algorithms, researching AI vulnerabilities, publishing research findings, and collaborating with experts in the field. Achieving relevant certifications and engaging in specialized training is critical to those who wish to excel in this role.

ML SECURITY ENGINEER

A machine learning security engineer is a specialized professional in the cybersecurity domain who focuses on integrating ML technologies to enhance threat detection and response capabilities. This role is critical in developing and refining ML-driven security tools, ensuring the robustness and effectiveness of cybersecurity measures. Key responsibilities include designing and implementing ML models for threat detection, analyzing and enhancing the efficiency of existing ML-based security tools, maintaining the integrity and security of ML systems, and collaborating with data scientists and engineers.

Designing and implementing ML models for threat detection involves creating sophisticated algorithms that are capable of dynamically identifying and responding to cyber threats. ML security engineers leverage their expertise in ML to develop models that can analyze vast datasets, identify patterns that are indicative of malicious activities, and adapt to evolving threat landscapes. This proactive approach helps detect sophisticated cyberattacks that might bypass traditional security measures.

ML security engineers continuously evaluate the performance of deployed ML models, identifying areas for enhancement. By fine-tuning these models and integrating the latest advancements in ML, the organization's security tools remain at the forefront of cybersecurity technology, offering an effective defense against emerging cyber threats.

Ensuring the integrity and security of ML systems is essential. As these systems handle sensitive data and play a critical role in security operations, maintaining their security and reliability is a priority. ML security engineers implement robust security protocols and conduct regular assessments to safeguard ML systems against tampering, exploitation, or data breaches, thus maintaining the trustworthiness and effectiveness of these systems.

Collaborating with data scientists and engineers fosters innovation and ensures the successful integration of ML in cybersecurity solutions. ML security engineers work closely with other technical professionals to share insights, develop joint solutions, and align ML initiatives with broader cybersecurity objectives. This collaboration enhances the organization's cybersecurity strategies' overall effectiveness and drives security technology advancements.

For aspiring ML security engineers, specialized training and certifications are crucial for acquiring expertise. Certifications in cybersecurity, such as CISSP or CISM, provide a solid foundation in security principles. Additionally, ML and data science certifications, such as the TensorFlow Developer Certificate or the NVIDIA Certified AI Data Scientist, offer specific skills in developing and implementing ML models.

Advanced courses in ML, AI, and cybersecurity are beneficial for understanding the intricate relationship between these fields. Training in ethical hacking, data analytics, and secure coding practices can also enhance an ML security engineer's ability to develop secure and effective ML-driven security tools.

The role of an ML security engineer is integral in leveraging ML technologies to strengthen cybersecurity defenses. Their responsibilities encompass developing ML models for threat detection, enhancing existing ML security tools, ensuring the integrity of ML systems, and collaborating with technical experts.

16

CYBERSECURITY ACROSS
DIFFERENT SECTORS

This chapter aims to illuminate the unique cybersecurity landscapes across various sectors by guiding individuals in identifying and pursuing career opportunities that align with their interests and expertise.

FINANCE SECTOR CYBERSECURITY

The finance sector—encompassing banking, investments, insurance, and other financial services—plays a critical role in the global economy. Its importance stems from its function in managing financial transactions, investments, and savings for individuals and businesses. The security of this sector is paramount due to the sensitive nature of financial data and the high volume of monetary transactions. Protecting this data against cyber threats is a crucial challenge, making cybersecurity an integral aspect of the financial industry.

Historically, the finance sector has been a prime target for cyber threats. The evolution of these threats has been significant, ranging from early phishing and scam attempts to sophisticated attacks like ransomware, advanced persistent threats, and targeted financial fraud. The sector's long history with cyber threats has made it a standard-bearer in developing and implementing robust cybersecurity measures.

The unique cybersecurity challenges in finance include protecting against data breaches, ensuring the security of online transactions, and guarding against insider threats. Financial institutions face the challenge of safeguarding their IT infrastructure against sophisticated cyberattacks while ensuring compliance with global financial regulations.

Regulatory compliance is a critical aspect of cybersecurity in the finance sector. Financial institutions must adhere to various regulations, such as the

General Data Protection Regulation in the European Union, which governs data protection and privacy, and the Payment Card Industry Data Security Standard, which sets the security standards for all entities handling credit card transactions. Compliance with these and other regulations is a legal obligation and is crucial for maintaining customer trust and preventing financial losses.

According to Cyberseek.org, the finance sector has experienced a remarkable growth in the demand for cybersecurity professionals. This reflects the industry's escalating need to fortify its defenses against cyber threats. In 2023, the sector reported a substantial 65,000 cyber job openings, a stark increase from the 6,200 openings that was recorded in 2010 (see Figure 16.1). This significant rise in job openings clearly indicates the burgeoning demand for skilled cybersecurity personnel within the finance sector. It underscores the industry's recognition of the critical need to protect financial data and systems in an era where cyber threats are becoming increasingly sophisticated and prevalent.

Parallel to the rise in job openings, there was a substantial expansion in the cybersecurity workforce that was employed in the finance sector. In 2010, the sector employed approximately 21,000 cybersecurity professionals, which grew more than six-fold to 138,612 by 2023. This exponential growth in the cybersecurity workforce within the finance sector is a testament to the increasing importance placed on cybersecurity. It reflects the sector's commitment to strengthening its cyber defenses and highlights the growing career opportunities for professionals in the field of financial cybersecurity.

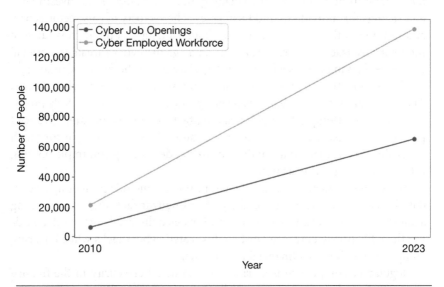

Figure 16.1 Finance sector cyber job openings and employed workforce: 2010 versus 2023.

Cybersecurity in the finance sector is of the utmost importance due to the sensitive nature of financial data and the sector's attractiveness as a target for cybercriminals. The sector has faced various cyber threats, leading to unique cybersecurity challenges and stringent regulatory compliance requirements. The growth in cyber job openings and the employed workforce in this sector underscores the increasing emphasis on cybersecurity. Professionals aspiring to enter this field must navigate a landscape where technical expertise, understanding of financial regulations, and awareness of evolving cyber threats are essential.

GOVERNMENT AND PUBLIC SECTOR CYBERSECURITY

The government and the public sector play a vital role in national security, infrastructure, and the well-being of citizens. Cybersecurity in this sector is paramount due to the sensitivity of the data involved and the potential impact of cyber threats on national security and public services.

National security considerations are at the forefront of cybersecurity in the government and public sector. Cyber threats in this domain can have far-reaching implications, including risks to national defense systems, confidential government data, and critical decision-making processes. Therefore, cybersecurity measures in this sector are closely tied to national security strategies, focusing on protecting against espionage, cyber warfare, and terrorism.

Protecting critical infrastructure is another crucial aspect. This includes securing systems and networks that facilitate essential public services such as utilities, transportation, and emergency services. The disruption of these services due to cyberattacks can have severe consequences for public safety and the functioning of society. Consequently, robust cybersecurity protocols and resilient infrastructure are essential to safeguard these vital systems.

Policy development for public sector cybersecurity is critical in establishing standards and guidelines for protecting government digital assets and infrastructure. This involves formulating comprehensive cybersecurity policies that address risk management, incident response, and data protection. These policies are integral in guiding government agencies and public sector organizations in implementing effective cybersecurity practices.

Challenges of cybersecurity in government systems are numerous and complex. These include managing a vast array of legacy systems that may be more vulnerable to cyberattacks, navigating bureaucratic hurdles that can slow the implementation of cybersecurity measures, and dealing with a diverse range of threats from domestic and international actors. Additionally, the public sector often faces challenges in attracting and retaining skilled cybersecurity professionals due to budgetary constraints and competition from the private sector.

Government and public sector cybersecurity is critical for national security and protecting essential public services. It involves addressing unique challenges such as protecting critical infrastructure, developing effective cybersecurity policies, and overcoming the inherent complexities of government systems. Ensuring robust cybersecurity in this sector is vital for safeguarding the integrity of government operations and maintaining public trust in digital services. As cyber threats evolve, the need for sophisticated cybersecurity measures and skilled professionals in the government and public sector becomes increasingly paramount.

HEALTHCARE CYBERSECURITY

Healthcare cybersecurity is a critical field that focuses on protecting sensitive patient data and ensuring the security of healthcare systems and technologies. In an era where healthcare data is increasingly digitized, cybersecurity plays a pivotal role in safeguarding this information against cyber threats and breaches. Protecting patient data is a matter of privacy, trust, and legal compliance. Healthcare organizations are entrusted with vast amounts of personal health information, making robust cybersecurity measures essential to protect against unauthorized access and data theft.

Compliance with health sector regulations—particularly the Health Insurance Portability and Accountability Act (HIPAA) in the United States—is a significant aspect of healthcare cybersecurity. HIPAA sets standards for protecting sensitive patient data and mandates that healthcare providers, insurers, and their business associates implement adequate safeguards to ensure the confidentiality, integrity, and availability of this information. Noncompliance with HIPAA can result in substantial penalties, making it imperative for healthcare organizations to adhere to these regulations rigorously.

Technology integration into healthcare has expanded the scope of cybersecurity to include medical devices and telemedicine. New cybersecurity challenges have emerged with the rise of connected medical devices and the increasing use of telemedicine, particularly heightened during the COVID-19 pandemic. While improving healthcare delivery and patient convenience, these technologies also introduce vulnerabilities that cyberattackers can exploit. Ensuring the security of these devices and telehealth platforms is crucial to prevent potential cyberattacks that could compromise patient care and safety.

According to Cyberseek.org, the healthcare sector has seen a significant increase in the demand for cybersecurity professionals. In 2023 there were 13,225 cyber job openings in the healthcare sector, a substantial rise from the 2,705 openings that were reported in 2010 (see Figure 16.2). This growth indicates the escalating importance of cybersecurity in healthcare and the expanding opportunities for professionals in this field. Similarly, the cybersecurity workforce that is employed in healthcare has seen a marked increase. In 2023, the employed workforce numbered 27,869, compared to 8,511 in 2010. This growth reflects the healthcare sector's commitment to bolstering its cybersecurity capabilities in response to the evolving cyberthreat landscape.

Healthcare cybersecurity is an increasingly vital field, underscored by the growing demand for professionals who are skilled in protecting patient data and securing healthcare technologies. With the rise in cyber job openings and the expansion of the cybersecurity workforce in healthcare, there are ample opportunities for individuals who are looking to pursue a career in this essential and dynamic sector. The focus on safeguarding sensitive health information, complying with stringent regulations, and the challenges presented by integrating technology into healthcare make cybersecurity a key priority in the industry.

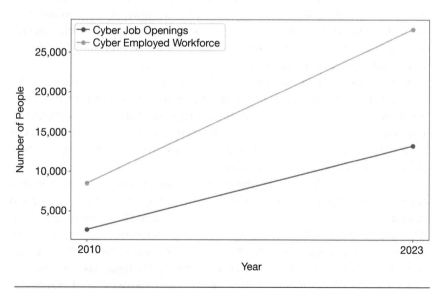

Figure 16.2 Healthcare sector cyber job openings and employed workforce: 2010 versus 2023 (final data).

RETAIL AND e-COMMERCE CYBERSECURITY

In retail and e-commerce, cybersecurity has become a cornerstone for ensuring the safe and secure handling of online transactions and the protection of customer data. With the rapid growth of digital retail and e-commerce platforms, the need for robust cybersecurity measures has never been greater. Securing online transactions is a critical challenge for retailers because it involves safeguarding against various types of cyberattacks, including phishing, identity theft, and payment fraud. These attacks pose a risk not only to financial assets but also to the reputation and trustworthiness of retail businesses.

Protecting customer data in retail is another significant aspect of cybersecurity in this sector. Retailers collect and store vast amounts of personal and financial information from their customers. Ensuring the security of this data is paramount since data breaches can lead to the exposure of sensitive customer information, resulting in legal repercussions and loss of consumer trust. Retailers must implement comprehensive data protection strategies to safeguard customer information, including encryption, access controls, and regular security audits.

Cybersecurity challenges in supply chain management are increasingly prominent in the retail sector. The interconnected nature of supply chains makes them vulnerable to cyberattacks that can disrupt operations and lead to financial losses. Retailers must secure their supply chain networks, including communication systems and logistics software, to prevent cyber threats that could impact the delivery of goods and services.

Case studies of cybersecurity breaches in the retail sector highlight the consequences of inadequate cybersecurity measures. These breaches often result in significant financial losses, brand reputation damage, and customer trust erosion. Learning from these incidents is crucial in order for retailers to understand the importance of investing in cybersecurity and adopting best practices to prevent similar occurrences.

The retail sector has seen a substantial increase in cyber job openings over the years. In 2023, according to Cyberseek.org, there were 16,633 cyber job openings in the retail industry, compared to 2,736 in 2010 (see Figure 16.3). This growth reflects the escalating need for cybersecurity expertise in the face of evolving threats targeting the retail and e-commerce sectors. Interestingly, the cybersecurity workforce that is employed in retail has not grown as quickly as the job openings. In 2023, the sector employed 10,740 cybersecurity professionals, an increase from 8,275 in 2010.

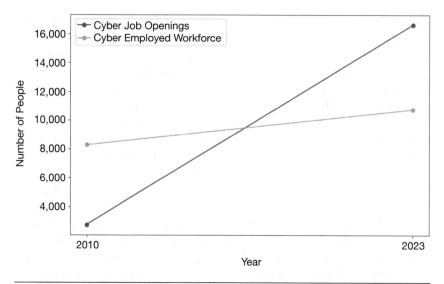

Figure 16.3   Retail and e-commerce sector cyber job openings and employed workforce: 2010 versus 2023 (new data).

Cybersecurity in retail and e-commerce is paramount, as evidenced by the growing number of cyber job openings. The challenges of securing online transactions, protecting customer data, and ensuring the security of supply chain networks are central to the success and trustworthiness of retail businesses. As cyber threats evolve, the retail industry must remain vigilant and proactive in its cybersecurity efforts to safeguard against potential breaches and maintain consumer confidence.

MILITARY AND DEFENSE SECTOR CYBERSECURITY

Cybersecurity is a critical component of national defense strategies and military operations in the military and defense sector. The sector faces unique cybersecurity challenges, given the sensitive nature of its operations and the potential impact of cyber threats on national security. Cybersecurity in this sector involves protecting sensitive and classified military information and safeguarding critical defense infrastructure from a wide range of cyber threats, including state-sponsored cyber warfare.

Protecting classified and sensitive military information is paramount in the defense sector. Cybersecurity measures are essential to prevent unauthorized access, espionage, and data leaks. Military cybersecurity teams work diligently to secure communication channels, databases, and information systems that handle sensitive data. The integrity of this information is crucial for national security because it includes strategic plans, personnel records, and other classified data that is vital to military operations.

Cyber warfare tactics and defense strategies form a core part of military cybersecurity. As cyber warfare becomes an increasingly common component of international conflicts, military organizations must develop sophisticated cyber defense strategies. This involves defensive measures to protect against cyberattacks and offensive capabilities to counteract and deter cyber threats from foreign adversaries. Cybersecurity teams in the military are continuously updating their tactics and technologies to stay ahead of evolving cyber warfare techniques.

Collaboration with government and private sectors is essential for a comprehensive national security approach. The military often works with other government agencies and private sector partners to enhance cybersecurity capabilities. This collaboration includes sharing intelligence, developing joint defense strategies, and leveraging private sector expertise and resources. Such partnerships are vital for building a resilient national cybersecurity infrastructure that is capable of withstanding and responding to diverse cyber threats.

Cybersecurity in the military and defense sector is critical to national security; it encompasses the protection of sensitive information, defense against cyber warfare tactics, and collaboration with other sectors. The nature of the threats that this sector faces demands a highly specialized approach to cybersecurity, focusing on both defense and offense. As cyber threats continue to evolve, the military and defense sector must remain vigilant and proactive in its cybersecurity efforts by adapting to new challenges and ensuring the safety and security of national defense operations.

MANUFACTURING AND INDUSTRIAL CYBERSECURITY

Manufacturing and industrial cybersecurity are increasingly critical as industries embrace digitalization, automation, and connectivity. The sector faces unique challenges in securing industrial control systems (ICS), Supervisory Control and Data Acquisition (SCADA), and the entire manufacturing supply chain. As manufacturing processes become more integrated with IT and operational technology, the potential cybersecurity risks escalate, necessitating robust protective measures.

Securing ICS and SCADA is a primary concern in manufacturing cyber-security. These systems are vital for the operational functionality of manu-facturing plants and are often targeted by cybercriminals who are seeking to disrupt operations. Protecting these systems involves implementing stringent security protocols, regular system audits, and continuous monitoring to de-tect and mitigate threats. Ensuring the security of SCADA systems that are used to control and monitor industrial processes is equally crucial. These sys-tems, if compromised, can lead to significant operational disruptions, safety hazards, and financial losses.

Addressing cybersecurity in the manufacturing supply chain is another significant challenge. The interconnected nature of supply chains makes them vulnerable to cyberattacks, which can compromise sensitive data and disrupt operations. Manufacturers must implement comprehensive cybersecurity strategies that extend to their suppliers and partners, ensuring that the entire supply chain is secure from potential cyber threats.

The risks associated with the Internet of Things (IoT) and smart manu-facturing are a growing concern. As manufacturers integrate IoT devices and intelligent technologies into their operations, they expose themselves to new cybersecurity vulnerabilities. These devices often lack robust security features, making them easy cyberattack targets. Ensuring the security of IoT devices and intelligent manufacturing systems is imperative to prevent data breaches and maintain operational integrity.

The demand for cybersecurity professionals in the manufacturing and in-dustrial sectors has seen a significant increase, according to Cyberseek.org. In 2023, there were 75,273 cyber job openings in the sector, a substantial rise from the 20,576 openings in 2010 (see Figure 16.4). Furthermore, the cyber-security workforce employed in the sector has grown substantially. In 2023, there were 66,427 professionals employed in manufacturing cybersecurity, compared to 21,000 in 2010. This growth indicates the sector's commitment to strengthening its cybersecurity posture in response to the evolving cyber-threat landscape.

Manufacturing and industrial cybersecurity is vital for protecting critical infrastructure, ensuring the integrity of the supply chain, and mitigating the risks associated with IoT and smart manufacturing. The significant increase in cyber job openings and the growth of the cybersecurity workforce in the sector highlight the escalating importance of cybersecurity in manufacturing. As the sector advances technologically, the need for skilled cybersecurity pro-fessionals is expected to grow, making it a promising area for career develop-ment in cybersecurity.

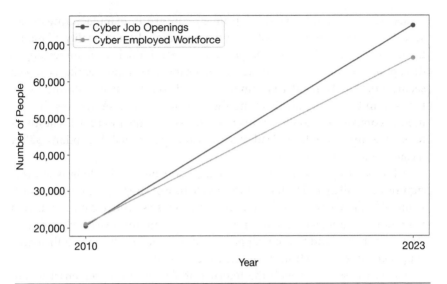

Figure 16.4   Manufacturing and industrial sector cyber job openings and employed workforce: 2010 versus 2023 (latest data).

ENERGY AND UTILITIES CYBERSECURITY

The energy and utilities sector faces significant cybersecurity challenges, particularly with securing energy grids and utility networks. This sector is fundamental to the functioning of modern society, and any disruption due to cyberattacks can have far-reaching consequences. The complexity of energy grids and the integration of digital technologies into utility networks have increased the sector's vulnerability to cyber threats. Securing these systems involves protecting critical infrastructure against various cyberattacks, from ransomware to sophisticated nation-state attacks. Ensuring the uninterrupted operation of these utilities is paramount, as they are essential for national security, economic stability, and public safety.

Risks associated with renewable energy technologies are also a growing concern. The cybersecurity landscape becomes more complex as the sector evolves to include more renewable energy sources, such as solar and wind power. These technologies often rely heavily on digital and connected technologies, introducing new vulnerabilities. Protecting these systems from cyber threats is crucial to ensure the reliability and efficiency of renewable energy sources.

Regulatory compliance, such as adherence to the North American Electric Reliability Corporation Critical Infrastructure Protection standards, is crucial to cybersecurity in the energy sector. These regulations are designed to enhance critical infrastructure security and protect the bulk electric system against cyber and physical security threats. Compliance with these standards is not only a legal requirement but also crucial for maintaining the operational integrity of energy utilities.

Incident response and recovery during energy sector breaches are essential to a robust cybersecurity strategy. Energy companies must have comprehensive plans to respond to and recover from cybersecurity incidents quickly. This involves regular drills, employee training, and collaboration with government agencies and industry partners in order to ensure a coordinated response to cyber incidents. Rapidly restoring services after a breach is critical to minimizing the impact on consumers and the economy.

Cybersecurity in the energy and utilities sector is of vital importance due to the essential nature of these services. The sector faces unique challenges in securing complex and evolving energy grids, managing risks associated with renewable technologies, complying with stringent regulations, and ensuring effective incident response. As cyber threats continue to evolve, the sector must remain vigilant and proactive in its cybersecurity efforts to safeguard critical energy infrastructure and maintain the reliability of utility services. The increasing focus on cybersecurity in this sector underscores the growing demand for skilled professionals to address these challenges.

TRANSPORTATION AND LOGISTICS CYBERSECURITY

Cybersecurity in the transportation and logistics sector is crucial for safeguarding the networks and systems that facilitate the movement of goods and people. This sector encompasses various modes of transport, including road, rail, air, and sea, as well as the logistic systems that support them. Securing these networks is vital, as disruptions can have significant economic impacts and compromise safety. Cybersecurity challenges include protecting infrastructure from cyberattacks that can disrupt operations, managing the vulnerabilities inherent in complex logistics networks, and ensuring the security of data transmitted across these systems.

Autonomous vehicles represent a burgeoning area within transportation that introduces unique cybersecurity considerations. These vehicles rely heavily on interconnected systems and data sharing for navigation and operation, thereby presenting new opportunities for cyberattacks. Ensuring the cybersecurity of autonomous vehicles is essential for their safe operation and public acceptance. This involves securing the vehicle's communication systems, protecting against unauthorized access, and safeguarding the data collected and transmitted by these vehicles.

Protecting against supply chain disruptions is another important aspect of cybersecurity in transportation and logistics. The supply chain is increasingly digitized and interconnected, making it vulnerable to cyberattacks that can cause significant disruptions in the flow of goods. Cybersecurity measures must be implemented to protect the integrity of supply chain systems, prevent data breaches, and ensure the continuity of operations.

According to Cyberseek.org, the transportation and logistics sector has seen a notable increase in the demand for cybersecurity professionals. In 2023, the sector had 5,339 cyber job openings, compared to 777 in 2010 (see Figure 16.5). This growth indicates an increased recognition of the importance of cybersecurity in ensuring the smooth operation of transportation and logistics networks. Additionally, the number of cybersecurity professionals employed in the sector has grown significantly. In 2023, 11,783 professionals worked in cybersecurity roles within the sector, a substantial increase from 2,376 in 2010. This growth reflects the sector's expanding commitment to cybersecurity as it evolves to incorporate new technologies and faces an increasingly complex cyber-threat landscape.

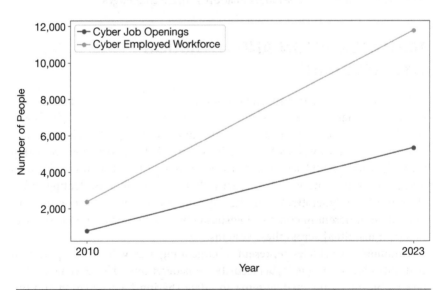

Figure 16.5 Transportation and logistics sector cyber job openings and employed workforce: 2010 versus 2023 (updated data).

Cybersecurity in the transportation and logistics sector is essential for the safe and efficient movement of goods and people. The sector faces unique challenges in securing networks and systems, particularly with the advent of autonomous vehicles and the increasing digitization of supply chains. The significant growth in cyber job openings and the expanding cybersecurity workforce within the sector highlight the increasing importance placed on cybersecurity. As the sector continues to evolve and integrate new technologies, the demand for skilled cybersecurity professionals is expected to grow, underscoring its commitment to safeguarding its critical infrastructure against cyber threats.

EDUCATION SECTOR CYBERSECURITY

Cybersecurity in the education sector is increasingly difficult due to the sector's unique needs and challenges. Educational institutions store vast amounts of sensitive data, including student records and academic research, which require stringent protection measures. The security of this data is paramount not only to protect the privacy of students and faculty but also to safeguard intellectual property and research findings. Effective cybersecurity strategies must be implemented to defend against data breaches, unauthorized access, and other cyber threats that can compromise the integrity and reputation of educational institutions.

The rise of remote and online learning, significantly accelerated by the COVID-19 pandemic, has introduced new cybersecurity challenges in the education sector. As learning moves beyond the traditional classroom and into the digital realm, securing online platforms and ensuring the safety of digital interactions becomes crucial. Cybersecurity measures must address vulnerabilities in remote learning systems, protect against cyberattacks that can disrupt online education, and ensure the privacy and security of online communications between students and educators.

Educating students, faculty, and staff about cybersecurity best practices, potential cyber threats, and safe online behaviors is crucial in building a culture of cybersecurity awareness. This education helps individuals recognize and respond to cyber threats effectively, reducing the risk of security incidents and fostering a secure learning environment.

Balancing open access with security in academic environments is a crucial challenge. Educational institutions often emphasize the free exchange of information and open access to resources, which can conflict with the need for tight security controls. Finding the right balance between ensuring open access to educational resources and maintaining robust cybersecurity measures is essential in order to support academic freedom and data protection.

According to Cyberseek.org, the education sector has witnessed a significant increase in the demand for cybersecurity professionals. In 2023 there were 17,454 cyber job openings in the sector, a substantial increase from the 3,269 openings in 2010 (see Figure 16.6). This growth indicates the escalating need for cybersecurity expertise in educational institutions. Additionally, the number of professionals in cybersecurity roles within the sector has risen notably. In 2023, 42,662 cybersecurity professionals worked in education, compared to 16,440 in 2010.

Cybersecurity in the education sector is vital for protecting sensitive student data academic research and ensuring the security of online learning environments. The sector faces unique challenges, including balancing open access with robust security measures. The significant growth in cyber job openings and the employed cybersecurity workforce within the sector underscores the increasing emphasis on cybersecurity in education. As digital technologies continue to play a crucial role in educational processes, the

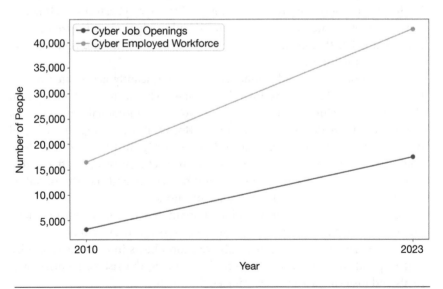

Figure 16.6   Education sector cyber job openings and employed workforce: 2010 versus 2023 (newest data).

demand for skilled cybersecurity professionals in the sector is expected to grow, highlighting the importance of cybersecurity in maintaining the integrity and safety of educational environments.

TELECOMMUNICATIONS CYBERSECURITY

Cybersecurity in the telecommunications sector is paramount due to its critical role in facilitating global communication networks and services. As the backbone of digital communication, the telecom industry faces the constant challenge of securing its vast and complex networks from cyber threats. This task involves protecting infrastructure from attacks that could disrupt services, managing the risks associated with the increasing volume of data transmitted, and ensuring the privacy and security of user communications. With the telecommunications network being a fundamental part of national infrastructure, its security is crucial for individual privacy and national security.

Addressing challenges with emerging technologies such as 5G and the IoT is a significant focus in telecommunications cybersecurity. The advent of 5G technology brings enhanced speed and connectivity but also introduces new cybersecurity vulnerabilities. These vulnerabilities require advanced security measures to protect against attacks and unauthorized access. Similarly, the proliferation of IoT devices, which often lack robust built-in security features, poses a challenge in ensuring the security of interconnected devices and networks. Telecommunications companies must implement comprehensive strategies to secure 5G and IoT technologies, considering their widespread use and potential for exploitation.

Telecom fraud, including identity theft, phishing, and financial fraud, can lead to significant financial losses and erode customer trust. Telecom companies must employ sophisticated fraud detection and prevention mechanisms to identify and mitigate these risks. Additionally, the sector is a target for data breaches, where sensitive customer information can be compromised. Implementing robust data protection measures and continuously monitoring potential breaches are vital in safeguarding customer data.

Best practices for ensuring data privacy and integrity in the telecom sector include implementing robust encryption protocols for data transmission, regularly updating and patching systems to address vulnerabilities, and conducting thorough risk assessments. Training employees in cybersecurity best practices and raising awareness about potential threats are essential in creating a security-conscious culture within telecom organizations.

As the sector continues to evolve with new technologies, robust cybersecurity measures become increasingly paramount. Telecommunications companies must remain vigilant and proactive in their cybersecurity efforts to protect their infrastructure and maintain customer trust in an industry that is foundational to modern digital communication.

17

FUTURE TRENDS IN CYBERSECURITY CAREERS

In this final chapter we explore the evolving landscape of cybersecurity careers and the future trends that will be shaping this dynamic field. The world of cybersecurity is in a constant state of flux, driven by rapid technological advancements and ever-changing threats. This environment presents both challenges and opportunities for cybersecurity professionals. The key to thriving in such a setting lies in understanding the nature of these changes and adapting to them proactively. This chapter will dissect the various aspects of these evolving roles and provide insights into how professionals can stay ahead in this fast-paced domain.

ADAPTING TO EVOLVING ROLES

The cybersecurity landscape continuously evolves, driven by rapid technological advancements and the ever-changing nature of cyber threats. This dynamic environment demands a deep understanding of current and emerging cybersecurity trends. Professionals must know how advancements in artificial intelligence (AI), machine learning (ML), and blockchain technology are reshaping cybersecurity. Additionally, staying informed about the latest types of cyber threats, such as sophisticated ransomware attacks or Internet of Things (IoT)-based vulnerabilities, is crucial. This continuous learning and awareness are vital in adapting to new challenges and staying ahead in the field. As cybersecurity becomes increasingly integral to various industries, the need for professionals who can navigate this complex and shifting landscape grows.

Keeping abreast of emerging technologies and threats is critical to adapting to evolving roles in cybersecurity. As new technologies emerge, they often bring new vulnerabilities and security challenges. Cybersecurity professionals must stay informed about these developments to protect against potential threats effectively. This involves understanding the technical aspects of new technologies and recognizing their potential implications for cybersecurity. Similarly, staying updated on the latest cyber threats is essential for developing effective defense strategies. This ongoing learning and staying informed requires continuous education and professional development. This dedication to staying current enables cybersecurity professionals to anticipate and respond effectively to new challenges.

As new threats emerge and technologies evolve, cybersecurity roles must adapt accordingly. This could mean a shift toward more specialized roles focusing on cloud security, IoT security, or cyber intelligence. It also implies a need for a broader understanding of how cybersecurity integrates with other business functions, such as risk management and compliance. Professionals must be prepared to adapt their skill sets and embrace new responsibilities as the field grows and changes. This adaptability is not just about acquiring new technical skills; it also involves developing a strategic understanding of how cybersecurity impacts and is impacted by other business areas.

Adapting to the future challenges of cybersecurity requires a proactive approach to skill development. As the field evolves, so too must the skills of cybersecurity professionals. This means staying ahead of the curve in learning new technologies and methodologies and refining existing skills to meet the demands of a changing landscape. Cybersecurity professionals need to be versatile and able to tackle various challenges. This versatility includes technical skills like coding and network security and soft skills like critical thinking and effective communication. The ability to quickly learn and apply new knowledge is essential in a field where *change* is the only constant. As cybersecurity grows in complexity and importance, the professionals who succeed will be those who can best adapt their skills to meet the needs of an ever-changing digital world.

ROLE OF AUTOMATION AND AI IN SHAPING CYBER ROLES

Automation and AI are increasingly prominent in shaping cybersecurity roles, fundamentally altering the field landscape. The impact of these technologies on traditional cybersecurity jobs is significant; they are automating routine tasks, freeing cybersecurity professionals to focus on more complex and strategic aspects of their roles. This shift is not without its challenges since it requires reevaluating the skills and knowledge that are necessary for success in cybersecurity. Professionals must now possess a deep understanding of both the opportunities and the potential risks associated with AI and automation in cybersecurity.

Upskilling to work alongside AI and automated systems is becoming necessary. As routine tasks become automated, the value of cybersecurity professionals will increasingly lie in their ability to interpret and manage AI outputs, integrate human insight with machine-generated data, and make strategic decisions. This shift demands a new set of skills, including an understanding of ML processes, proficiency in managing automated systems, and the ability to analyze complex data sets. The transition also involves developing a nuanced understanding of how AI can enhance cybersecurity strategies and how cybercriminals can potentially exploit it.

The opportunities and challenges presented by AI in cybersecurity are manifold. On the one hand, AI offers the potential to analyze vast quantities of data for threat detection, predict potential vulnerabilities, and respond to threats with more incredible speed and efficiency than ever before. On the other hand, the sophistication of AI systems also presents new vulnerabilities, as malicious actors can target or use them to carry out complex cyberattacks. Navigating this landscape requires a balanced approach that leverages the strengths of AI while remaining vigilant about its limitations and vulnerabilities.

Future-proofing careers in the age of AI and ML is thus a critical consideration for cybersecurity professionals. As the reliance on these technologies increases, the nature of cybersecurity work will continue to evolve. Professionals must be proactive in staying informed about the latest AI and ML developments and be willing to adapt their skills continuously. This might involve pursuing specialized training or certifications that focus on AI and cybersecurity, engaging in professional development opportunities, and staying connected with the broader cybersecurity community to share knowledge and best practices. In an age where AI and automation are becoming integral to cybersecurity, the professionals who will thrive are those who can seamlessly integrate these technologies into their skill set and strategic approach.

TRANSITIONING TO NEW CYBERSECURITY DOMAINS

Transitioning to new cybersecurity domains is becoming increasingly important as the field expands into specialized areas such as cloud security and IoT security. Identifying and moving into these growing areas requires a keen understanding of current trends and foresight into where the industry is heading. As organizations increasingly rely on cloud infrastructures and IoT devices, the demand for professionals who are skilled in these areas is surging. For cybersecurity experts who are looking to stay ahead, this means recognizing these trends early and acquiring the necessary skills to address these domains' unique challenges.

Building expertise in niche or emerging cybersecurity fields can be a strategic move for career advancement. As the cybersecurity landscape broadens, opportunities in specialized fields like cryptocurrency security, AI defense, and quantum computing security are emerging. Professionals who are willing to delve into these niche areas can position themselves as leading experts. However, gaining expertise in these areas often requires targeted learning and practical experience, which might involve pursuing advanced training, certifications, and hands-on projects. This specialized focus can set a professional apart in an increasingly competitive job market.

Developing strategies for successful career transitions within cybersecurity is essential for those who are looking to navigate this dynamic field effectively. Transitioning to a new domain within cybersecurity can be challenging; it often involves stepping out of one's comfort zone and embracing new learning curves. Strategies for a successful transition include staying informed about industry developments, networking with professionals in the desired domain, and seeking expert mentorship or guidance. Additionally, engaging in continuous learning through courses, workshops, and self-study can provide the foundational knowledge that is needed to break into a new area of cybersecurity.

Balancing domain expertise with a broad understanding of cybersecurity is crucial in these transitions. While specialization can provide a competitive edge, a comprehensive understanding of the broader cybersecurity landscape is invaluable. This broader perspective enables professionals to see how their specialized skills fit into the larger picture of an organization's security strategy. It also allows for more effective collaboration with other cybersecurity professionals and teams who may focus on different areas of the field. Maintaining this balance between specialized knowledge and a holistic understanding of cybersecurity can help build a versatile and resilient career.

LIFELONG LEARNING AND SKILL DEVELOPMENT

Lifelong learning and skill development are fundamental to navigating the rapidly evolving field of cybersecurity. In an industry that is characterized by constant technological advancements and shifting threat landscapes, the importance of continuous education cannot be overstated. For professionals in cybersecurity, staying informed and up-to-date is not just a matter of professional development but also a necessity for ensuring the effectiveness and relevance of their skills. This ongoing learning process is critical to adapting to new challenges, technologies, and methodologies that emerge in the field.

Engaging in ongoing professional development is critical to this continuous learning journey. This can take many forms, from attending industry conferences and seminars to participating in hands-on workshops and training sessions. These activities provide opportunities to learn about the latest cybersecurity trends, tools, and best practices. They also offer a platform for professionals to refine and acquire new skills, ensuring that their expertise remains current and applicable in a rapidly changing environment.

Leveraging online courses, workshops, and webinars has become an increasingly popular and accessible means of skill development in the digital age. Today's vast online learning resources allow cybersecurity professionals to tailor their learning experiences to their specific needs and interests. Online platforms offer flexibility, enabling learners to engage with content at their own convenience and on their own schedule. These online resources are crucial in facilitating continuous education and skill enhancement, from foundational courses to advanced training in specialized areas.

Certifications and advanced degrees in cybersecurity are also necessary. Certifications provide a structured way to acquire and validate professional skills, often focusing on specific areas such as penetration testing, cybersecurity analysis, or network defense. They are highly regarded in the industry as a benchmark for professional competency. Similarly, pursuing advanced degrees in cybersecurity or related fields can deepen the understanding of complex concepts and prepare cybersecurity professionals for higher-level organizational roles. These formal educational achievements are vital in demonstrating commitment and expertise in the field.

Engaging with other professionals provides invaluable opportunities to exchange ideas, share experiences, and gain insights from the expertise of others. This can be achieved by joining professional associations, participating in online forums, and attending industry events. Networking not only aids in staying informed about the latest developments but opens doors to collaborative opportunities, mentorship, and career advancement.

Lifelong learning and skill development are essential for success in the cybersecurity profession. Continuous education, professional development activities, leveraging online learning resources, obtaining certifications and advanced degrees, and networking with industry peers are all critical elements that contribute to maintaining and enhancing the expertise required in this dynamic and demanding field.

KEEPING SKILLS RELEVANT IN A FAST-PACED INDUSTRY

Keeping skills relevant is a continuous challenge for professionals, given the rapid technological advancements and evolving cyber threats. This process is crucial to identifying and learning about emerging cybersecurity technologies. As new tools and technologies are developed, they often bring many new security challenges and opportunities. For cybersecurity professionals, staying informed about these developments is important. This might involve dedicating time to research, attending industry-specific training sessions, or experimenting with new technologies in a controlled environment. Being proactive in understanding and utilizing these emerging technologies enhances one's technical skill set and ensures a deeper understanding of the latest cybersecurity landscapes.

Regularly updating technical and soft skills is equally important in maintaining relevance in cybersecurity. Technical skills, such as network security, ethical hacking, and cryptography, are foundational to a career in cybersecurity, but they need regular updating to stay effective against new types of cyberattacks. Soft skills such as critical thinking, problem-solving, and effective communication are increasingly recognized as vital in this field. These skills aid in understanding complex systems, devising strategic solutions, and collaborating effectively with teams and stakeholders. Regular training through formal courses or self-learning is vital in keeping these skills sharp and current.

Participation in community events and cybersecurity forums is another way to ensure that skills remain relevant. These platforms provide opportunities for professionals to engage with peers, share knowledge, and learn from the experiences of others. Community events, such as conferences, workshops, and meetups, offer insights into current best practices and emerging trends in cybersecurity. Online forums and discussion groups can also be valuable resources for staying connected with the global cybersecurity community, providing a space for real-time discussions on current challenges and developments.

Staying ahead of industry trends and standards is essential for maintaining relevance in the rapidly changing cybersecurity landscape. This involves keeping up with technological advancements and staying informed about changes in industry regulations, standards, and best practices. Cybersecurity professionals must be aware of global and regional regulatory changes that could impact their work—such as data protection laws and compliance requirements. Additionally, staying attuned to industry standards helps align security practices with recognized benchmarks, ensuring that the measures implemented are up-to-date and effective.

Keeping skills relevant in the fast-paced industry of cybersecurity requires a multifaceted approach. It involves actively learning emerging technologies, continuously updating technical and soft skills, participating in community events and forums, and staying ahead of industry trends and standards. This ongoing process of learning and adaptation is crucial for professionals to remain effective and competitive in the ever-evolving field of cybersecurity.

MENTORSHIP AND KNOWLEDGE SHARING

Mentorship and knowledge sharing are integral components of professional growth and development in the cybersecurity field. Finding and working with mentors who have established themselves in this domain can be a transformative experience for burgeoning cybersecurity professionals. A mentor can provide guidance, share invaluable insights from their experiences, and offer advice on navigating the complexities of a cybersecurity career. One can look toward professional networks, industry events, or even within their current organization to find a mentor. Building a relationship with a mentor involves open communication, respect for their time and knowledge, and a willingness to learn and take feedback constructively. Effective mentorship can accelerate learning, provide direction, and open up new opportunities for professional advancement.

Conversely, sharing expertise through mentoring others is equally enriching. As professionals grow in their careers, they accumulate a wealth of knowledge and experience that can be invaluable to those who are just starting. Becoming a mentor not only contributes to the growth of others but also reinforces the mentor's understanding and skills. It encourages staying updated on the latest trends and challenges in the field since mentoring requires *experience* and *current knowledge*. Mentoring can take various forms, from formal mentoring programs to informal guidance and support. It is an opportunity to give back to the community and shape the future of the cybersecurity field.

Learning through teaching and community involvement is another facet of professional development in cybersecurity. As a speaker or instructor, engaging in community events, workshops, and seminars allows professionals to share their knowledge and insights. This process of teaching can be a powerful learning experience. It challenges individuals to articulate their knowledge clearly and effectively, often leading to new insights and a deeper understanding of the subject. Community involvement also facilitates networking with other professionals, staying abreast of industry developments, and contributing to the collective knowledge base of the cybersecurity community.

The role of mentorship in professional growth and development cannot be overstated. Mentorship provides a learning framework that is rooted in real-world experience and tailored guidance. It can help you navigate career paths, make informed decisions, and avoid common pitfalls. For mentors, it offers a sense of fulfillment and the opportunity to shape the next generation of cybersecurity professionals. In an industry as dynamic and challenging as cybersecurity, mentorship and knowledge sharing play crucial roles in individual growth and strengthening the overall cybersecurity community.

BALANCING SPECIALIZATION AND VERSATILITY

In an industry encompassing a wide range of technologies and threats, professionals often choose between developing deep expertise in a specific area or maintaining a broad range of skills.

Developing a core specialization involves delving deeply into a particular aspect of cybersecurity, such as network security, ethical hacking, or digital forensics. This specialization allows professionals to become experts in their chosen niche, often making them highly sought after for specific roles. Developing this specialization may require focused education, certifications, and hands-on experience in the chosen area. Specializing allows the cybersecurity professional to work on more complex problems and contribute significantly to cybersecurity.

However, building a versatile skill set is equally essential in addition to specialization. Cybersecurity is interconnected and issues often span across various domains. Hence, having a broad understanding of different areas can be highly beneficial. Versatility allows professionals to adapt to various challenges and work effectively in cross-functional teams. It involves staying informed about cybersecurity topics and continuously updating skills to include new technologies and methods.

Integrating specialization with broad knowledge allows for a well-rounded career in cybersecurity. This integration involves using one's core expertise as a foundation while understanding how it fits into the larger cybersecurity landscape. Professionals who combine their deep specialized knowledge with a broad understanding of the field can often provide more comprehensive solutions and strategies. This holistic approach enables them to see the bigger picture and understand how different aspects of cybersecurity interact and affect each other.

Career path planning for long-term cybersecurity success should consider specialization and versatility. As the field evolves, so may the relevance of specific specializations. Maintaining a balance between deep expertise in a specific area and a versatile skill set can provide more stability and opportunities for advancement. It allows professionals to pivot as needed, adapting to changes in the industry and taking advantage of new trends and technologies. Thoughtful career planning should involve setting specialization and broad skill development goals, seeking opportunities that align with these goals, and being open to continual learning and adaptation.

Balancing specialization with versatility is crucial for a successful and sustainable career in cybersecurity. Combining deep expertise in a specific area and a broad understanding of the field enables professionals to remain adaptable and relevant in an ever-changing industry, positioning them well for long-term success.

PLANNING FOR CAREER LONGEVITY AND SATISFACTION

Planning for career longevity and satisfaction in cybersecurity involves a multifaceted approach that focuses on professional development, personal well-being, and job fulfillment. As the cybersecurity industry rapidly evolves, adapting to these changes is crucial for maintaining a long and satisfying career.

Adapting to industry changes for career longevity requires a proactive mindset. The cybersecurity landscape is continuously shaped by new technologies, evolving threats, and shifting regulatory environments. Professionals must be willing to learn and adapt in order to stay relevant and practical. This might involve regular training and certification, staying abreast of industry news, or even shifting specializations as the market demands. Adapting to industry changes also means being flexible in one's career path by recognizing that the routes to success and satisfaction in cybersecurity are diverse and may change over time.

Work-life balance in cybersecurity is essential, given the work's often high-pressure and demanding nature. Cybersecurity professionals can face long hours, especially during critical security incidents. Finding a balance that allows for professional dedication without compromising personal well-being is essential. This balance might involve setting clear boundaries between work and personal time, pursuing hobbies or interests outside of work, and ensuring sufficient rest and downtime. Employers who recognize the importance of work-life balance and who support their employees in achieving it will contribute significantly to job satisfaction and employee retention.

Finding fulfillment and satisfaction in your career is about more than just professional accomplishments; it involves engaging in meaningful work that aligns with personal values and interests. For many in cybersecurity, this might mean working on projects that significantly protect people and organizations from cyber threats. Satisfaction can also come from continuous learning, overcoming challenging problems, and seeing the tangible results of one's work. Regular self-reflection on career goals, achievements, and aspirations can help maintain a sense of fulfillment and direction in one's career.

Networking and community involvement are also critical components of a satisfying and long-lasting career in cybersecurity. Building a professional network provides support, opens new opportunities, and can lead to valuable collaborations. Networking can occur in various settings, such as conferences, workshops, online forums, or local meetups. Whether through mentoring, volunteering, or participating in community events, involvement in the cybersecurity community can provide a sense of belonging and contribution. These connections and community interactions often bring additional satisfaction and enrichment to a cybersecurity career.

INDEX

Note: Page numbers followed by "*t*" refer to tables.